NOBODY'S CHILDREN

NOBODY'S CHILDREN

Abuse and Neglect, Foster Drift, and the Adoption Alternative

ELIZABETH BARTHOLET

Beacon Press   Boston

Beacon Press
25 Beacon Street
Boston, Massachusetts 02108–2892
www.beacon.org

Beacon Press books
are published under the auspices of
the Unitarian Universalist Association of Congregations.

05 04 03 02 01 00 99   8 7 6 5 4 3 2 1

This book is printed on recycled acid-free paper that contains at least 20 percent
postconsumer waste and meets the uncoated paper ANSI/NISO specifications
for permanence as revised in 1992.

Text design by Elizabeth Elsas
Composition by Wilsted & Taylor Publishing Services

Library of Congress Cataloging-in-Publication Data

Bartholet, Elizabeth.
    Nobody's children : abuse and neglect, foster drift, and the adoption
alternative / Elizabeth Bartholet.
        p.   cm.
    Includes bibliographical references.
    ISBN 0-8070-2318-3 (cl)
    1. Child welfare—Government policy—United States.   2. Child abuse,
neglect, and maltreatment—United States.   3. Children—Institutional
care—United States.   4. Foster home care—United States.   5. Adoption—
United States.   6. Kinship care—United States.   I. Title.
HV741.B315   1999
362.76'0973—dc21   99-22976

For Michael, Christopher, and Derek

CONTENTS

NOBODY'S CHILDREN

INTRODUCTION

This book is about the children who are growing up without true families—without, that is, families that are functioning to provide the kind of care and nurture that is essential to well-being. It is about victims who are the children of victims. It is about children born to parents who are themselves the products of inadequate parenting, of poverty and unemployment, of drugs and alcohol, of violence at the hands of their mates or of strangers. It is about black children and white children, Latino, Native American, and Asian children. It is about children growing up in homes in which they are physically brutalized or sexually exploited. It is about children born damaged by the drugs and alcohol their mothers used during pregnancy, children in need of very special parenting to overcome the damage, who are sent home to parents whose first love is their drug. It is about children who grow up parenting themselves and their siblings as best they can because the adults in their home are not mentally or emotionally capable of parenting. This book is about the children left to grow up in inadequate homes, but also about the children removed only to be placed in inadequate foster or institutional care. It is about those who will spend the rest of their childhood in state custody, and

about those who will spend it bouncing back and forth between foster care and their homes of origin. These are *Nobody's Children*.

This book is also about the culture that makes it possible to see
children as *Nobody's*, or *Somebody Else's*, and certainly *Not Ours*. It
tells the story of how our child welfare policies came to place such a
high value on keeping children in their families and communities of
origin without regard to whether this works for children. It envisions
a new culture in which the larger community assumes responsibility
for the well-being of its children, a culture in which we understand
children born to others as belonging not only to them, and not only
to their kinship or racial groups, but to all of us.

KINSHIP AND COMMUNITY

"It takes a village to raise a child," is a popular cry among child welfare professionals. The reference is to an African tradition in which
the child is seen as the responsibility not simply of the family but of
the entire village. Also popular is Carol Stack's work, *All Our Kin*, in
which she describes the African-American family as an extended kin
network, with various members standing in as substitute parents as
needed.

These images have tremendous appeal. It feels good to think of
children nestled in their parents' arms, with supportive family members ready to help in good times and bad, and with the village community there for the child and the family from day one. It fits with
our intuition that in the best of circumstances nuclear family units
can't be expected to provide everything that a child needs all the time.
And it fits with the reality that in modern America huge numbers of
children are growing up in family situations that are far from ideal—
in families torn apart by poverty and drugs, in neighborhoods characterized by violence, unemployment, and despair.

For our children to thrive, they *do* need a community which takes
significant responsibility for their care and nurture, rather than leaving them dependent on their nuclear family unit's ability to make it
in the competitive struggle. But our country has traditionally been
more reluctant than many to assert responsibility for its children,
because of the value placed in our culture on individual and family

autonomy, and on the free market. We do far less than most countries in Europe, for example, to support parental leave from work, to subsidize community child care, or to make health care generally available.

Many in the child welfare world have argued for decades that our government should do more to provide children with *support*, but they too have been resistant to incursions on family autonomy. When the individual family unit breaks down, and the child is subject to abuse or neglect, they tend to resist the notion that the state should intervene in the family to assume *responsibility* for the child. They resist, for example, efforts to punish the parents, or to remove the child and find another family that can provide adequate parenting. They contend that extraordinary efforts should be made to keep the child first within the family of origin, and next within the kinship group, and next within the racial or community group of origin, the local "village." They argue that children's best interests should be understood in terms of their connection to and continuity with their past—their birth heritage and racial group heritage. I discuss in chapters 1 and 5 some of the reasons why we have come to treat children as belonging, in an essentialist sense, to their blood kin and their racial group, and why these policies so often end up preventing children from truly belonging anywhere.

I want to enlarge the understanding of "kin" and "village." Children will be able to thrive in our society only if we begin to think of children born to other people, and to other racial groups, and to poor people, and to people who live elsewhere, as in some sense "ours." When a child's parents prove unfit, their blood kin will sometimes be the best candidates to take over parenting responsibilities. There will sometimes be advantages for the child in maintaining continuity with its past and its heritage. But this will depend on what those kin and that past and that heritage look like. It will depend on the reality of the child's particular family and local community. Often the blood kin are plagued by the same problems and victims of the same circumstances as the child's parents. And rarely does the local community look like the cozy village envisioned by the African proverb. Many parents who abuse or neglect their children suffered the same maltreatment[1] as children themselves; they are parenting as they

were parented. And, while abuse and neglect occur at all socioeconomic levels, they are most highly concentrated among the most disadvantaged. Accordingly, the victims of maltreatment tend disproportionately to live in neighborhoods characterized by poverty,
unemployment, drugs, crime, and violence, neighborhoods which
are the least supportive environments for children and families.[2]

We need to stop romanticizing "heritage" and recognize that
while children's lives may be enriched by maintaining some continuity with their past, children's vital needs are for parents who are committed to and capable of caring for them today and in their future. It
does take a village to raise a child, but we have to look to the entire
community to be that village—to provide support in the first instance and, in the event that things go terribly wrong, to provide protection and alternative parenting.

THE RACE/CLASS PROBLEM

But there's a problem in looking to the entire community to take care
of all its children. We live in a society in which that community is
segregated along race and class lines. The local villages are often black
or latino or white villages. The families in trouble, in which children
are threatened with abuse and neglect, and from which children are
removed to foster care, are disproportionately poor, and they come
disproportionately from racial minority groups. If the state, representing the larger community, steps in to protect children, it intrudes
on the lives of those who are already oppressed. If the state takes their
children away, it takes the only thing many of these families feel they
have in this world. If the state moves their children to families in the
larger community, families outside the local village, families which
may be in a better position to parent because they enjoy the luxury
of decent jobs and housing and schools, is this the larger community
stepping in to help those in need? Or is this the ultimate form of exploitation? Is this class and race warfare? Chapters 5 and 10 address
these questions.

There's another problem also. In a class and race segregated society, how do you get the well-off groups to care about the children
who most need care—children it may be easy to think of as foreign

"others." How do you get funds devoted to programs designed to prevent child maltreatment? How do you get people to step forward to offer their homes and their hearts, to become foster and adoptive parents to the children in need?

Race and class issues dominate policy in this area, although the issues are rarely addressed honestly in a way that illuminates for on-lookers their power. Change is impossible unless we can face up to the issues. Debate has been silenced, and potential actors paralyzed, by fear of opening up wounds and triggering rage, fear of proposing or taking action which would victimize already victimized groups, and fear of being accused of racism and classism.

Addressing these issues is not easy. In the first place, the answers are not easy. Many smart people who have committed their lifetime careers to civil rights, or poverty rights, or children's rights, or to making the child welfare system work, are convinced that the kind of family preservation policies challenged in this book are appropriate policies. They think we should do better by poor families and their children, but they are suspicious of using child removal or adoption except in the most extreme cases. These people obviously care deeply about improving children's lives, and they are convinced that family preservation policies serve that purpose, even if the current system leaves much to be desired.

It's also not easy if you see yourself as someone who is committed to racial and social justice, to take positions which trigger claims that you are promoting racial genocide, and that you have deserted the war on poverty for the new war on the poor. I write as someone who has devoted most of my career to civil rights work and to work on behalf of some of society's ultimate outcasts, people dealing with substance abuse and with AIDS.[3] I understand the concerns that lead some to equate state intervention to protect and remove children with class and race warfare. But I don't see things that way. I think it's important that those of us who understand ourselves as liberals concerned with social justice speak out, rather than being silenced by doubt and fear. In recent years it has been conservatives who have pushed most zealously for changes in law and policy designed to pro-tect children against abuse and neglect, for limits on family preser-vation policies and for the expanded use of adoption as a way of shielding children from harm and providing them with nurturing homes. But unless liberals join with conservatives to promote children's interests, there will be no real change.

The starting point for honest and meaningful debate has to be the recognition that racial and social injustice is at the core of child abuse and neglect. The parents who treat their children badly are themselves victims, and if we want to stop the vicious cycle, we need to create a society in which there is no miserable underclass, living in conditions which breed crime, violence, substance abuse, and child maltreatment.

But at the same time we need to recognize that children who are abused and neglected, children who are growing up in foster and group homes, are also victims. Like their parents, they are often black and brown-skinned victims, and most of them are poor. Keeping them in their families and their kinship and racial groups when they won't get decent care in those situations may alleviate guilt, but it isn't actually going to do anything to promote racial and social justice. It isn't going to help groups who are at the bottom of the socioeconomic ladder to climb that ladder. It is simply going to victimize a new generation. Moving those children into nurturing homes will give them, at least, a chance to break the cycle.

These homes might be with kin, they might be with same-race nonkin, they might be with other-race parents from the other side of town. What matters is that the children get into homes where they can thrive. But if we want to find truly nurturing homes for all the children in need, we have to reach out to the entire community. Most of the local villages at issue are not going to have enough good homes to spare. Encouraging people who are in a position to provide good parenting to step forward, without regard to race or class or membership in the local village, encouraging them to see children born to others as children they are responsible for, can be painted as a form of vicious exploitation. But that's not how I see it. It seems to me that if more members of the larger community thought of all the community's children as their responsibility, we'd have a much better chance of creating the just society that is our goal.

BLOOD BIAS AND FAMILY AUTONOMY POLITICS

At the core of current child welfare policies lies a powerful blood bias—the assumption that blood relationship is central to what family is all about. Parents have God-given or natural law rights to hold on to their progeny. Children's best interests can be equated with those of their parents because parents have a natural inclination to care for their young. These beliefs are deeply entrenched in our culture and our law. And they are common to the thinking of people from one end of the political spectrum to the other, although left and right may articulate different concerns. Some speak of children's rights to their roots and heritage. Others speak of adults' rights to procreate and of parents' rights to guide and control the children they produce. But most share a deep sense that children belong with and to their biological parents.[4]

Also at the core is the related idea that the state must be kept from interfering with parent-child relationships and family privacy. Again left and right tend to agree on the overriding goal, while emphasizing different reasons and motivated by different issues. Those concerned with the interests of the poor and of minority groups are afraid that state intervention will discriminate against these groups, resulting in even greater oppression. Those concerned with women's interests are concerned that state intervention will discriminate against women, since they do most of the parenting. They welcome state intervention to protect women and children against violence by adult males, but oppose state intervention that might interfere with women's authority over their children. They promote women's privacy rights to protect against state intervention in parenting as in pregnancy, and for many of the same reasons. Those concerned with individual liberty rights see the state's intervention in the relationship between parent and child as a threat to individual autonomy.

But just as left and right have joined in supporting the current system, individuals and groups from all parts of the political spectrum have come together in recent years to promote change, questioning the supremacy of family preservation policies and promoting adoption as an important option for children. Prospects for real change in child welfare policies in the future depend on whether powerful new political coalitions can be built based on new understandings of the meaning of family and the role of the state. There should be potential for left and right agreeing that true parenting is defined more by social bonds than by blood. There should be potential for left and right agreeing that children have liberty interests as well as adults, and that, like adults, they may need the state to protect them against oppression.

In dealing with violence against women, women's rights advocates have forced the larger society to recognize that the concept of family privacy was being used to bolster men's power over women in the home. They have forced us to recognize that violence and oppression are not private, but public issues, and that women deserve protection by the state. They have taught us that family preservation is not always the answer—that where women are being oppressed, liberation from their oppressors is what they may need, and a chance for a new start elsewhere. We need to apply these lessons, discussed in chapter 2, to the situation of children today.

Change is in the air, and change is possible. But it's clear from looking at today's child welfare landscape, that we're not there yet.

TWO STORIES OF A FAMILY AT RISK FOR CHILD MALTREATMENT

There is no "typical" story of child maltreatment. Each story involves a unique family situation. Child welfare policies vary significantly from state to state and agency to agency and are defined in significant part by individual workers' judgments as they apply policies to the facts of particular family situations. But there are basic scenarios that get repeated over and over. There are regularly occurring family situations that put children at unusually high risk for abuse and neglect. And when maltreatment occurs and is reported, states respond in ways that fall into repetitive patterns. "Linda," whose story I tell below, is not a real person. But while her story is made up, it is made up from the bits and pieces of thousands on thousands of real people's stories. It is a story that fits a common pattern. I tell her story below in two forms. "The Current Story" describes what would typically happen to Linda and her children in today's child welfare world. "An Alternative Story" describes what might happen in a radically reformed child welfare world, one in which the larger community asserted greater responsibility for the well-being of its children.

The Current Story

Linda gets pregnant with her first child at the age of sixteen. By the time she is twenty she has two children at home, aged one and three, and a third child on the way. As a single, unemployed parent, she fits a classic profile for abuse and neglect. She has been reported in the past to the state Child Protective Services (CPS) agency for physical abuse of her older child. On two different occasions CPS investigated and found that the alleged abuse had occurred: the child had been severely beaten both times, resulting in severe bruises, swelling, and lacerations. His injuries had required hospital treatment and over-night stays for observation. But CPS could not determine whether it was Linda or her then boyfriend who had been directly responsible, and since the child had suffered no permanent physical impairment, CPS decided that removal of the child was not warranted. After the second incident CPS arranged for Linda to attend parenting classes, which she attended one time and then dropped. CPS was aware of this but took no action since there were no further reports of abuse. CPS subsequently closed the case. CPS's actions in this case were consistent with practice common throughout the nation, as discussed in chapter 4. Agencies are likely to investigate only on the basis of fairly serious allegations, and even then they are likely to do little more than investigate. Even if they find that severe maltreatment occurred they are unlikely to remove the child except as a last resort or in the most extreme cases. If they leave the child in the home after substantiating the maltreatment they will only sometimes provide supportive services to prevent it from recurring; frequently such services are unavailable. Even when agencies do provide services, they will only sometimes put the parents under significant coercive pressure to accept them, to cooperate in any suggested treatment regimen, and to improve their parenting practices, by making the parents' continued custody of the child conditional upon their satisfactory performance and by carefully monitoring that performance.

Linda's third child Jonah is born six weeks premature, showing classic signs of exposure to drugs during pregnancy. Hospital tests and interviews with Linda reveal she has been taking crack/cocaine and drinking alcohol on a relatively regular basis throughout pregnancy. There is no father in the picture.

Different versions of this story could be told. These are only some of the drugs that parents use in ways that injure their children. Most substance abusers abuse a combination of drugs, and cocaine and alcohol are a particularly popular combination. But Linda could be abusing alcohol alone, or heroin and alcohol, or some other combination of licit and illicit drugs. The central element in the story is that Linda is abusing substances that can have an adverse impact on her child's mental and physical development, by virtue both of their damaging effects during pregnancy, and their impact on her parenting capacity after the child is born. Seventy to eighty percent of the CPS caseload consists of cases in which a parent's substance abuse plays a role. As discussed in chapters 3 and 9, parental substance abuse is wreaking havoc on an entire generation of children and has thrown the nation's child welfare system into a state of unprecedented crisis.

After one month in the neonatal unit Jonah is released from the hospital and sent home with his mother, who has visited him only infrequently during that month. He is a fragile, difficult, demanding infant, as is often the case with babies exposed to drugs and alcohol during pregnancy. The hospital provides Linda with instructions as to the special care he will need during the next months and remedial help he may need during later years. Research shows that babies like Jonah are at risk for a variety of developmental and other problems. As infants they present parenting challenges which make it hard for parent and child to develop an appropriate relationship. This in turn makes it hard for parents to provide the special care that these babies need. The research also shows that *with* special parenting care these babies have a good chance of developing relatively normally, at least as compared with others in comparable socioeconomic situations.

Since Jonah was born showing signs of drug exposure, and tests confirmed his mother's use of cocaine and alcohol during pregnancy, CPS is alerted to the situation under relatively recent policies that require the hospital to report these cases. CPS refers the case to its Intensive Family Preservation Services (IFPS) program, which is designed to provide intensive support services for a six-week period to families at risk of having children removed for abuse or neglect. IFPS programs were introduced in the 1970s and are now a regular feature of many states' child welfare systems. The idea is to provide an extraordinarily intense form of CPS supervision and services, albeit for a brief period of time, in order to prevent children from having to be removed from the home.

The IFPS worker meets on a near-daily basis with Linda, helping her adjust to Jonah's needs and encouraging her to confront her substance abuse. The worker arranges for Linda's admission to an outpatient poly-drug treatment program and helps her work out a plan for her sister to take care of Jonah and the two older children during the day when Linda has to attend the program. Linda agrees to enter treatment. She sticks with the treatment regimen during the next two weeks, at which point the IFPS program ends and the worker departs. Within a week Linda has dropped out of treatment and returned to using cocaine and alcohol. The dropout rate at substance abuse treatment programs is very high, as studies reviewed in chapters 3 and 9 show.

CPS takes no action as a result of Linda's return to drugs. Indeed it is not likely anyone there is aware of this development, as the regular CPS social worker now on the case is only scheduled to visit Linda once every few months.

Linda's drug-dominated lifestyle leaves her with little energy to meet her children's needs and often enraged at their demands. When under the influence of drugs or alcohol she often reacts to their presence with anger and sometimes with violence. The situation with Jonah deteriorates rapidly: his demands are particularly annoying to her as he is a very difficult baby, constantly screaming and difficult to calm even when she picks him up; unlike the older children, he can't get out of her way when she is angry. His demands escalate as she fails on a regular basis to meet them, and one day when he is six months old she shakes him violently and then slams him down in his crib to stop the crying that has become nearly constant. He ends up in the hospital for a week recovering from internal injuries. Hospital workers report the case to CPS as involving suspected abuse, and CPS goes to court to remove Jonah from Linda's home on at least a temporary basis. CPS takes no action to remove the older children as no recent maltreatment reports have been filed on them.

Jonah is placed in an emergency foster home while CPS figures out what to do next. As chapter 3 describes, Jonah fits the classic profile for a child in foster care. The overwhelming majority of children in the state's care have parents with substance abuse problems. A disproportionate number enter the state's system as infants, many born showing the effects of their mothers' use of drugs or alcohol during pregnancy. These children are likely to stay in foster care for disproportionately long periods of time.

Linda's CPS worker concludes that to get Jonah back home Linda is willing to make an effort to deal with her crack/cocaine habit and serious drinking problem. She decides that Jonah should be placed in foster care with a plan for his return home when Linda has shown signs of progress. The other two children will be left with Linda. They show signs of chronic neglect but do not appear to have suffered any recent injuries.

In looking for a foster home the CPS worker is guided by agency policies which require that she look first to the extended family. Only if no relative is available who satisfies minimum standards can she consider nonrelatives. Accordingly she reviews the extended family situation and decides that Linda's mother is the best prospect for a temporary home among the relatives. She lives nearby and seems willing, if not especially eager, to take Jonah. She has barely enough money to get by on but says she thinks she can afford Jonah's care if she gets a foster-parent stipend; she's already licensed as a foster parent because she took in Linda's sister's kids a couple of years back when they also were removed on the basis of abuse and neglect charges.

The CPS worker is not too happy about this as a placement for Jonah: the grandmother is fifty-three years old and has some health problems; she seems worried about the special demands that Jonah represents, on top of the two grandchildren she's already caring for; and she doesn't know if she would want to keep him on a long-term basis. The household looks pretty chaotic, and the worker sees no evidence of an especially good relationship between the grandmother and the grandchildren she's already fostering. But the agency's strong kinship preference policy encourages placement with relatives unless there is evidence of their actual unfitness to parent. As discussed in chapter 3, this is typical of kinship preference policies common throughout the nation.

The agency also has a strong policy of placing children for adoption or foster care with families of the same race. These policies, too, are common throughout the nation, as discussed in chapter 5. For Native American children the Indian Child Welfare Act applies, requiring that agencies try to place Indian children within their tribe first, within the Indian community next, and with non-Indians only as a last resort. Recent federal legislation has made it illegal to use race as a basis for decision-making in foster and adoptive placement. But as yet this legislation has had little impact on practice, given the enormous commitment within the child welfare world to the idea that children should be kept within their racial community of origin. Race-matching policies have gone underground to some degree, but their influence still holds sway.

Whatever Linda's racial or ethnic group, these matching policies would limit the number of potential foster homes for Jonah. They also limit the number of potential adoptive homes should the worker conclude that Linda's parental rights should be terminated and Jonah moved on to adoption. Indeed, the limited prospects for finding a good adoptive home entered into the CPS worker's calculus when she made her decision about whether the appropriate plan for Jonah should be his eventual return home or adoption.

If Linda is African-American, same-race matching policies will severely limit the availability of appropriate foster and adoptive homes. The proportion of children in foster care who are African-American—some 59 percent as of 1998—is much greater than that of African-Americans in the general population. This makes it very hard to find qualified and interested same-race families for all the children in need of foster or adoptive homes. This situation has increased the pressure on CPS agencies to look to kinship homes; since kin are almost always of the same race or ethnic background as the parents, kin placements satisfy the same-race matching goal.

So the CPS worker places Jonah with the grandmother. Even if this placement has problems, the hope is that Linda will soon be able to take Jonah back home. Arguably, there are benefits in the meantime to having him with relatives. Linda is again referred to parenting classes and to substance abuse treatment. She understands that if she gets her drug and alcohol problems under control, Jonah will be returned home. In the meantime she has her two other children, and she can see Jonah as much as she wants since her mother lives nearby. CPS may set limits on her "visits" with Jonah—requiring supervi-

sion by the grandmother, or requiring sobriety during visits, or preventing access to Jonah by the boyfriend Linda said was responsible
for beating the older children—but CPS is extraordinarily unlikely
to monitor compliance with any such rules.

Our story stops here. Linda may enter treatment, and she may
stay in treatment. She may rid herself of her crack/cocaine habit and
get her drinking under control. She may get Jonah back and prove a
good mother to all three of her children. But statistics indicate that
this scenario is very unlikely. If she does enter treatment she is likely
to drop out. If she does get off cocaine for a period she is likely to
relapse. If she ever conquers her substance abuse problem it is likely
to be years from now, after many unsuccessful attempts. In the meantime she will almost certainly not be up to the job of parenting any of
her three children. And she will be quite likely to get pregnant again.

Linda's two older children will probably continue to live with her
anyway, unless someone subjects them to severe physical abuse, or to
sexual abuse, and it is reported and demonstrated to the satisfaction
of CPS authorities, and Linda is found either directly or indirectly
responsible. Jonah may be returned home, or he may continue to live
with his grandmother, or he may move on to another foster home. If
he goes home he stands a good chance of being bounced back into
care as a result of new findings of abuse or neglect, or related concerns: almost one-third of all children reunited with their birth parents reenter foster care.

Jonah is in any case extremely unlikely to be adopted, although at
this stage of his life it would be relatively easy to find an adoptive
home for him. The CPS system simply won't consider this an option
without first giving Linda every opportunity, over a period of years,
to get free of drugs. As those years go by Jonah will likely become
increasingly difficult to parent, and adoptive homes will get increasingly hard to find. As discussed in chapter 8, a new federal law called
the Adoption and Safe Families Act looks as if it's designed to prevent
children from languishing in foster care. But the law doesn't directly
address drug problems, or give CPS agencies any direction in how to
deal with them. It seems to encourage moving children on to adoption when they can't safely go home, but at the same time it says that
children need not be moved on if they are living with kin, or if the
state hasn't done enough to help parents get their lives together so

that they can keep their children. So while states could take advantage of the new federal law to make some changes in our story, they don't actually have to.

Jonah and his siblings will grow up without what you might call true parents—the kind of "good enough" parents who, although they fall short of the ideal as almost all parents do, are doing their best most of the time, and are there for their children every day in a way that lets them know they matter, enormously, to someone. Although the research tells us that loving, nurturing treatment could help Jonah overcome the damage caused by the combination of prenatal substance exposure and postnatal abuse he suffered, so as to live a relatively normal life, Jonah is extremely unlikely to get that kind of treatment. He is at high risk for emotional and cognitive problems that will make it very hard for him to develop normal human relationships, to do well in school, to get a job, or otherwise to function as a happy and contributing member of society. Linda's older two children are also at high risk. While healthy at birth, at least one has been subject to physical abuse, and both have grown up in a state of chronic neglect, with no one there for them in the way that research confirms is essential to healthy brain development and to healthy emotional development.

An Alternative Story

In this story Linda never gets to be a twenty-year-old, single, unemployed mother of three, with a cocaine habit and a drinking problem. She lives in a state which has established a system of universal home visiting for first-time mothers, during the period of pregnancy and early infancy. State legislators had been impressed by the research, reviewed in chapter 7, indicating that certain carefully designed, intensive home visitation programs might have a meaningful impact on the problem of child maltreatment. They noted that some of these programs had apparently helped reduce the incidence of prenatal damage, had helped get the young mothers off welfare and into employment and, as a result of these and other factors, had helped reduce the number of subsequent pregnancies and the rates of child abuse and neglect. The legislators were convinced that money spent up front to support families in order to help prevent trouble from developing would save the state money in the end. They decided that it made no sense to wait until children had been seriously abused to provide intensive support services. They also thought that, for families already in trouble, home visitors would help protect infants and young children against abuse and neglect by their very presence and would be in a position to alert CPS if more intervention were necessary to protect the children.

When at the age of sixteen Linda first discovers she is pregnant, she is referred to the Home Visitor program by her health care provider and is assigned a worker who meets with her on a regular basis throughout the rest of her pregnancy, counseling her about prenatal care and the importance of avoiding substances that might damage her fetus, like tobacco, alcohol and drugs. The Home Visitor advises Linda about adoption, and about educational and employment opportunities, and helps her think through her decision as to whether to keep the baby or place it for adoption at birth. Linda decides to keep the baby in our story, so the worker helps her make a plan for supporting the child and caring for it, while she pursues her high school education and explores employment prospects.

Linda's child is born healthy and goes home with her from the hospital. The Home Visitor arrives the next morning to begin what will be a five-year program of visits designed to help Linda ensure that her child gets off to the best possible start. The visits will be weekly at first, but as time goes by the worker will decide whether Linda can manage with less frequent visits, or whether she's having difficulty and needs more frequent visits. The visits will be designed primarily to give Linda a variety of parenting and life skills, educating her about infant and child rearing, advising her about contraception, helping her plan and pursue educational and employment goals, and helping her connect with other community resources which she might not know of or be capable of pursuing on her own. The visits will also enable the worker to monitor the child's well-being during the period of life when children are most vulnerable to maltreatment, and when most child fatalities take place.

Things go well for the first couple of years. Linda feels good about parenting but also is committed to preventing another pregnancy until she gets her life together. She works on finishing her high school degree while holding down a part-time job.

Things may continue to go well. Early results of the research on intensive Home Visiting programs indicate that when support is provided early to vulnerable young mothers it can make a real difference, enabling them to get started on parenting in a way that works for them and the child, enabling them to get parented themselves in ways that help them feel good about themselves, and encouraging them to develop educational and work skills that help keep them on track.

But let's assume that Linda falls off the track. She had a hard start in life, with a family that subjected her to a certain amount of abuse and not much in the way of attentive caretaking, and she finds the strain of single parenting overwhelming despite the Home Visitor's best efforts. Linda falls into a problematic relationship with a boyfriend who's into drugs, and prone to violence, and she starts to use crack/cocaine on a regular basis and to engage in some heavy drinking. The Home Visitor, who had been visiting only once a month since Linda's child turned one, increases her visits to once a week, so that she can try to get Linda to deal with her problems and so that she can monitor the situation with Linda's now two-year-old child.

Linda becomes pregnant for the second time. The Home Visitor tells her that if she continues to abuse cocaine and alcohol during her pregnancy she risks serious damage to the child. The worker warns that if she suspects ongoing substance abuse she will report this to CPS, and CPS might go to court to request removal of both the child to be born and the two-year-old. Terrified at this prospect, and concerned for her future child's health, Linda agrees to enter a poly-drug treatment program, and manages to stick with the treatment regimen during the rest of her pregnancy, with only minor and occasional relapses. Her child is born full-term and apparently healthy.

One month after the child goes home with her Linda drops out of drug treatment and is soon using crack/cocaine regularly. The worker, who has continued to visit weekly, and who had been monitoring Linda's compliance with the drug treatment regimen, concludes that the situation at home has deteriorated to the point where the two children are suffering extreme forms of neglect. Linda has left them alone on many occasions, with only the two-year-old in charge of the baby. Linda and her boyfriend seem to be in a heavily drugged state much of their time at home. The worker has arrived several times to find both children crying, and hungry, and the refrigerator entirely empty. The house looks increasingly chaotic. The worker worries also that the children are at risk of physical harm from both Linda and the boyfriend. Linda seems unwilling or unable to make a serious commitment to deal with her substance abuse problem, or to deal with the separate risks that the boyfriend poses to the children. At the worker's urging CPS intervenes to remove both children.

The court ruling in Linda's case gives her a maximum of twelve months from the time her children were removed to get her life together if she wants her kids back. The state has recently adopted a family court drug program modeled on one being tried out in New York City. Linda must immediately enter a drug treatment program, and by law any state or state-funded programs must provide priority access to clients referred by the court. Linda must stay in treatment and stay clean of drugs, after a brief initial period of adjustment. If she does not live up to these conditions her parental rights will be terminated forthwith so that the children can be adopted as soon as possible. If she does live up to these conditions the children will be sent home by the end of the twelve months to live with her on a probationary basis for the next twelve months. During that probationary period the Home Visitor will monitor the situation, reporting any evidence of drug use or child maltreatment to CPS and the court. Significant drug use or child abuse or neglect will trigger removal of the children again, followed by immediate termination of her parental rights and prompt finalization of adoption with adoptive parents chosen pursuant to the state's recently initiated "concurrent planning" program.

Concurrent planning is one of the promising reform initiatives discussed in chapter 8. It is designed for children who have been removed from their parents and whose prospects for returning home are limited. In these programs CPS proceeds on two tracks simultaneously, working with the parents toward family reunification, while at the same time developing an appropriate adoption plan. In the event reunification efforts fail, the children can be adopted without delay; usually the disruption of another move is avoided since the children will typically have been living during the foster care period with the prospective adoptive family.

When Linda's children are removed, the court assigns her case to the concurrent planning program at CPS's request. CPS workers canvas a wide range of possibilities in considering placements for Linda's children. Their goal is to find a home that will work both as a temporary placement, in case Linda resolves her problems, and as a permanent adoptive home, in case CPS decides it has to terminate Linda's parental rights.

CPS exercises no automatic preference for kinship or for same-race placements, telling workers simply to look for placements that will work well for the children. CPS workers are also told that federal law and state policy forbid any state-imposed preference for same-race families.

Workers can take kinship into account. They can count it as a plus if a grandparent or aunt or uncle is interested in serving as a substitute parent. But they won't take blood as a proxy for caring relationship. They won't presume that simply because someone is kin they will have the child's interests at heart and will provide a good home. They must instead assess kin in comparison with nonkin in the prospective parent pool and make an individualized decision in the end as to which placement is most appropriate. The child's interests should count the most in that decision, although adult interests in maintaining their relationships with the child can also be considered. If the workers find a loving grandmother who has a meaningful, positive relationship with the child, that relationship will of course be a major factor in the final decision. If the grandmother doesn't have the financial wherewithal to support the child, they will inform her of the foster parent stipends, special needs adoption subsidies, and free medical care and other services that exist to help provide support for the child. They won't count poverty against the grandmother, but will take advantage of whatever programs exist to put her in a position to afford to care for the child, so long as she demonstrates that she is truly concerned with the child's welfare and interested in providing parenting. At the same time they won't offer financial stipends to encourage relatives who might not be truly interested in parenting to take on responsibility for the child.

Applying these guidelines, CPS assesses Linda's kinship network for parenting prospects at the same time that it looks to a pool of prospective parents previously recruited for their concurrent planning program. CPS workers find that Linda's mother is the only possible prospect in the kinship pool, and they conclude that there are many better parenting prospects in the concurrent planning pool. They are concerned that Linda's mother has never demonstrated especially positive parenting qualities either in raising her own children or in fostering the two grandchildren already in her care. She does not seem highly motivated to parent Linda's children, and she is not willing to commit to keeping the children permanently in the event Linda's rights are terminated.

The CPS agency will have recruited on a broad basis for its concurrent planning parent pool, giving the workers involved in Linda's case a wide range of prospective parents to consider. The workers will look to Linda's neighborhood to see if there are friends or neighbors with a meaningful connection to the children, people who are truly interested in parenting them and seem able to provide a nurturing home on a permanent basis. They will not count poverty against otherwise promising candidates, but they won't automatically exclude from consideration people who live outside Linda's neighborhood, people who live in neighborhoods which might offer the child more in the way of safety, stability, and good schooling.

In the end CPS selects from the concurrent planning pool a couple who have successfully raised several birth and adopted children and have one young foster child now at home. These parents seem to have the time, energy, resources, and motivation to provide the kind of superior parenting that children who have taken lots of knocks in their early lives desperately need. They could be black or white or latino, or of some other race or ethnicity. CPS is not looking for parents who will match the children's racial background, but for parents who are motivated to provide a good home for these children and seem capable of doing so. Under federal law, which CPS is committed to following, generalized assumptions that race is relevant to parenting capacity are now clearly prohibited.

These parents might live in Linda's neighborhood or they might live elsewhere. The CPS workers would have thought about many factors in assessing the advantages and disadvantages of moving the children outside their neighborhood. They would have considered whether they had meaningful, positive connections with people or institutions in their neighborhood. They would have also considered whether it seemed likely that in the end the children would be adopted, in which case they might weigh their past connections less heavily, and place greater emphasis on factors related to their future opportunities.

The children are placed with the chosen foster parents, with the understanding that Linda will have supervised visits with them until a decision is made whether they will return home to live with her or will be freed for adoption.

I'll stop Linda's new story here. We don't know for sure what will happen. The clear signals she is given, and the threat that she will lose her children if she doesn't stick with the drug treatment regimen, probably give her the best chance she has at freeing herself from substance abuse at this point in her life. If she can, the children will be placed back with her, probably not much damaged by virtue of the disruption in their lives, given the quality parenting CPS workers feel they can expect from the foster family chosen. If she can't, it may be a devastating blow for her, but it may also help her understand that if she sticks with the drugs and alcohol they will destroy her life. In any event the children should be all right. They will of course have suffered pain—pain from their early experiences and deprivation, and pain from being separated from the mother that they nevertheless attached to in significant ways. But they were removed from Linda early enough so that the chances of irreparable damage are limited. They will stay with and be adopted by the foster parents with whom they have been developing a relationship, people chosen because of their potential as permanent parents. If it seems important for the children to maintain a relationship with Linda or other relatives from their family of origin, that can be worked out by the adoptive parents as the years go by, or if it seems appropriate, guidelines for such a relationship can even by laid down by the court at the time of the adoption.

There is much talk today about changing the child welfare story for children born in the twenty-first century. Some call for increased support to all families to protect against trouble developing. Some call for earlier and more active intervention in families as soon as children are identified as victims of abuse or neglect.

But while few defend all aspects of the current story, there is tremendous commitment to certain of its features, and tremendous resistance to the alternative story told above. Family support is a hard sell in an era of hostility to big government and to welfare spending. Family autonomy remains overwhelmingly popular. Home Visitor programs are spreading, but virtually *no one* suggests that they should be made mandatory like early childhood education, even though it is generally recognized that the most troubled families are also the most unlikely to participate in voluntary Home Visitor programs. Intervention by child welfare authorities to remove children victimized by abuse and neglect, and the placement of children outside of their kinship and racial groups, are regularly denounced as forms of class and race warfare.

NEW DIRECTIONS FOR THE TWENTY-FIRST CENTURY?

The Apparent Sea Change

There has been an apparent sea change in attitudes toward family preservation, adoption, and related issues of children's rights, in these final years of the twentieth century. Popular reaction to the "Baby Jessica" case is illustrative. Jessica was placed for adoption shortly after birth and lived with the prospective adopters for two and a half years while they fought over her future in court with the birth parents. In the end the courts ordered her removed and sent to the birth parents in deference to their biological rights, without giving any legal recognition to the relationship between Jessica and the people who had nurtured her since birth, or to their interests in preserving that relationship. The only court that considered Jessica's interests found that she would be best off staying with the parents with whom she had been living. But the highest courts of two states found Jessica's interests irrelevant, and allowed blood rights to trump social bonds, and the Supreme Court of the United States refused to intervene.[5] While the court rulings were consistent with the value American law traditionally has accorded biological parents' rights, they triggered an overwhelmingly hostile public response. It seemed that the law was out of synch with popular understanding of the meaning of family, and the value that should be placed on the child's interest in a nurturing parental relationship. On the streets and in the polls, on the talk shows and in newly formed activist groups,[6] people demonstrated their belief that real parenting had more to do with social bonds than with biology, and expressed their concern that Jessica's interests be weighed at least equally with those of the adults who gave birth to her.

The 1990s have also seen an enormous upsurge in interest in adoption among prospective parents, and related attention by the media, with some reporting that adoption has really turned a corner, shedding the stigma of the past.[7]

Simultaneously, criticism has been leveled at the family preservation policies that keep some children in abusive homes, keep others in foster care, and keep still others bouncing between foster homes and their homes of origin, or from one foster home to another. Persuasive new research, reviewed in chapter 5, has called into question the claims made for the success of Intensive Family Preservation Services (IFPS) programs, claims that helped popularize these programs during the last two decades. Policy-makers in some states and localities have begun to introduce changes designed to free more children up from abusive families and move more children stuck in foster limbo on to adoptive homes. Leading scholars in the child welfare research community have made a powerful case for limiting the excesses of family preservation policies and for placing a higher priority on children's developmental needs, and on permanency and adoption as the way to meet those needs.[8]

The federal government has intervened dramatically, passing legislation that has radically changed the rules of the game. The Multiethnic Placement Act, known as MEPA, was passed in 1994 with the goal of eliminating the racial barriers that stood in the way of placing black children in need of foster and adoptive homes. MEPA was strengthened in 1996 to prevent federally funded agencies from using race *at all* in foster and adoption decision-making.[9] Given that the near-universal policy and practice throughout the nation had been for child welfare agencies to place children with same-race families if at all possible, this law was truly revolutionary in concept.

Even more significant is the Adoption and Safe Families Act (ASFA) enacted in 1997.[10] This Act was designed to undo some of the damage that Congress perceived had been done by the 1980 federal law requiring states to make reasonable efforts to preserve families before removing children on a temporary or permanent basis. Many felt that the earlier law had been interpreted as a mandate to preserve the family at all costs, even when children had suffered horrendous maltreatment and there seemed no possibility that they could ever live safely at home. ASFA places a much higher value on protecting children against abuse and on giving them a permanent nurturing home at the earliest possible point. ASFA tells child welfare agencies that they must make reasonable efforts *not only* to preserve families, *but also* to move children on to a permanent home when preservation is not appropriate. ASFA, for example, says that in cases of torture or other extreme forms of abuse, or if parents have murdered a sibling, *no* effort to preserve the family need be made, and states should take action to terminate parental rights. ASFA creates strict time deadlines to limit the period children can be held in foster care for family reunification efforts before they are moved on to adoptive or other permanent homes. ASFA also creates a new emphasis on adoption as a positive option for children. It offers states financial bonuses for increased adoption rates, and it threatens them with financial penalties if they fail to live up to its various new rules.

Adoption is enjoying new popularity, and family preservation policies are under attack from a variety of different directions. But it remains unclear as we enter the twenty-first century whether the sea change is more apparent than real, and whether the child welfare system will actually undergo fundamental rather than cosmetic reform.

Traditional Undercurrents

Family preservation has always been the dominant modus operandi in the child welfare system. The pendulum has swung back and forth, but always within a narrow scope. The choices for children have, accordingly, been defined narrowly. When the pendulum swings in the family preservation direction we try to avoid removing children from their families at all costs and to return children who are removed as quickly as possible. When the pendulum swings in the opposite direction, we intervene more readily to protect children, removing them to foster or institutional care, and leaving them there for long periods, formally tied to their parents, who retain parental rights and the opportunity to regain custody.

Adoption, severing the birth parents' rights and providing new parents for the child, has never been treated as a serious policy option.[11] From the beginnings of modern child welfare systems in the latter nineteenth century through today, adoption has been seen as an arrangement suitable only for the truly exceptional situation, rather than as a normal and appropriate way to provide for children whose birth parents cannot or will not care for them. Family preservation has been regularly promoted and defended on the basis of the claim that the only alternative for children is foster and institutional care. Out of the more than half a million children in foster care in 1997, no more than 27,000 were placed in adoptive homes. President Clinton's Adoption 2002 initiative, billed as a major effort to promote adoption, set as a goal the doubling of that figure in five years.[12] This seems a modest goal in light of the scope of the problem. The foster care population has more than doubled in size since the latter part of the 1980s, reaching historic highs.[13] Upwards of three million children are victimized by serious maltreatment each year.

Experience with the 1980 federal legislation targeted by ASFA also cautions against assuming too readily that ASFA or any other of the new legal initiatives will result in radical change. This 1980 legislation, the Adoption Assistance and Child Welfare Act,[14] grew out of concern with the increase in the foster care population during the 1970s and the lengthy periods many children were spending in care. It was designed to further the goal of permanency for children *either* in their home of origin *or* in an adoptive home. Family preservation was the first priority, with states mandated to make reasonable efforts to keep children in their homes and to return children who had to be removed. But the Act was also designed to ensure that children move promptly on to adoptive homes if their birth parents could not adequately care for them. Accordingly the Act set deadlines for establishing a Permanency Plan for each child in foster care and for court review of the progress in achieving permanency. The 1980 Adoption Assistance Act was thus remarkably similar to the new ASFA in its general design and goals, even though ASFA is obviously intended to change the situation that the 1980 Act helped create.

Something went wrong as the Adoption Assistance Act moved from the design to the implementation stage. The family preservation piece of the Act took over while the adoption piece largely disappeared. The Act came to be read by many as requiring efforts to preserve families at all costs, regardless of whether the efforts were "reasonable" given the nature of the family and the seriousness of the maltreatment. While initially the Act may have stimulated efforts to move children on to adoption, these initiatives died an early death. And the deadlines stipulated by the Act were routinely ignored. Its requirements regarding permanency planning and court reviews proved inadequate to accomplish the goal of moving children into permanent adoptive homes promptly and eliminating foster limbo.

So a law designed to give new life to adoption as an alternative for children ended up functioning primarily as a family preservation law. How could this happen? Presumably in significant part because the child welfare workers, judges, and others in a position to implement the law on a daily basis were committed to family preservation and averse to adoption, and because the law was written in such a way as to enable them to subvert some of its apparent goals. And in significant part because those in the federal bureaucracy responsible for enforcing the law were similarly committed to traditional ways.

Radical as MEPA and ASFA might seem, there is good reason to wonder what impact they will have on child welfare policies. MEPA has already triggered enormous resistance. State social service agencies tend to be committed from top to bottom to race-matching. Private foundations and nonprofit child welfare groups have joined forces with public agencies to promote kinship care, in part to help ensure that children in need of homes remain within their racial group. "Cultural competence" is one of the code phrases in the post-MEPA era for assessing whether agencies remain sufficiently committed to same-race matching and are doing enough to recruit families of color to make same-race placement possible. The United States Department of Health and Human Services, responsible for enforcing MEPA, is peopled with child welfare traditionalists imbued with the race-matching ideology, and it has done little to date to ensure that federally funded state adoption agencies live up to the MEPA mandate. MEPA *may* someday have a significant impact, but for now, as discussed in chapters 5 and 8, race matching by the state is alive and well.

ASFA was enacted with broad political support, which can be read as a demonstration of the nation's commitment to give new priority to children's interests and to adoption as a way to serve those interests. But the broad support also signals political compromise.

The child welfare establishment had fought MEPA behind the scenes and tried to weaken its mandate. Its members were heavily involved in the lobbying over ASFA also, and their support for the version that emerged indicates that they felt they had achieved much of what they wanted. Analysis of ASFA's specifics shows why. The Act reauthorizes federal funding for family preservation and increases the amounts to new levels. The Act's emphasis on moving children promptly to adoptive homes if they cannot safely stay in their original homes is subtly undermined by a series of exceptions and loopholes. States are exempted from the requirement to free children for adoption if the state has failed to provide family preservation services or if the children are in kinship care. The Act's title and opening preamble seem to make *adoption* a primary goal, but the Act's key operative provisions make *permanency* primary, equating adoption with other permanency options like guardianship, which from the child's perspective may not be at all equal. While ASFA's emphasis on the child's safety seems to give the child's interests a new priority, the safety focus means that the bill excludes from specific coverage the overwhelmingly important, and contentious, "neglect" category. Many assume that neglect cases are minor "dusty house" or other cases in which middle-class social workers inappropriately impose their personal standards on parents from other classes or cultures who are doing a fine job of raising their children. But in today's child welfare world, neglect cases that result in children being removed are typically cases of severe, chronic neglect in which the children are effectively without functioning parents, or are for other reasons at serious risk. The overwhelming preponderance of children in foster care have been removed from parents with serious substance abuse problems. Most of these cases get categorized as neglect cases, and in most of these cases the children are at serious risk—at risk of physical abuse, as well as at risk of going without adequate food, clothing, housing, or supervision. They are extremely unlikely to receive the affirmative parental attention children require. ASFA's failure to specifically address either neglect or drugs exempts these cases from some of the Act's most important protective provisions. In the negotiations over ASFA's language some child advocates fought to make the child's *well-being* rather than *safety* central. When they gave up well-being as the governing standard they gave up a lot.

The child welfare establishment is hard at work today pushing for the development of new programs and the expansion of old ones that are consistent with the family preservation tradition. Foundations that played a key role in developing and promoting Intensive Family Preservation Services programs are now putting their resources into promoting "community partnerships." The community partnership concept is designed to divert from the state CPS system a huge percentage of the abuse and neglect cases that now trigger CPS investigations to determine whether to provide services or take more coercive action. Community partnership advocates contend that families will do better if services are provided on a voluntary basis by local community groups. "Family group decision-making" is being promoted as a way of empowering the extended family unit to decide how to deal with abuse and neglect, and as a way of ensuring that more of the children involved are able to stay with their families rather than being removed. Many advocate expanding kinship foster care, and creating subsidized permanent guardianship arrangements in which kin and other caretakers would be paid the equivalent of foster parent stipends without being subject to the state supervision that goes with foster parenting. These and other recent initiatives could be applied in ways that bring real benefits for children and their families. But, as discussed in chapter 6, they also hold the potential for drastically undermining current efforts to create a more child-friendly care and protection system. They may function to provide convenient end runs around MEPA, ASFA, and related policies that place greater emphasis on children's need to be protected against abuse and neglect and to be provided with nurturing homes as early in life as possible.

So while change is in the air, it may not really happen.

The Challenge Presented: America's "Orphans"

Today's climate presents an extraordinary opportunity to move in new directions. There does seem to be a new level of popular support for taking children's interests seriously, and for rethinking the meaning of family.

We need to seize the opportunity. Abuse and neglect rates continue to rise, and experts believe that the statistics reflect real increases, not simply changes in consciousness or reporting practices. The most serious maltreatment cases quadrupled between 1986 and 1993. Homicide is a leading cause of childhood death, and *the* leading cause of childhood death due to injury. Huge numbers of children are born damaged by the drugs and alcohol their mothers used during pregnancy. Huge numbers are growing up with parents whose abuse of drugs and alcohol make them incapable of providing the kind of care that is essential for children to thrive. The foster care population has doubled in little more than a decade, and the children coming into foster care are more damaged than in previous years. Infants are coming into care in disproportionate numbers; they are destined to stay in care for longer periods than the older children, and they are more likely to be living in group homes or institutions. Each year 25,000 children graduate from state care because they turn eighteen and go forth into the world on their own, never having had a permanent family.

These are America's modern-day orphans, growing up effectively without parents. They have no chance to enjoy what are supposed to be the pleasures of childhood. And they emerge into adulthood with limited prospects for life. In grossly disproportionate numbers they will go on to homelessness, unemployment, crime, substance abuse, and maltreatment of the next generation of children.

Safety and permanency are the mantras of the day. But children need more than protection from physical or sexual violence. And they need more than permanency. They need permanent parents who can give them the kind of love, attention, and on-going commitment that enables human beings to thrive.

HISTORY AND POLITICS

1. THE INHERITED TRADITION: PARENTING RIGHTS AND STATE WRONGS

AUTONOMOUS FAMILIES
A Man's Home Is His Castle
•

Historically in the United States, as in other Western nations, the family was seen as a mini-state in which the father ruled over his wife and children as a near-absolute monarch. His power to impose his will through physical force sometimes had the formal backing of the law. The Massachusetts Stubborn Child Statutes of 1646 even allowed him to order the execution of rebellious or stubborn sons over fifteen. Even as the law changed to limit his formal power, family privacy doctrines developed to protect against any challenge to his abuse of power. So while he might no longer be *allowed* to beat his wife and children, the law made it difficult to challenge what he did in the privacy of his home.[1] The social understanding was that with this power went economic responsibility. The family was to function as an independent economic unit.

This traditional model of the family has undergone dramatic change with respect to women, as they have gained significant economic independence and political power. Women's rights advocates have challenged the patriarchal family model and the misuse of privacy doctrine to protect men's abuse of power in the home. The battered women's movement has mounted an effective campaign to address the problem of male violence against women.

The model has changed far less for children. As naturally dependent creatures they of course cannot fight for their rights to economic support and to protection from harm. State and federal governments have stepped in to assume greater responsibility for children, but they have not stepped very far. So we have a welfare system, but it is a not a system designed to provide for the welfare of all children. Instead it is designed only for those fringe families that don't fit the autonomy model and consequently aren't able to make it on their own. AFDC—Aid to Families with Dependent Children —our longest-standing welfare program, was not a family entitlement made generally available, but a stigmatizing stipend designated only for the eligible poor.[2] Its replacement, TANF—Temporary Assistance for Needy Families—is yet more restrictive.[3]

As for child maltreatment, the good news for children is that child abuse was "discovered" in 1874, with the Mary Ellen Wilson case, and "rediscovered" in 1962 by the radiologist C. Henry Kempe, who coined the phrase "battered child syndrome."[4] The bad news is that family autonomy and privacy functioned to make child maltreatment so invisible during the nineteenth and twentieth centuries that *discovery* was seen as the appropriate word when someone finally paid attention.

Mary Ellen was viciously abused for years by her stepmother. At the time there were no laws protecting children against abuse, so her rescuers had to rely in court on the law that protected animals against cruel treatment. The lawyer arguing Mary Ellen's case went on to form the first Society for the Prevention of Cruelty to Children. The case became a cause célèbre, inspiring the development of comparable organizations elsewhere and the passage of laws to protect children against abuse and neglect. Private and later public agencies used these laws to intervene in the family, often removing children to orphanages or to foster care.

But by the 1960s, child abuse was again so invisible that Henry Kempe's work could be seen as revolutionary. Kempe was a physician who became concerned about the injuries he was seeing in young children brought into the hospital for treatment. While most doctors had been accepting without question parents' innocent explanations for such injuries, Kempe used the then-new x-ray technology to demonstrate that many of these children had suffered multiple broken bones in the past. With his publication of *The Battered Child Syndrome* in 1962, he forced the world to recognize that many parents were guilty of physically abusing their children on a systematic basis.

Kempe's work helped trigger a new wave of concern about abuse and neglect. Reporting laws were passed throughout the country mandating professionals who came in contact with children—police officers, teachers, physicians, and others—to report suspected maltreatment to child protection authorities. Abuse and neglect laws were expanded, and protective efforts newly energized. However, the family autonomy model shaped the state's response to child maltreatment in important ways. Under the new child protection system, the state would intervene only if necessary and would remove children only on the basis of a powerful showing of parental unfitness. The strong presumption was that parents would care for and protect their children.[5]

"Poor Joshua!"

Justice Blackmun, dissenting from the U.S. Supreme Court's 1989 decision in *De Shaney v. Winnebago County Dept. of Social Services*,[6] wrote:

> Poor Joshua! Victim of repeated attacks by an irresponsible, bullying, cowardly, and intemperate father, and abandoned by [the Department of Social Services] who placed him in a dangerous predicament and who knew or learned what was going on, and yet did essentially nothing. . . . It is a sad commentary upon American life, and constitutional principles—so full of late of patriotic fervor and proud proclamations about "liberty and justice for all"—that this child, Joshua De Shaney, now is assigned to live out the remainder of his life profoundly retarded.

Joshua DeShaney was repeatedly beaten by his father, until, at the age of four, he was beaten so severely that he suffered brain damage and was committed to an institution for the profoundly retarded, where he was expected to spend the rest of his life. A court had awarded custody to the father after Joshua's parents divorced, and state child protective authorities had investigated Joshua's situation and been monitoring his case as a result of a series of abuse reports. But Joshua was never removed from the home until after his final beating. Emergency brain surgery revealed a series of hemorrhages caused by traumatic injuries to the head which had been inflicted over a long period of time. The father was subsequently tried and convicted of child abuse. Joshua and his mother sued, claiming that the state should be held responsible for his injuries, by virtue of its failure to intervene to protect him from his father. The United States Supreme Court found that the state bore no responsibility for Joshua's fate.

The Court's reasoning shows the family autonomy model at work. Joshua was his father's responsibility, and it was his father who injured him. The state had nothing to do with it. True, the state got a little involved by sending a caseworker into the home, and true, the caseworker was aware of the risk to Joshua, which had been duly recorded in her notes. But the state didn't actually remove Joshua to a state-sponsored home, in which case it might have been responsible, says the Court. The Court notes that had the state removed Joshua it might have been charged with unconstitutionally intruding into the parent-child relationship. By contrast, the state risks nothing by not intervening, since there is no affirmative constitutional duty to protect Joshua from harm so long as he is in the care of what the Court refers to as his "natural" father. The Court talks of Joshua operating in a "free world" as if the brutalized child were a free agent.

The Court's decision seems shocking because of Joshua's tragic fate, and because of the level of state involvement in his case. But the philosophy expressed is quite consistent with our nation's general approach to child maltreatment. Families are supposed to take care of children, and the state assumes little direct responsibility for their well-being. Even the dissenting Justice Blackmun argues for state responsibility largely on the ground that the state had effectively *assumed* responsibility through the involvement of its child protection program.

So the state denies direct responsibility for its children, both in terms of basic economic support, and in terms of protection against harm. It is only if parents prove unfit to provide for their children that the larger society sees itself as obligated to step in with either welfare or child protective services.

The support and protection problems are intertwined. Poverty is a powerful predictor for child maltreatment. Employment and other social programs are the best measures we could take to prevent maltreatment. And early support and prevention programs work a lot better than after-the-fact attempts to treat abusive parents, or abused children. We know all this and have known it for decades. But we continue with the policy of doing "too little too late," providing only very limited support to families up front, and waiting to provide more until after children have been abused and neglected, when the still relatively limited services made available will be inadequate to what is now a far more overwhelming task.

Alternative Visions
"Mankind owes to the child the best that it has to give . . . "
—*League of Nations, Declaration on the Rights of the Child*, 1924

Developments in the international community demonstrate that things here don't have to be the way they are. Many Western nations take a more activist role in supporting families and providing for the welfare of children. In Europe and Scandinavia parents and children are typically supported by a network of social services that includes health care, paid parental leave from employment, and child care for working parents.[7] Home visiting services for new parents and their children are provided on a universal basis in Great Britain and Denmark, serving as a main source of preventive health information and care for young children. A number of countries make their national governments directly responsible for the welfare of the nation's children, through constitutional or legislative language establishing the legal relationship, giving parents duties with respect to their children and giving children related rights. Other countries give national "ombudsmen" authority and responsibility for ensuring children's welfare.[8]

An international treaty called the *Convention on the Rights of the Child* demonstrates that throughout the world there is general agreement at least on the *principle* that the entire community is responsible for ensuring the welfare of its children. The *Convention* was adopted by the United Nations Assembly in 1989 and ratified as of early 1999 by 191 parties, including all nations of the world except the United States and Somalia. Article 19 of the *Convention* requires that nation states take action to protect children from abuse or neglect, and to that end that they develop appropriate support and prevention programs, as well as effective systems for dealing with instances of child maltreatment.[9] This notion that states have an affirmative responsibility to protect their children from abuse and neglect is quite inconsistent with the *DeShaney* world described above. Moreover, since the treaty is intended at least as a formal matter to create legally binding obligations on all nations which ratify, it means that the larger community of nation states are asserting their common responsibility to the children of all those nations, and are giving those children legal rights enforceable, at least in theory, in international tribunals. This is a far cry from the understanding so common in the United States that children belong to their parents, and next to their extended families, and next to their racial or tribal groups, and next to their local village. It is an assertion that in the beginning and the end the *entire community* must take responsibility for its children. While there are many reasons why the United States has failed to ratify the *Convention*, concern for family autonomy and parents' rights has played an important role.[10]

FAMILY PRESERVATION POLICIES AND PRACTICES

In this country government does little to prevent the problems that give rise to abuse and neglect, intervening only in crisis, when the family is effectively falling apart. At that point, family preservation is the overwhelming priority, shaping everything the government does as it responds to claims of child maltreatment.

History shows that family preservation achieved priority status early. In response to the extensive use of institutional care in the late nineteenth and early twentieth centuries, the first White House Conference on Children in 1909 declared, "home life is the highest and finest product of civilization" and argued that children should not be removed "except for urgent and compelling reasons":

> No child should be removed from the home unless it is impossible so
> to construct family conditions or to build and supplement family
> resources as to make the home safe for the child.[11]

Theorists offered powerful support for family preservation efforts. Writing in the 1970s and 1980s, Joseph Goldstein, Anna Freud, and Albert J. Solnit combined their backgrounds in law and psychiatry to produce what remain the best-known and probably most influential works in the history of child welfare: *Beyond the Best Interests of the Child* (1973), *Before the Best Interests of the Child* (1979), and *In the Best Interests of the Child* (with Sonja Goldstein, 1986).[12] These books argued for making the child's interests central, telling readers, "put yourself in the child's skin." They challenged the practices of the day, which condemned large numbers of children to foster limbo, arguing that children needed continuity in parenting and were injured by uncertainty and disruption. But while their perspective was child-centered, and they emphasized the psychological aspect of parenting over the biological, one of their central claims was that children's interests were best served by placing a high priority on family autonomy and family preservation. They argued that the state should intervene to protect children only in cases of severe physical abuse, because, while they recognized the harm that might come from emotional abuse or severe forms of neglect, they felt that more harm would come to children in the end from incursions on family autonomy.[13] Even in cases of severe abuse they contended that every effort should be made to avoid removing the child. Goldstein, Freud and Solnit had little empirical support for their claims, speaking essentially on the basis of their belief system,[14] a system that was entirely consistent with the American tradition. But they spoke with the authority of their impressive reputations and backgrounds, and they had enormous influence.

The entire child-protection system was shaped by the family preservation priority. The enforcement of child-protection legislation was turned over almost entirely to child welfare workers. Police and prosecutors were brought in only in the most egregious cases. Child welfare workers, trained as helping professionals, tend to understand both the parent and child as victims of circumstance; their approach is to work things out through therapy and mediation, and their vision of success is a resolution that keeps the family together. Police and prosecutors are more likely to focus on children as the victims of maltreatment and on parents as the perpetrators; their approach is to deter maltreatment using criminal penalties and to prevent it by incapacitating parents in prison and removing children from harm's way.

The United States Supreme Court created a framework of constitutional rights which simultaneously reflects and reenforces the family preservation bias. The rights of biological parents are the starting point for analysis, and usually the ending point also: these rights are so powerful that children's rights, or the rights of competing "social parents," don't count at all unless the biological parents are first demonstrated to be unfit. The *DeShaney* case, discussed above, helps set the stage—a natural rights universe in which parents rule over their families until and unless the state intervenes. Other Supreme Court cases set limits on the state's power to intervene, making it clear that parents have constitutionally protected rights to hold onto their progeny unless the state makes a powerful case that they are unfit. In *Santosky v. Kramer*[15] the Court dealt with a case in which three children had been removed from their parents for what the dissent characterized as "shockingly abusive treatment." The children were kept in foster care for four and a half years, at which point New York terminated parental rights, freeing the children to be placed for adoption. The Supreme Court found this unconstitutional, ruling that states cannot terminate parental rights without satisfying a higher than normal burden of proof as to the parents' unfitness. States must, according to the Court, provide clear and convincing evidence of unfitness. The Court found this higher standard necessary to properly protect "the fundamental liberty interest of natural parents in the care, custody, and management of their child." The Court claimed that this standard simultaneously served children's interests, arguing that parents and children have a common interest in preserving the family until and unless the parents are proven unfit. But the Court failed entirely to face up to the concern that by setting the proof standard so high it might prevent findings of unfitness in cases where the parents are in fact unfit and the child would be best served by adoption. The unstated assumption is consistent with the Goldstein, Freud, and Solnit premise: keeping families together without investigating too carefully whether they actually serve children's best interests will in the end best serve those interests.

Not surprisingly, in light of *DeShaney* and *Santosky*, the Court has failed to accord children any constitutionally protected rights to be properly parented, and has failed to accord foster or preadoptive parents any right to challenge the biological parents' claims.[16] State court rulings in the famous "Baby Jessica" case produced shock in the press and public when they ordered that Jessica should be returned to her biological parents without any consideration of her interest in remaining with the only parents she had known for her two and a half years of life, and without any consideration of her preadoptive parents' interests. But those court rulings were entirely consistent with our legal tradition in treating the rights of the biological parents as absolute until and unless those parents are clearly shown to be unfit.[17]

State and federal legislation flesh out the picture in ways consistent with the family preservation theme. After the 1960s and 1970s, when many critics thought that legislation had given child welfare authorities too much discretion to remove children from families, laws were rewritten to limit the grounds on which children could be removed to more clearly defined forms of abuse and neglect, with more serious implications for the health and safety of children. Procedural protections for biological parents were increased, giving indigent parents free legal assistance and better defined rights to be heard in court.

Programs and policies designed to provide services to help preserve families are also an important part of the picture. These come in both a traditional and a more recent intensive form. The underlying idea is the same: as families fall apart, and children are threatened with maltreatment, the social welfare system responds with services designed to enable families to do better and keep their children. These services may be provided either to prevent children from being removed to foster care, or to enable those who have been removed to be reunited with their families (often called "family reunification").

While our society espouses family preservation as the goal, we have failed to provide the resources to really make it work. We don't support families up front in ways designed to ensure their success, waiting instead until families are in such trouble that preservation efforts are often doomed. We are more generous by far in our talk about family preservation services than we are in the funding. Foster limbo ends up being the societal compromise of choice: removing children from their parents prevents some of the most egregious

abuse and neglect; keeping them in foster care allows us to avoid finally terminating the parents' rights and preserves the family in a
technical if not a real sense. The Supreme Court's *Santosky* decision
encouraged this compromise, making it far harder constitutionally
to finally terminate parental rights than to "temporarily" remove
children to foster care. The irony is that foster care turns out to be an
expensive way of caring for children. And therefore when the foster
care population builds up, the pressure to find another way builds
up simultaneously.

By the 1970s, growth in the foster care population had produced
pressure for change, resulting in a renewed emphasis on family preservation and family reunification services as the solution to foster
limbo. Child welfare advocates argued that many children languishing in foster care could be living safely at home if only support
services were provided to their families. Fiscal conservatives could
take satisfaction in the savings that would result from reducing the
foster care population. Congress passed the 1980 Adoption Assistance and Child Welfare Act,[18] which required states to make reasonable efforts to provide family-support services both to avoid removing children and to "reunify" families if children had already been
removed. This Act, as interpreted by social workers, judges, and the
child welfare establishment, helped produce an atmosphere in which
the removal of a child and termination of the parents' rights came to
be seen as system failures. It ratcheted up the pressure on child welfare agencies to preserve families at all costs. Many interpreted the
federal law as requiring family preservation efforts even when the
family seemed hopelessly dysfunctional, or when children had been
subjected to extreme forms of abuse such as intentional torture. This
is why Congress felt it necessary in the 1997 Adoption and Safe Families Act (ASFA) to specify that reasonable efforts were *not* required
in such cases.

In the late 1970s and the 1980s, new support for family preservation came in the form of "Homebuilders" and related programs fea-
turing "intensive family preservation services" (IFPS). In the Homebuilders model, social workers with extremely limited caseloads were
assigned to work with families at risk of losing their children to foster
care, providing intensive services on a daily basis for a short, six-week
period of time, with the goal of enabling the family to overcome the

problems that had precipitated the threat of child removal. IFPS pro-grams brought new funds and new energy to family preservation efforts. The Edna McConnell Clark Foundation made IFPS a major priority, contributing significant resources to funding programs and encouraging government agencies, advocacy groups, and other foundations to join in promoting IFPS programs. By the 1990s most states had such programs in place.

While there is much talk today about the recent backlash against family preservation, financial support for traditional and intensive forms of family preservation programs has continued to expand. The federal government significantly increased its funding in 1993 with the passage of the Family Preservation and Support Services Act, al-locating $1 billion over a five-year period to support state efforts at family preservation.[19] The Congress that passed ASFA simulta-neously reauthorized and expanded funding for family preservation, providing $275 million for fiscal year 1999, $295 million for fiscal year 2000, and $305 million for fiscal year 2001.[20]

2. THE POLITICS

THE LEFT-RIGHT COALITION: AN UNHOLY ALLIANCE?
The Puzzle

Our society's response to child abuse and neglect is something of a puzzle, however much tradition may lie behind it. While there is evidence indicating that it would be cost-effective to support families up front to prevent problems from developing,[1] we wait until families have deteriorated and children have been damaged. We then pour money into investigating abuse and neglect charges, into family preservation services, and into foster and institutional care for children. We know that at this point our efforts will be largely ineffective. We know that many of these children will grow up permanently damaged by their lives at home and in institutional care, damaged in ways that will result in huge future costs to society in terms of unemployment, substance abuse, crime, and future child abuse.[2] We say we care about children, and much of our child welfare law indicates that the best interest of the child is our guiding principle. Yet we wait until children have been subjected to severe forms of abuse and neglect to address their concerns, and we then make it our primary goal to keep children within the families which have mistreated them. We choose to define children victimized by abuse and neglect as "at risk of removal," when we know that removing children from their parents will often be their only salvation.

Why is it that family preservation policies have had such on-going appeal? Why have there been so few voices advocating for children's right to grow up in loving, nurturing homes and their related right to be removed from homes that don't fit that description?

Left and Right Perspectives

Left-leaning political groups tend to see poor and minority race families and communities as their constituency. They are committed to fighting class and race injustice and see child abuse and neglect as the end-product of such injustice. They tend to see the removal of children from troubled families for placement in more privileged foster or adoptive homes as one of the ultimate forms of exploitation. They also know that issues involving child abuse, child removal, and family preservation are politically potent. They can be used as rallying cries to unite and energize the politically powerless and to appeal to the politically powerful. Political passions can be roused by describing adoption as a form of child purchase or theft and by equating transracial adoption with racial genocide. Comparisons can be drawn to the days of slavery when black children were put up on the auction block for whites to buy. The threat that children will be victimized by abuse and neglect can be used to gouge money out of a reluctant political majority: those too stingy and short-sighted to invest appropriately in supportive social programs may react viscerally at the thought of a small child being tortured and untie the purse strings for programs that sound in child protection terms. Abuse and neglect can thus be the vehicle for getting some level of support for the poor, so long as family preservation reigns supreme.

Right-leaning political groups tend to be true believers in family autonomy. They want to limit government's intrusion on individual freedom, and they want to keep government expenses down. Their members don't like the idea of government interfering with their own parenting rights and are not inclined to assert responsibility for other people's children.[3] On the other hand, no one likes to see children suffer abuse or neglect, and everyone knows that there are long-term social costs involved when children do. Responding to child maltreatment with family preservation services has a lot of appeal.

Individuals and groups across the spectrum who do focus on children's interests tend at the same time to share many of the above values and political concerns. They worry about dealing with child maltreatment in a way that will have a discriminatory impact on poor people and on people from racial minority groups. They believe that limiting state intervention in the family helps protect individual freedom and societal diversity in ways that are important to the entire society. They also think that state intervention in too many cases may do more harm than good to the children involved, given the limited resources now devoted to CPS agencies, and the related risk that they may do little more than disrupt parenting relationships without actually improving children's situations.

Politics at Work

Our history with family preservation shows these politics at work. Time and again left and right have agreed that the proper way to respond to perceived crises in child abuse and neglect, and in the child welfare system, is to devote increased efforts to keeping children in their families of origin or, if that is impossible, then in their extended families, or their racial or ethnic groups, or their local communities.[4] The result has been to channel at least some increased funding and social services to those families, groups, and communities.

Thus in the 1970s there was agreement across the political spectrum on the nature of the foster care crisis and on the appropriate direction for change. Foster care was seen as damaging to children, given children's needs for continuity in nurturing relationships; and it was seen as unduly expensive. It was a time of fiscal constraint, with limited funding being made available for services to families. There was broad agreement that the appropriate solution was to make more efforts to keep more children at home. Left and right support enabled passage of the 1980 Adoption Assistance Act, which provided significant federal funding for state child welfare operations, and which required that as a condition for receiving this funding states respond to child maltreatment in the first instance with social services designed to support the family, rather than by removing the child and terminating parental rights.

There was also broad political support for the proposition that if children had to be removed from their biological parents, they should be placed with kin as a first preference, and if not with kin then within their racial group and their local community. From the late 1970s on kinship preference policies have become increasingly prevalent, with roughly one-third of all foster children in kinship care today. During the same period race-matching policies have required public agencies to place children in same-race foster and adoptive homes if at all possible, placing across racial lines only as a last resort, if at all. Foster care policies developed during this period have favored selecting foster families from the same community as the child's family of origin. Adoption policies developed that give preference to foster parents who have established a relationship with their foster child; in many communities today adoptions by foster parents account for more than half the adoptions out of the foster care system.

All these preference policies have helped channel funding and social services to impoverished families and communities during a period when general welfare and social service funding was being cut back. The children removed from families on grounds of abuse and neglect come disproportionately from the poorest families and communities in our society; they come disproportionately from racial minority groups. Accordingly, when money is devoted to family preservation services, money is channeled to these families, communities, and racial groups. When foster and adoptive stipends are paid to abused children's kin, neighbors, and racial look-alikes, these stipends are going disproportionately to the relatively poor and to racial minority group members. The services and stipends may seem far from generous. But they compare well to what exists in their absence. Foster parents are paid stipends that are significantly more generous than typical welfare stipends. Adoptive parents of "special needs" or "hard-to-place" children are entitled to adoption subsidies that roughly match foster stipends; and most children adopted from the foster care system qualify for these subsidies either by reason of mental or physical disability, or simply by reason of their minority race status.

The Intensive Family Preservation Services (IFPS) programs that became popular during this same period are a product of the same politics. IFPS was promoted by liberals as a way to do better by poor families and children without spending money. The idea was to work intensively for a relatively short period of time, devoting human and other resources to helping the family address its problems. IFPS was sold on the basis of a claim that it would keep children out of foster care; the reduction in foster care costs was supposed to more than pay for a few weeks of intensive services. Success was judged in the early days solely in terms of whether or not the programs succeeded in keeping children from being removed from their homes, without regard to whether they were still being abused or neglected, or any other measures of the children's well-being. This focus seems odd if IFPS is understood as a child welfare program, since the issue of well-being would obviously seem central. Also, since the primary goal of IFPS was to keep children from being removed, it seemed predictable that the very existence of the programs would be likely to reduce the number of removal decisions.[5] But this focus makes total sense if IFPS is looked at as political deal-making with respect to the allocation of scarce resources for poor people's services. If the foster care savings more than paid the costs of the family preservation services, then fiscal conservatives, social-welfare oriented liberals, and family values traditionalists could unite in celebration.

In 1993 The Family Preservation and Support Services Act was pushed through by child welfare groups in cooperation with others to provide significant new funding for family preservation.[6] One observer describes the dynamics of the ad hoc committee convened in connection with this effort by the Clinton Administration:

> The ad hoc committee was, however, decidedly less interested in specific child abuse and neglect services. Child abuse and neglect emerge from the committee's deliberations only as indicators of a need for family preservation services. . . . [F]amily preservation was firmly established as the future paradigm for serving families at risk of child abuse.[7]

Similar politics are at work in connection with new proposals promoted as child welfare reforms. Liberals press for subsidized guardianship as a long-term option for children who cannot return home. This would mean transforming kinship or other foster parents into permanent guardians who would be paid the equivalent of foster stipends but would be freed from the kind of monitoring that is supposed to go with foster parenting. The selling pitch includes the obvious money savings that would result from the elimination of monitoring.

Liberals press for the transformation of much of the current child protective system into a new "community partnership" system. The idea is to divert most of the abuse and neglect cases now dealt with by the formal state system to an informal, community-based system. Funds that have supported centralized government agencies would be freed up to support community-based agencies, and those agencies would devote their new resources to supporting families rather than treating parents as perpetrators. These kinds of new program proposals seem likely, if implemented, to significantly increase the resources for poor and minority communities in the form of family preservation services, foster, adoptive, and guardianship stipends, funding for community organizations, and employment opportunities working for these organizations. But it's not so clear that they will reduce child abuse and neglect.

With welfare reform, the appeal of this kind of political deal-making increases. The AFDC program—Aid for Families with Dependent Children—has functioned as the most significant family preservation and family support program this nation has ever had. In 1996 Congress changed it in order to move many parents off the welfare rolls. Many states had passed legislation along similar lines. As welfare stipends are reduced or cut off, the pressure increases to find other ways to channel support to the poor. It's no surprise that at child welfare conferences in recent years, talk of the impact of welfare reform has sometimes been coupled with talk of the potential support to be found in *child welfare* programs. It's no surprise that the 1997 Adoption and Safe Families Act, which received support across the political spectrum in Congress, provides new funding for family preservation, kinship care, and other traditions from our past, even as it seems to push in new directions.

Who Represents the Children?

There's no problem with political deal-making, so long as the important interests are being represented and served. But it's not clear that children's interests are being represented, or served. Once children are identified as victims of serious abuse or neglect, it is likely that

their interests would be better served by a system that placed a much
higher priority on moving them out of the homes in which they have
been victimized and placing them promptly in permanent adoptive
homes, with parents selected primarily on the basis of their ability to
provide a loving and safe environment.

People talk of a children's rights movement. But the brutal truth
is that children are economically and politically powerless. They are
dependent on adults, and adult political groups have generally not
taken up their cause.

LESSONS FROM THE BATTERED WOMEN'S MOVEMENT

Women, in contrast, have developed the kind of political and economic strength that powers social reform. As a result they have, in
the last few decades, transformed our society's understanding of the
problem of violence against women and radically changed our policies for dealing with such violence.

In the not too distant past, women's power situation in the family
had many parallels with their children's situation. Women were subject to men, as children were subject to their parents. Men who battered women were protected, as were abusive parents, first by doctrines of legal right, and later by doctrines of family autonomy and
privacy. Women were only marginally more free to leave the family
than were children, bound as they were by economic dependence
and social convention. Societal efforts to intervene in marital affairs
favored a therapeutic approach, with the goal being preservation of
the marriage and the family.

Starting in the 1970s, the battered women's movement set out to
challenge this state of affairs. Women's advocates argued that if men
were abusing their mates and making the home more like hell than
haven, this should not be understood as a private family affair. They
argued that society was responsible for women's dependent state and
should accordingly take responsibility for their protection. They argued that criminal laws used to deter men from assaulting strangers
on public streets, and to punish those who committed such assaults,
should be applied to men who beat on women in the privacy of the
home. Women's advocates were suspicious of social workers and
therapists, and suspicious of mediation and treatment as approaches

to achieving marital harmony. They worried that such soft approaches would reinforce the status quo and leave women at risk for continued victimization. They put their faith in police, prosecutors, and power. They argued that women had a right to be liberated from the men who abused them. They challenged the assumption that all marriages can and should be preserved, and argued that instead women should be empowered to escape abusive relationships. They pressed for legal and policy changes that would give women the ability to throw men out of the marital home and keep them out, and they promoted the creation of a shelter system that would give women the ability to leave the marital home safely.

Women's advocates have successfully pushed for many policy changes in this new direction over the past couple of decades. They have gotten changes in the criminal law so that men can be held criminally responsible for marital rape. They have gotten mandatory arrest policies in many jurisdictions, designed to force police to arrest men for assaults against their mates. They have gotten new prosecutorial policies designed to increase the likelihood that male batterers will be criminally convicted and punished. Battered women's shelters have been created so that women will have a place to go to escape abuse, where they can be kept safe from their mates and where they can be given support in constructing a new life on their own. Women's advocates have also persuaded legislatures to authorize, and courts to issue, protective orders designed to keep male abusers out of women's homes and lives. New "stalking" laws have been enacted to deter and punish men who refuse to leave women alone. Some jurisdictions have created special units which coordinate law enforcement activities with shelter and other supportive efforts in order to better protect and empower women.[8]

Research so far provides no definitive evidence that women are better off as a result of this new direction. This is not surprising, since the policies are relatively new, and social science in this area is complicated. Even when mandatory arrest policies exist they may not be enforced, and if enforced they may not be followed up by effective prosecution and punishment.[9] Indeed, for all the progress women's advocates have made, it is clear that they have only begun to change the traditional pattern of official unresponsiveness to male battering. So there is no way yet that research *could* tell us much about what the impact of systematic policies penalizing male batterers and protecting their victims would be.

But there has been little dispute within the battered women's movement, or more generally, that these steps in the direction of punishing male perpetrators and liberating their female victims are a move in the right direction for women. Women's advocates don't feel they need to wait for more definitive research, or that they can afford to. Doubts about the strategy are voiced only at the periphery. There is dispute, for example, about whether "no-drop" prosecution policies, which mandate the prosecution of male perpetrators whether or not their victims want to press charges, are consistent with the new emphasis on women's empowerment. There is doubt about the relative efficacy of certain criminal penalties, as compared, for example, to employer sanctions for employees who batter. But there is no doubt about the fundamental direction of the movement.[10] No one argues that the appropriate response to wife battering is to redouble efforts to keep the wife in the home and her marriage intact.

"Domestic violence" is the phrase commonly used to describe the problem that the battered women's movement has taken on. But the fact is that women have not mounted a generalized challenge to violence in the home. They have focused their efforts on violence against *women*, largely ignoring violence and other forms of maltreatment involving *children*. The battered women's movement tends to pay attention to children only when, as is often the case, the man's violence is directed against both a woman and her child, or when children witness violence against their mothers. In these circumstances the movement has challenged men's rights to abuse power, and to parent, while at the same time trying to protect women's rights to parent. Thus women's advocates have argued that when families separate or divorce, male batterers should be denied custody in favor of their wives and their visitation rights should be limited if not extinguished; they have argued that when children are abused by their fathers, or their mothers' boyfriends, the state should punish the actively abusive male. But women's advocates have opposed removing children from the mother's custody solely on the grounds of her failure to protect them against abuse, and even in cases when the mother is directly responsible for abuse.

So while women's advocates have radically changed attitudes and policies concerning violence against women, their movement has left the world of child maltreatment relatively untouched. Here attitudes remain largely mired in the past. Parents who abuse and neglect children are treated largely as victims in need of services and treatment, not perpetrators in need of incapacitation and deterrence. Families are to be preserved not separated. Children victimized by their parents are described as children "at risk of removal," rather than children in need of liberation. As discussed in chapter 6, many new child welfare programs designed to address abuse and neglect place renewed emphasis on the old values. These programs encourage social workers to focus on family strengths, as opposed to family dysfunction, and to see all parents as capable of providing good parenting so long as they are given appropriate support. While women press for criminalization of male violence against women, "Community Partnership" advocates argue that we should avoid stigmatizing parents as perpetrators by investigating them for maltreatment, or listing their names on child abuse registries.

Women's reluctance to directly address child abuse and neglect is understandable. Women are the primary custodians for children in our society. This is particularly true in poor and racial minority groups, where single parenting is the norm, and where abuse and neglect rates are highest. Not surprisingly, women are disproportionately responsible, as compared to men, for child maltreatment, and are responsible for three-fourths of all fatal and very serious injuries, although men are disproportionately responsible for certain forms of physical abuse and for sexual abuse.[11] Even when men commit physical acts of abuse, a woman will often be in some sense responsible, in that the child was formally in her custody and she failed to provide protection. Advancement of children's interests in being protected against abuse and neglect may easily be seen as in conflict with women's own interests as parents.

Child maltreatment and woman battering are not, of course, exact equivalents. There are differences other than power politics that might explain the differences in our social attitudes and policies. Children are *necessarily* dependent. We can't expect them to make new lives for themselves by simply separating them from their abusers and finding them shelter and employment. If the state takes them from their parents then the state will have to figure out what to do with them.

But in the end the parallels seem more powerful than the differences. For the state to provide real help to any given battered woman, it will usually have to play a variety of supportive roles over a significant period of time. At the same time, if the state steps in to remove a child from one set of parents, it can step out again. The state doesn't have to assume the parenting role on an ongoing basis, as it does when it keeps children in long-term foster or institutional care. It can instead transfer the child to a new set of adoptive parents, giving them full parenting responsibility.

Richard Gelles, Research Director of the Center for the Study of Youth Policy, at the University of Pennsylvania School of Social Work, argues that people commit unspeakable acts against weaker members of their families in large part because they can get away with it.[12] They can get away with it because it happens behind closed doors, and because they suffer none of the penalties that would apply if they committed comparable acts upon nonfamily members. We need to change this reality for children just as we do for women.

POLITICS FOR THE FUTURE

The traditional left-right deal-making in child welfare matters doesn't seem to have served either side's interests very well. The left has gotten some increased resources for impoverished families and communities but they are still far too limited. Even in the face of children threatened with abusive treatment, the right is far more ready to write requirements for family support services onto paper than it is to fund them.

The right may have thought that it was managing to promote family values without having to spend much money, but it seems to have made a poor bargain. Intervention after the fact of child maltreatment is costly. Family preservation services and related treatment programs, foster care, and group homes are expensive, as are the court costs related to removing a child and monitoring the CPS system's compliance with the law during a child's life in foster care.[13] Direct government expenditures for child welfare amounted to about $11.2 billion in 1995, including investigations, casework services, foster care, and adoption assistance. Per capita costs of foster care placements, group homes, and residential treatment centers taken together approach $22,000 per year.[14] Long-term costs are even more significant. Studies link child maltreatment with an increased risk of low academic achievement, drug use, teen pregnancy, juvenile delinquency, and adult criminality. The cost consequences include mental health and substance abuse treatment programs, police and court interventions, correctional facilities, public assistance programs, and lost productivity. Child abuse and neglect are problems not just for the children who suffer, but for the society that will pay the costs of their foster and institutional care, and of their future unemployment, drug use, criminal activity, and maltreatment of the next generation.

New political understandings and alignments may be in the works. Left and right have joined forces in recent years to pass laws and promote policies that seem to place a new priority on ensuring that children grow up in loving, nurturing families. The Multiethnic Placement Act has eliminated—at least on paper—racial barriers to foster and adoptive placement. While the Adoption and Safe Families Act has some significant flaws and gaps, there's no denying that it represents a new spirit at work in Congress. Throughout the country there seems to be widespread support for making child welfare policies more truly child-centered.

Children have no voice and no vote. The challenge is to figure out how nonetheless to ensure that their interests count.[15] Liberals should recognize that children deserve protection as much as the other powerless and exploited groups whose interests they have promoted. Conservatives should recognize that policies which do more to support families and prevent child maltreatment are more truly cost-effective than the programs of the day.

THE PROBLEM

3. MODERN-DAY ORPHANS

Huge numbers of children are growing up in this country without what all children need—true parenting. Almost all of them have parents in the legal sense—people who by virtue of procreation have the legal rights and responsibilities of parents. Many of them also have foster parents, or group home parents, or other institutional caretakers. But however many official parents they may have, they are without the parents they need. They are living in various states of abuse and neglect, without the nurturing care that children require to thrive.

In 1990 the U.S. Advisory Board on Child Abuse and Neglect issued its first report, a report that designated child abuse and neglect in the United States a "national emergency."[1] Things have gotten worse since. Increasing numbers of children are subject to brutal forms of physical abuse resulting in serious injury, disability, and death. Increasing numbers are subject to extreme forms of neglect that are often equally destructive of body and mind. Increasing numbers are growing up in foster care, and in group homes or institutions.

How do we decide how much abuse and neglect is too much? Civilizations throughout history have subjected some of their children to various forms of horrible abuse.[2] And in this country today many adults as well as children live in daily fear of physical abuse and other forms of maltreatment.

But there are particular problems involved in subjecting our children to maltreatment. Since children need good parenting to grow up healthy and whole, when we mistreat them we risk not only destroying their childhood but damaging their entire future lives. Their loss is thus arguably greater than when adults are abused, and the damage to the whole community is more devastating. Children subject to abuse and neglect are high-risk children, unusually likely to suffer in the future and to inflict suffering on others. In vastly disproportionate numbers they will show up as adults in prisons and homeless shelters and in the ranks of the unemployed. They will have a propensity to turn to alcohol and drugs for comfort and will be unusually likely to live the troubled lives characteristic of those who struggle with substance abuse. In their adult relationships many will become perpetrators or victims of domestic violence. As parents many will perpetuate the cycle of abuse and neglect. As the U.S. Advisory Board on Child Abuse and Neglect said in that same 1990 report: "Protection of children from harm is not just an ethical duty: it is a matter of national survival."[3]

We could do something about it. We could do more in the way of prevention. And when we fail in prevention, we could do more to protect children against ongoing abuse and neglect, and do more to enable them to overcome the early damage they suffered. And we know what to do, if these are our goals. The child welfare experts have long known that children subject to abuse or neglect do better when removed to foster or institutional care than they do in their families of origin. They do better yet when placed in adoptive homes. The earlier they are removed from damaging homes and placed in permanent nurturing homes, the better they do. The reasons that early removal and early adoptive placement work best are obvious and well-supported in the research. Children require active nurturing and healthy parenting relationships in their early months and years, in order to develop normally, both intellectually and emotionally.

All this remains a relatively well-kept secret, however, since those in the know have generally chosen not to call attention to information that gives the lie to claims that family preservation and family reunification policies serve children's best interests.

ABUSE AND NEGLECT
The Amount

The available statistics give some sense of the extent and nature of the child maltreatment problem. Taken together, the different measures of abuse and neglect provide a sobering picture.

Estimates indicate that more than three million children a year are subjected to serious forms of abuse and neglect. There are no hard figures available: available instruments for measuring the over-all level of maltreatment are flawed and limited; definitions of mal-treatment vary, and decisions as to whether maltreatment has oc-curred involve subjective judgment.[4] But those who make it their business to collect and analyze the data tell us that the number is in the three million range, and growing. This number is based both on studies that rely on community surveys to assess the actual incidence of maltreatment, and on studies that rely on official statistics maintained by the various states' Child Protection Services (CPS) systems.[5]

The most important "incidence" studies are the National Inci-dence Studies conducted by Westat for the National Center on Child Abuse and Neglect in 1979–80 (NIS-1), 1986 (NIS-2), and 1993–94 (NIS-3). The NIS-3 study indicates that in 1993 close to three million children, one in every twenty-four children in the United States, were victims of child maltreatment.[6]

Over three million children a year are reported to state CPS au-thorities as a result of suspected abuse or neglect.[7] While only about one million of these cases are "substantiated" as actually involving maltreatment, the evidence indicates that this one million figure rep-resents a gross underestimate of the actual amount of serious mal-treatment, and that the NIS-3 incidence figure of three million is closer to the real amount. Only a portion of all cases of serious mal-treatment are ever reported to CPS: most instances of abuse and ne-glect occur in the privacy of the home, and many of them never come to the attention of the professionals and public officials with man-dated reporting obligations; also many mandated reporters fail to re-port suspected cases of abuse and neglect.[8] Fewer than half of the children who have died as a result of maltreatment had come to the attention of state authorities before their deaths.[9] The latest National

Incidence Study reveals that CPS investigated only a minority of the cases of children NIS found abused or neglected, only one-third of the cases of children found demonstrably endangered by abuse or neglect, and only slightly more than one-fourth of the children who were seriously harmed or injured by abuse or neglect.[10]

Of the maltreatment cases that are reported, only a portion of those that in fact involve serious maltreatment end up officially designated as substantiated. CPS authorities have limited resources to investigate cases, and even more limited resources to provide services to families when abuse and neglect claims are substantiated. CPS will often simply not substantiate cases unless the maltreatment is particularly egregious or immediately threatening to the child's safety. Even in these more serious cases, the facts may be hard to prove with the degree of certainty that laws and policies favoring family preservation require. As maltreatment reports have increased in recent years, without any comparable increase in CPS resources, the agencies have resorted to triage, by raising the threshold for substantiating maltreatment claims. While reports of abuse and neglect have skyrocketed, the number of CPS investigations have remained stable.[11] Twenty years ago, two-thirds of all reported cases were substantiated, whereas today only one-third are.[12] The Child Welfare League of America reports that 45 percent of state administrators say that triage policies have caused child abuse and neglect reports to go uninvestigated that would have been investigated five years ago.[13] Some indication of the "under-substantiation" problem is revealed by the fact that *fully 60 percent* of the parents named in cases of suspected but unsubstantiated maltreatment show up in the CPS system again, based on new allegations.[14]

Self-report surveys indicate that parents are responsible for much higher rates of physically abusive behavior than either the NIS or the CPS systems reflect—sixteen times higher than the rates of physical abuse reported to CPS officials.[15]

Rates have been rising at a dramatic rate in the last two decades. Maltreatment rates as measured by the National Incidence Studies *doubled* between 1986 and 1993.[16] Significantly, it is the most serious maltreatment cases that are growing at the most rapid rate, having *quadrupled* between 1986 and 1993.[17] Homicide is among the leading causes of childhood death in the United States today.[18] Roughly two thousand children are estimated to die annually as a result of abuse and neglect.[19]

Experts believe that although some portion of this rise might be due to a change in public consciousness about maltreatment, and in related reporting practices and rates, much of it reflects an *actual* increase in maltreatment caused by increases in poverty and substance abuse during this period.[20]

The youngest children are those most at risk. Since it is the youngest children who have the least opportunity to be observed by those who might suspect and report maltreatment, it is likely that they are subject to even more disproportionate rates of maltreatment than the reports reveal.

Homicide is *the* leading cause of infant death due to injury. Infant homicide rates have been growing significantly in the last two decades, and studies indicate they are significantly underreported even though death gives the related maltreatment more visibility than maltreatment that results in nonfatal forms of injury.[21] *Roughly 80 percent of maltreatment-related fatalities involved children under five years of age, and 40 percent involved infants under one year.*[22]

About one-half of the maltreated children are officially categorized as neglected, and one-quarter as physically abused, with smaller percentages categorized as sexually abused, as emotionally abused, and as suffering other forms of maltreatment. Official reports show that 53 percent of all victims are white, 27 percent African-American, and 11 percent Hispanic. These reports indicate that African-American and Native American children are abused and neglected at a rate of almost twice their proportions in the national population, a fact that is not surprising given the strong correlation between poverty and maltreatment.[23] (See chapter 10.)

The Severity

Measures of the amount of abuse and neglect mean little if we don't know what is included in these categories. After all, no parent is perfect. Many parents that most would agree satisfy the "good enough" standard are guilty at times of what some might term "abuse" or "neglect." Family preservation advocates argue that parents are often reported and investigated, and their cases substantiated, on the basis of minor concerns that should not trigger abuse and neglect charges or findings. They argue that CPS workers impose middle-class white standards in judging impoverished parents from other races and cultures. They assert the importance of cultural sensitivity to different traditions of child discipline, implying that many cases categorized as physical abuse amount to nothing more than disciplinary spankings imposed by loving parents who have only their child's best interests at heart. They note that the majority of maltreatment cases are cases of neglect, which they belittle as involving little more than dirty houses or latchkey children who are on their own for a few hours after school solely because their parents cannot afford child care. They say that neglect charges are often based on nothing more than the circumstances of poverty characterizing the parents' lives.

Assessing the severity of child abuse and neglect, as reflected in CPS reports and other measures, is far from an exact science, but the best available information indicates that the above claims miss the mark. Obviously mistakes get made. And obviously poverty pushes some parents into situations in which it is difficult to provide adequately for their children however hard they may try. But there are many reasons to conclude that when CPS substantiates abuse or neglect, or NIS studies conclude children are demonstrably endangered, it is more typical than aberrational to find children who have been subject to brutal forms of physical abuse, or to destructive forms of sexual exploitation, or to forms of neglect that deny the fundamentals necessary for children to thrive.

First, state law has defined abuse and neglect in ways that are designed to exclude all but the more serious forms of maltreatment. Legislators and judges have together narrowed the definitions in reaction to earlier eras when many thought the categories were overly vague and inclusive. Statutes in the majority of states limit child abuse to acts that cause or threaten to cause lasting harm to the child. Neglect is generally defined in ways that limit it to abandonment, or extreme forms of parental negligence or incompetence that similarly put the child at risk of lasting harm.[24] Second, NIS and other systems designed to measure actual maltreatment use definitions that are similarly strict. Third, some measures rely on cases in which children have suffered damage that is impossible to minimize, such as death.

Finally, informed experts from both inside and outside the CPS system testify to the fact that the abuse and neglect cases substantiated by today's CPS workers are far more serious than those of earlier eras and typically involve severe forms of harm and deprivation. They cite increases in poverty and decreases in social services, together with increases in substance abuse, particularly the abuse of crack/cocaine, as causal factors. They also cite the CPS system's inability to process the increased number of maltreatment cases and its resulting concentration on only the most serious. A 1997 study in Alameda County, California gives a flavor for the nature of today's CPS caseload:

> Most alarming is the complexity of the cases coming to the attention of the child welfare services system. These are not families who need assistance with their parenting practices alone. Instead, the majority of these cases are deeply troubled by substance abuse, criminal histories, mental health challenges, and housing problems.[25]

Neglect

Neglect is generally defined as involving negligence or omissions to act that threaten the child's health or welfare. It includes emotional as well as physical neglect, and may involve abandonment, delay or refusal of health care, inadequate supervision, inadequate nutrition, or starvation.[26] The Association for Children of New Jersey reviewed a sample of cases in which the children were placed in foster care over a one-year period (April 1992 to April 1993). In the report on their findings, *Stolen Children*, some "typical cases" are described briefly—"neither the best nor the worst cases but . . . the average situations" that trigger decisions to remove a child. Two of them help illustrate what this kind of neglect looks like:

Tyrone—Age 8
Tyrone was placed into foster care with his three younger siblings on an emergency basis. The Department of Youth and Family Services received a call from neighbors saying that four young children had been left alone for several days, a frequent occurrence. When the DYFS

caseworker arrived at the apartment with the police, they found 8-year-old Tyrone in charge of his three younger siblings, ages 4, 2 and 1. The apartment was in a shambles, there was no food, and the children couldn't remember when they last saw their mother. His younger siblings called Tyrone "Mommy."

Before taking the children to a foster home, the caseworker drove Tyrone around the neighborhood to try to locate other family members. At his grandmother's apartment, they learned she had moved out of state. They left a note for Tyrone's father at his apartment. While looking for another relative, they saw Tyrone's mother coming out of a bar. She refused to talk to the caseworker, telling her to do what she wanted with the children. The children were placed. . . .

Betsy—Age 10

Ten-year-old Betsy and her younger brother had been homeless with their mother for several weeks, living with friends, relatives and on the street, when their mother sent them to stay with a friend across town. When they got there, they discovered that the friend had moved away. Uncertain of what to do and how to find their mother, the two children spent three days in the hallway of the apartment building until someone noticed them and called DYFS. It wasn't the first time that DYFS had gotten involved. In fact, Betsy and her brother had been known to DYFS off and on for six years, after at least four complaints that they were being neglected, left alone or physically abused by their mother.

DYFS took the children to a foster home and began to search for their mother and other relatives. Two weeks later, their mother finally contacted the DYFS office but refused to give her address or to see her children.[27]

Many who concede the seriousness of physical and sexual abuse contend that the neglect category sweeps in all sorts of "minor problem" and "mere poverty" cases. Family preservation advocates often treat it as self-evident that neglect cases are insufficiently serious to warrant state intervention, citing the fact that neglect accounts for a majority of all substantiated cases as proof that the CPS system intervenes unduly in the family.

Tragic mistakes do get made. And parents are sometimes charged with neglect when the circumstances of poverty have kept them from providing the kind of supervision or housing that social workers deem essential. But available evidence indicates that the great preponderance of today's neglect cases pose extremely serious threats to children's welfare. Many cases involve a combination of abuse and neglect, or circumstances that could fall into either category. CPS workers often opt to use the neglect category because the requisite proof is easier to make out. But even in cases of pure "neglect," the type of neglect today's CPS workers take seriously is likely to be extreme and chronic, and as a result to cause harm.[28]

Infants and young children require attentive, active care simply to survive, much less thrive. They also require social interaction with a responsive caretaker to develop normally, both cognitively and emotionally. Developmental psychology has been delivering the same message from Bowlby's era to date: children's relationships with nurturing parent figures are essential to their development. (See "The Impact on Children" below.)

Outcome studies have confirmed that children deprived of active nurturing don't do well, giving the lie to any notion that neglect should be thought of as minor. Neglect causes permanent emotional damage and cognitive deficits. The immediate and long-term damage is comparable to that caused by physical and sexual abuse.[29] Neglect causes problems that are thought particularly difficult to remedy.[30] *And neglect cases account for almost half of maltreatment-related deaths.*[31]

Substance abuse cases account for an overwhelming percentage of all CPS cases, including the neglect cases. A look at the substance abuse piece of the problem is helpful in understanding the seriousness of the maltreatment problem generally and of the neglect category in particular.[32]

SUBSTANCE ABUSE: AT THE HEART OF THE PROBLEM

Substance abuse is at the heart of the problem. It causes or exacerbates abuse and neglect in the overwhelming majority of cases. And it has had a catastrophic impact on the child welfare system's capacity to protect children. A recent two-year national study of the relation between substance abuse and child maltreatment, conducted by the National Center on Addiction and Substance Abuse (CASA), finds:

> Parental drug abuse and alcohol addiction has triggered an explosion in child abuse and neglect that has thrown the child welfare system into a state of chaos, collapse and calamity, leaving behind a wreckage of millions of children.[33]

The CASA Report finds the child welfare and family court systems completely inadequate to the task of addressing the problem. And it concludes that the children of drug- and alcohol-abusing parents have been left with "no safe haven," calling them "the most vulnerable and endangered individuals in America."[34] Alcohol and crack/cocaine are the chief offenders. Methamphetamine and marijuana also contribute significantly. Multiple drug use and abuse is the common pattern, with alcohol abuse usually combined with illicit drug abuse.[35]

Experts with a variety of perspectives on the CPS system join forces in pointing to substance abuse as one of the key factors responsible for the increase in severe forms of abuse and neglect. Informed estimates indicate that 70 to 80 percent of the CPS caseload consists of cases in which the parents are abusing drugs or alcohol or both.[36] The overwhelming preponderance (88 percent) of CPS programs surveyed in 1997 named substance abuse as one of the top two problems in families reported for maltreatment.[37] The CASA Report found substance abuse "the chief culprit" accounting for "at least 70 and perhaps 90 percent" of child welfare costs.[38] Many women are abusing legal and illegal drugs during pregnancy in ways that affect the health and development of their fetuses. Many children who have been exposed to drugs in utero are affected in ways that make them difficult to parent, which in turn increases their risk of being maltreated. Many are born impaired by drugs in ways that will negatively affect them for life, even if they receive superior parenting. Many children are growing up with parents whose parenting capacities are drastically affected by substance abuse.

The Impact of Drugs on Children Exposed During Pregnancy

The rates of alcohol and drug use during pregnancy vary enormously depending on the area, and on the socioeconomic status of the group involved; good hard numbers are generally unavailable. But experts provide rough estimates that give a sense of the scope of the problem.[39] Surveys indicate that roughly 11 percent of all pregnant women use illicit drugs during pregnancy. One-half to three-quarters of a million infants are thought to be born each year who have been exposed to one or more illicit drugs in utero. When the legal drugs alcohol and tobacco are added, the figure rises to more than one and a half million.[40]

The CASA Report found prenatal substance use and abuse on the rise; a study in Sacramento County, California, found that the percentage of women whose newborns tested positive for alcohol and drugs increased from 9.2 percent to 15.2 percent between 1990 and 1992.[41]

Relatively recent statewide surveys indicate a rate of cocaine use among pregnant women ranging from a low of 0.7 percent in Utah to a high of 2.6 percent in Rhode Island. Surveys at selected hospitals show much higher rates: 46 percent in San Francisco, 18 percent in Boston, 10 percent in New York City.[42] One report on births in the United States from 1984 through 1992 indicates that 1–2 percent, or 35,000 to 70,000 infants were born cocaine-exposed; other estimates indicate that as many as 375,000 babies exposed to cocaine in the womb are born in the United States each year.[43] Recent indications that crack/cocaine use is going down do not seem to apply to inner city minority groups, where prevalence rates range up to 50 percent of women of child-bearing age.[44]

Use and abuse of legal drugs such as alcohol and tobacco is significantly more prevalent than illicit drug use and overall has a greater impact on fetal health and development.[45] As noted above, poly drug abuse is typical, with those who abuse alcohol or cocaine often abusing it in combination with one or more other licit or illicit drugs.

How *much* harm all this drug use does to the growing fetus depends on the extent of use, as well as the drug or drugs involved. Occasional light use of alcohol, tobacco, or illicit drugs may have no harmful impact. Heavy or continuous use of one or more of these drugs puts the growing fetus at risk for significant harm. We don't know much about the rates of *serious* substance abuse, but we know enough to know that all too many babies are affected by their mothers' substance abuse during pregnancy in ways that put them at risk for lifelong problems. A recent governmental report sums up the research as to the impact of substance use and abuse during pregnancy as follows:

> Research has shown that illicit drug use during pregnancy is associated with poor pregnancy outcomes and child development problems, including preterm delivery, increased incidence of stillbirth and neonatal mortality, low birth weight, decreased size for gestational age or head circumference, incidence of sudden infant death, and long-term developmental neurobehavioral disabilities in infants. Alcohol use during pregnancy has also been correlated with a number of adverse obstetric and neonatal consequences, such as spontaneous abortions, low birthweight infants, and infants with fetal alcohol syndrome. Additionally, hazards associated with cigarette use during pregnancy include low birth weight, fetal and neonatal mortality, fetal distress, and long-term mental and growth retardation.[46]

Cocaine blocks the flow of oxygen and nutrients to growing fetal tissue and can affect neurological development. Cocaine use is associated with higher than average rates of spontaneous abortion, premature birth, cardiac abnormalities, small brain hemorrhages, and other abnormalities. Infants exposed to cocaine before birth tend to be smaller, and in some studies they are reported to have smaller than average heads.[47] Women who use crack/cocaine are "more than twice as likely to deliver a low birth weight infant (very early, very wasted or both) than socially matched controls. Users are three times as likely to . . . deliver an infant with a low . . . Apgar score." After delivery the babies of crack users are less autonomically stable, have poorer fine and gross motor function, and have more abnormal reflex reactions. The more cocaine used, the worse the short-term neurological outcome.[48] Crack babies may have permanent changes in their brain-wave patterns with unknown long-term results.[49]

The research to date gives us only limited information about the developmental prospects for children exposed to cocaine in the womb. Recent research has tended to negate some of the more hysterical claims made a decade ago, when the crack baby phenomenon hit the nation's consciousness, and newspapers featured stories indicating that these children were permanently brain-damaged in ways that would inevitably affect their future learning and development. Controlled studies following cocaine-exposed infants into their early childhood years have failed to confirm the kind of dramatic harm predicted. But these studies, relying on comparisons with control samples of children in similar socioeconomic circumstances, can't negate the concern that cocaine exposure puts children at significant risk. The children in the control groups are subject to all kinds of harmful substances and other influences themselves, making it extremely hard to identify the impact that cocaine might have had. No long-term outcome studies are yet available. And the existing research, discussed below, provides reason for concern as to the children's long-term prospects. Taken as a whole, the research indicates that while we don't know everything we could know about the long-term impact of prenatal cocaine exposure, there is reason to believe that these children are at risk for developmental problems, and that they will need special parenting care in order to prosper. (See also chapter 9.)

Studies of children exposed to cocaine during pregnancy indicate certain behavioral differences during early infancy and childhood that give reason for concern. And all these differences pose parenting challenges which in turn increase the risk of developmental problems, as well as of maltreatment.

As newborns they tend to be "unresponsive and cranky—stiffening at a mother's touch, crying at the sound of voices." As they grow older there may be other problems:

They often have symptoms of attention deficit disorder—impulsiveness, distractability, and hyperactivity. They have been described as intolerant of frustration, easily startled, and both difficult to arouse and too easily overexcited once they are aroused. One study found impaired habituation—inability to ignore a repeated stimulus and recover interest when a new one is introduced.[50]

A recent study at Brown University analyzing available research indicates they suffer from slowed language development, learning disabilities, and slightly reduced IQ.[51] The research also shows that prenatal cocaine exposure has an impact on behavior at the preschool age, indicating that the children are at risk for ongoing developmental problems.[52] The recent Toronto Adoption Study helps separate out the effects of prenatal cocaine exposure from the effects of the negative environment to which most cocaine-exposed infants are subject when they go home with their drug-using parents. This study compared infants exposed during pregnancy and placed with adoptive parents soon after birth, with unexposed infants growing up with parents who were matched for socioeconomic, IQ, and other relevant characteristics. It also controlled for the effect of prematurity, which may itself be caused by cocaine use in pregnancy. The study concluded that prenatal exposure caused clinically significant language delay and decreased IQ in preschool age children.[53]

There is only one longitudinal, prospective study of school-age children prenatally exposed to cocaine and other drugs. A controlled study, involving two groups of 4- to 6-year-old children growing up in the Chicago inner city, it assesses the impact on children in the experimental group of their mothers' use of cocaine during pregnancy, together with the other drugs most of these women had also used, including marijuana, alcohol, and/or tobacco. It found the IQ scores for both groups at the lower end of the normal range, with a steady decline over the three-year period, reflecting the negative effect of the impoverished environment. Continued drug use by the mother after pregnancy had a negative impact on IQ scores. It found that prenatal drug exposure had a significant impact on behaviors that were troubling in terms of the children's potential for learning:

> The picture of the drug-exposed child that emerged . . . was one in which the child is poorly organized, has trouble regulating his behavior, has trouble staying on track and completing a task, has higher activity levels, has low frustration levels and poor tolerance for stimula-

tion . . . , and experiences more anxiety and depression. These children also are reported to not respond to traditional behavioral interventions, especially those with negative connotations.

The study found "a strong direct effect on the children's behavior at four to six years of age, with prenatally exposed children showing much higher rates and levels of behavioral problems with low thresholds for stimulation, a low tolerance for frustration, and difficulty with self-regulation."[54]

Of all the drugs commonly used during pregnancy, alcohol may present the clearest case of destructive impact.[55] Drinking during pregnancy is the primary cause of preventable mental retardation in this country. Fetal alcohol syndrome is also associated with distinct facial malformations, microcephaly and severe learning disorders.

Heroin use can lead to neonatál addiction. The resulting withdrawal syndrome can lead to death if not treated.[56]

Extensive use of tobacco during pregnancy affects fetal development, causes low-weight babies, and puts the child at risk for mental disabilities. But it does not have the kind of devastating impact on the mother's capacity to care for the baby after birth that alcohol and illicit drugs have. And it is the interaction between substance-exposed children's special parenting needs and their parents' impaired capacity that is central to the most serious problems that substance abuse poses for children.

The Impact of Drugs on Parenting

Most drug- or alcohol-exposed babies will go home from the hospital with their mothers, unless their mothers choose not to take them home. The parents will often be provided with little or nothing in the way of treatment or other services.[57] Many of the children will be subsequently removed because of abuse and neglect. A recent California study of infants entering foster care during their first year of life showed that 69 percent were prenatally exposed to drugs, with 86 percent of this group exposed to cocaine. This study revealed that substance abuse was the dominant problem in cases in which infants were removed from home: 84 percent of the mothers were abusing alcohol or drugs, with crack/cocaine the primary drug of choice. Almost all the cases—97 percent—in which infants had been removed, then returned to their mothers, and then were removed again to foster care, involved mothers with substance abuse problems prior to the initial removal of the baby.[58] Surveys in Washington state reported that over 40 percent of children placed in foster care were born to mothers who abused alcohol or other drugs during pregnancy.[59] Recent research indicates that drug-exposed children may now constitute a majority of all children in foster care.[60]

A 1994 governmental report indicates that 12.8 million children under eighteen years of age, or 18 percent of all in this age group, live with a parent who has used illicit drugs in the past year. Approximately 6 million, or 9 percent, live with parents who have used illicit drugs in the past month.[61] A 1996 national survey indicates that 8.3 million or 11 percent of all children in the United States live in households in which at least one parent is either alcoholic or abusing illicit drugs or both.[62]

Experts on substance abuse often describe those trapped in patterns of abuse as inherently unfit to provide the basics of what parenting demands. Barry Zuckerman, Chief of Pediatrics at Boston Medical Center, Professor and Chairman of Pediatrics at Boston University School of Medicine, and an expert on drug addiction and related child welfare issues, writes:

> Heavy use of drugs—especially actual addiction—interferes with a mother's ability to provide the consistent nurturing and caregiving that promote children's development, self-esteem, and ability to regulate their affect or impulses.[63]

Judy Howard, a professor of pediatrics at UCLA who has done extensive research over the years and worked in connection with projects promoting comprehensive services for pregnant addicts and their offspring, writes:

> Parents who use drugs heavily comprise a group that has enormous difficulty consistently engaging with their children. . . . The nature of addiction, in and of itself, propels users to consider their own needs first—obtaining their next fix is their primary goal. Thus, attending to

the ongoing and daily basic physical requirements of a newborn infant or young child, not to mention the child's emotional need for nurturing, seems incompatible with the heavy use of drugs.[64]

A 1997 federal government report writes:

Parental drug abuse is associated with an increased risk of maladjustment in children. Research has provided empirical evidence that children with drug-abusing parents—in particular with drug-abusing mothers—are at greater risk than their peers for alcohol and drug use, delinquency, poor school performance, as well as depression and other psychiatric disorders. . . . Studies have shown that parents who abuse drugs tend to provide inadequate nurturing and guidance, and to provide their children with maladaptive models of coping skills.[65]

Many say that neglect is almost inevitable in these families.[66] The CASA Report states:

Many alcoholics and addicts neglect their children because they can think of only one goal: getting their next high. Addicts develop a "relationship" with alcohol and illegal drugs and their energy and resources focus on maintaining that relationship. Crack addicts who are in recovery report that when they wanted to get high, they could think of nothing else and would stop at nothing, including selling their bodies or their children's, in order to get the drug and use it. Commonly, children end up "parenting" their own parents, taking care of them and running the household.[67]

One study found that 100 percent of children living with drug-using mothers showed insecure attachments, a finding previously seen only in children already identified as abused and neglected.[68]

Physical abuse is also a problem. A recent study of domestic violence showed that 92 percent of the assailants had used drugs or alcohol on the day of the assault.[69] Half of all violent crime is connected with alcohol abuse.[70] In 1994, for example, a study found that in almost three quarters of New York City's cases of child abuse fatalities, one or both of the child's parents were drug-addicted; almost 30 percent of the fatality cases involved babies who had tested positive for drugs at birth.[71]

Cocaine is thought to have a particularly virulent impact on parental functioning:

> [T]he reality is that crack—more than almost any other factor—nullifies a woman's maternal instincts, causing her to neglect the most basic needs of her children, in both the prenatal and postnatal stages. In New York, for instance, the introduction of crack set off a horrifying epidemic of child abuse and neglect, with the number of reported cases soaring from 36,305 in 1985 to 59,353 in 1989.[72]

In the District of Columbia Family Court, drug tests of families with abused and neglected children in 1995 revealed that two in three parents tested positive for cocaine.[73]

The Interaction Between the Drug-Exposed Infant and the Drug-Abusing Parent

Although studies indicate that babies born drug-exposed or drug-impaired can very likely do relatively well in life with early intervention and supportive services (see chapter 9), *this research should not be taken to mean that these babies are problem-free. Many of them will be difficult to parent, which will increase their risk of being maltreated. Many will need much more care and special treatment than the average child, not just during infancy but throughout childhood, if they are to overcome some of the damage caused by early drug or alcohol exposure. Many will be damaged for life even if they receive superior parenting. None of them are likely to get the kind of special parenting they need from their birth parents.*

Experts on drug-exposed and drug-impaired infants describe babies who would present a major parenting challenge in the best of circumstances. These babies often shrink from human contact rather than instinctively engaging in the kind of social interaction that triggers a parent's response and affection. They are unusually cranky, needy, and demanding. Ira Chasnoff, one of the nation's leading experts on the impact of prenatal substance abuse, sums up the picture:

Infants prenatally exposed to drugs may be difficult to care for because of significant feeding and sleeping problems, hyperirritability, and hypersensitivity to touch, movement and eye contact. They may spend their time in bouts of inconsolable crying, being very irritable, or being unresponsive in a deep sleep.[74]

To match such children, whose care demands exceptional patience, effort, emotional maturity, and fortitude, with drug-abusing parents, even those with the best intentions, seems a recipe for disaster. Yet this is the match that family preservation policies provide on a systematic basis. Experts regularly describe these children as subject to the double jeopardy of prenatal damage and postnatal maltreatment.[75] A medically trained director of child abuse programs describes the problem as follows:

Although mothers often promise to cease use of drugs if their infant is discharged home with them, it is rare for women to stop drug use after delivery. The postpartum period is in fact a time of increased risk for drug use. It is frustrating and unrewarding for parents to care for babies who are irritable, sleep less than an hour, do not cuddle, do not suck or swallow well, avert their gaze from their mothers' faces, have shrill penetrating cries, and are difficult to console. Trained nurses find these infants difficult to care for in 8-hour shifts. A newborn infant is a stress to any family. If a difficult infant is given to a mother who is anxious about her ability to parent, guilty about the harm her addiction has caused her baby, and who copes with stress by turning to drugs or alcohol, are problems not to be expected?[76]

Barry Zuckerman illustrates the dangerous interaction between the drug-exposed infant and the drug-abusing parent as follows:

Consider, for example, a child born to a cocaine-using mother who did not eat well during her pregnancy and received minimal prenatal care. Following a three-day hospitalization, the infant has difficulty remaining alert and is minimally responsive. The child's passivity engenders maternal feelings of inadequacy that may deepen already existing depressive symptoms and promote continued reliance on cocaine to alleviate these painful feelings. During the first year, the mother's at-

tempts to get her infant's attention lead to overstimulation, general
irritability, and at times, inconsolable crying. The mother's feeling of
inadequacy and depression increases, and she continues to use drugs
and alcohol to self-medicate these painful feelings. In the second year
of life, as the child strives for independence, struggles develop between
the mother and her toddler. The mother sets unusual or inconsistent
limits, and most interactions with her child are negative and involve
commands, especially on the days following a drug or alcohol binge.
At two years of age, the child is hyperactive and impulsive, with de-
layed language development.[77]

Studies of children brought up by drug-abusing parents reveal the
harmful impact. The CASA Report summarizes:

The human costs are incalculable: broken families; children who are
malnourished; babies who are neglected, beaten and sometimes killed
by alcohol-and crack-addicted parents; eight-year olds sent out to steal
or buy drugs for addicted parents; sick children wallowing in unsani-
tary conditions; child victims of sodomy, rape and incest; children in
such agony and despair that they themselves resort to drugs and alcohol for relief.

And these children are at risk of continuing the cycle when they become parents. As the CASA Report finds, "the parent who abuses
drugs and alcohol is often a child who was abused by alcohol- and
drug-abusing parents." The CASA Report concludes:

It is the children who pay the exorbitant price. They are beaten by mothers and fathers high on alcohol or cocaine. They are left to suffer mal-
nutrition and disease because they lack food and heat. Children of
substance-abusing parents suffer low self-esteem, depression, self-
mutilation, suicide, panic attacks, truancy and sexual promiscuity, and
in later life mimic the drug and alcohol abuse problems that they witness in their parents. For most of these children, we offer no safe port
from the storm of parental drug and alcohol abuse and addiction that
has engulfed their lives.[78]

The Successive Pregnancy Problem

Many substance abusing mothers give birth on successive occasions to drug-affected or drug-impaired children, each of whom will typically be sent home at birth, even if the mother has demonstrated her inability to care for previous children. A study of births in San Francisco in early 1991 found that 95 percent of all cases of infant prenatal exposure involved women who had given birth to drug-exposed babies in the past.[79] A report by the U.S. General Accounting Office (GAO) to Congress entitled "Parental Drug Abuse Has Alarming Impact on Young Children" states that cocaine abusing mothers have an average of three to five children apiece.[80]

A case study from a research report on infants removed to foster care in California illustrates the problems for children inherent in this situation. The case study was selected specifically because it was "representative" of the kinds of problems that are most commonly found, rather than as an unusually egregious case:

In 1988, Nell had her first baby, a girl named Joyce, who was born cocaine exposed. A CPS investigator interviewed Nell in the hospital and carefully reviewed the case. Nell had no prenatal care prior to the delivery and had smoked crack cocaine throughout her pregnancy. At the end of her investigation the social worker determined that Joyce could go home with her mother.

In 1989, Nell had her second child, also a girl whom she named Beth. Like Joyce, Beth was born exposed to cocaine. A CPS report was filed and a social worker investigated the case. Beth, too, was allowed to return home with her mother. No further services were offered.

In 1990, Nell had her third baby girl and named her Crystal. Crystal was born with a toxicology screen that showed positive for cocaine. A child abuse report was filed by medical personnel and a social worker investigated the case. This worker, too, closed the case. . . .

In 1991, the child welfare agency received an anonymous complaint that Nell was using crack and was leaving her babies unattended. The child welfare worker assigned to the case found Nell's home "messy," but did not find Nell. The case remained open for two months while the social worker "searched" for Nell; this included two additional unannounced visits to the home when no one was there. When Nell could not be located, the case was closed.

In 1992, Nell gave birth to Patrick, who was also drug-exposed and who was also reported to the child welfare agency. When this report was received, a social worker investigating the case removed Patrick from his mother's home.[81]

Treatment and Relapse

People caught up in patterns of abuse and addiction can free themselves, and many do. *But drug-abusing parents are not likely to free themselves soon enough to salvage the lives of their children.* Experts in drug treatment testify that drug addiction generally, and cocaine addiction in particular, are chronic, relapsing conditions.[82] The classic path to rehabilitation for those who make it down that path involves a series of failed attempts to get off drugs and stay clean, repeated over a period of years.[83]

The federal government is now in the process of conducting the first major study of drug treatment outcomes, known as the Drug Abuse Treatment Outcome Study (DATOS). Early results show that while treatment can be helpful, it is helpful only for addicts who are willing and able to get into and stay in treatment. Most addicts are not willing and able to do this, even when treatment is available. While they may eventually come to treatment, "relatively long intervals pass, on average more than 5 years, before drug abusers become drug abuse treatment patients." And for those addicts who do pursue treatment, success claims are based on the percentages who reduce drug use for periods of time. Abstinence is rare, and ongoing abstinence even rarer. The results of the treatment outcome study confirm earlier findings that most of those who achieve even relative rehabilitation will relapse, following a pattern of "repeated cycles of addiction and treatment that interrupt rather than terminate addiction careers. . . . [G]iven the chronic, relapsing course of drug dependence, multiple treatment episodes may be better understood as parts of a cyclic process of recovery than as categorical failures. . . . [T]reatment for drug dependence may require an extended intervention involving staged recovery efforts that are not usually possible in a single treatment episode."[84]

It should be no surprise that children from families involved with alcohol and other drugs remain in care longer than other children.[85] If kept with or reunited with their parents, they are even more likely to suffer repeated abuse and neglect than other maltreated children.[86]

FOSTER AND INSTITUTIONAL CARE

Increasing numbers of children are growing up in foster and institutional care. Almost all of them are there because they have suffered abuse and neglect in their homes of origin.

Most of them have parents in a technical sense, since their original parents' rights have not been terminated. As a practical matter this means that they are not free for adoption, and in the current system most never will be free. They will instead either remain in foster or institutional care for the rest of their childhood, or they will be returned to their homes of origin. Either way they won't fare very well in terms of parenting. If returned home, close to one-third will be removed again. If left in foster or institutional care, studies indicate that most of them will do better than children who are returned to their parents but less well than children who are adopted, or children in the general population. (See below, "The Impact on Children.")

The Exploding Population

In the 1970s concern over the large numbers of children growing up in foster and institutional care led to calls for reform. Child advocates pointed to the evidence from developmental psychology to demonstrate the harm children suffered from growing up without permanent parents. The permanency movement pushed to make foster care the temporary solution it was originally intended to be. Policies were changed to keep children in their homes of origin if at all possible, and to move children placed in state care either back to their original homes or on to adoptive homes as promptly as possible.

The number of children in state care is now roughly double what it was during the 1970s. Over half a million children are in foster or institutional care.[87] While the number dipped for a period, it then escalated rapidly, roughly doubling since the 1980s.[88]

Infants in Care

Infants and children under four are the fastest growing population in the state care system, with infants under one making up 20–25 percent of the children who have entered care in recent years, a dramatic increase. Infants have been placed in disproportionate numbers in group homes or institutions, rather than with families, and spend disproportionate periods of time in state care as compared to other children.[89] Many of them were damaged by their mother's substance abuse during pregnancy. While these babies may do better in foster and institutional care than with drug-abusing parents, only limited numbers will get the kind of parenting they need.

Length of Stays

Efforts have been made to reduce the duration of children's stays, but many children today spend long periods in state care, and some graduate to adulthood without ever getting a permanent family. Children spend an average of from three and a half to five and a half years in out-of-home care. Over one-third stay in care for more than two and a half years. Those freed for adoption have been in state care an average of almost four years, and those that get adopted will typically spend almost one more year from when they are legally free for adoption until they are placed in an adoptive home.[90] Each year roughly 25,000 children turn eighteen and graduate out of the state care system without having had a permanent family.[91]

Reunification and Reentry Rates

While lengthy stays are not good for children, current approaches to reducing stays may be even more harmful. The primary method of reducing the length of stay in foster care has been to return children to their original parents, rather than moving them on to adoptive parents. *It is not at all clear that increased reunification rates benefit children overall.* These are the parents who originally subjected the children to abuse and neglect. They will typically have received little in the way of services to help them improve their parenting. There is no evidence that such services even if provided are successful in reducing maltreatment rates. *Studies indicate that in close to one-third of all cases in which children are reunited with their parents they later reenter the state care system, typically because of repeated abuse or neglect, or because their parents have failed to stick to drug treatment or to live up to other requirements imposed as a condition of the child's return home.*[92] Given the CPS system's limited capacity to detect abuse and neglect, and limited inclination to remove children even when it does, it is likely that the rates for maltreatment of reunited children are higher than this reentry rate.

Recent research on death rates of children leaving foster care to return to their families shows children dying at home as a result of violence at three times the rate of children in the general population and one and a half times the rate of children in foster care. The authors conclude:

> [W]hen we reunify children into their homes and communities we need to conduct careful assessments of the potential lethality of those homes and communities. We do need to continue to counter our over-optimism about the benefits of returning children home to the often hazardous families and communities they left.[93]

A research report on infants who were reunited with their families hints at some of the many risks for children inherent in reunification programs:

> It is arguable whether the families who "succeed" in the child welfare system, by achieving the goal of having their children returned home and remain at home for at least two years would generally be labeled so by the public at large. Over one-third of the mothers were still using drugs when their children were returned to their care, 55 percent had continued mental health problems, 21 percent had engaged in more criminal behavior during their children's absence, and 36 percent had new or continuing housing problems. Even if the mothers were viewed

as successful by virtue of sufficiently meeting the requirements of their case plans, the likelihood that their infants would thrive under such circumstances . . . is slim.[94]

A case study contained in this report helps illustrate the problem. It is a real-life story, which, like "Nell's" case above, was selected because it is representative of many reentry cases:

Angela was born in 1965 to a teenage mother. . . . At age fourteen, Angela gave birth to her first child, Alex.

When Alex was one year old, Angela's mother reported him to the social services agency. She told the child welfare worker that Angela was pregnant with her second child, that she was involved with drugs, and that Angela and her baby could not live in her home. Angela's case file provides few details about the next ten years of her life, but shows that she gave birth to her second child, Lisa, in 1980; to Daniel, Mark, and Francis two years apart; and to Gina in 1987. All her children were removed from her home for "general neglect," "parental incapacity," and "drug abuse." . . . In 1990, Stacie was born, also exposed to drugs, and was immediately reported to child welfare by medical personnel [and removed for placement]. . . .

During Stacie's stay in care, her parents made efforts toward reunification. Her father, Scott, had a history of abusing alcohol, crack, and heroin. He had been arrested for drug possession, forgery, stolen property, and parole violations and was often violent towards Stacie's mother. Shortly after Stacie's birth, Scott married another woman, broke up with her a few months later, and reunited with Angela. Scott and Angela's relationship, however, was punctuated by frequent arguments, fighting, and domestic abuse. Angela moved numerous times, first from Scott's home and then to his mother's home and was homeless on several occasions. After some months, Scott and Angela told their social worker that they had finally ended their relationship and Scott began to make earnest efforts to gain custody of Stacie. . . .

When Stacie was nineteen months old, she was reunified with her father. One month later, Scott was arrested for drug possession. The social worker assigned to the case discovered that Scott and Angela had lived together for the month after Stacie had been returned to home. Angela was again using drugs heavily, and Stacie was removed from her care and placed in an emergency foster home.[95]

"Permanence" within the Foster and Institutional Context

Efforts have also been made to try to provide children with some level of permanence within state care. These efforts take as a given that children will spend significant periods in foster care, and try to turn that vice into a virtue. While foster parents used to be discouraged from forming powerful attachments with their foster children, they are now often encouraged to do so; if children are freed up for adoption, foster parents who have developed such attachments are generally given priority as adoptive parent prospects. Nationally, one-half of adoptions out of state care are by foster parents, and in many urban areas today 80–90 percent of all such adoptions are. There has also been an increasing tendency to place children with kin for fostering purposes, an arrangement which typically results in longer-term foster placements than nonkin foster care.

Still, many children in kin and nonkin foster care continue to bounce from home to home. And even when foster care might seem stable, it often turns out not to be stable in the way that legally permanent homes are. Recent studies by Richard Barth, and the Child Welfare Research Center at the University of California at Berkeley School of Social Welfare, show that even when foster care lasts for an unusual number of years, it often does not last for the child's entire childhood.[96] Barth points out that children who graduate from a childhood spent in foster care are often without the lifetime anchor that family provides other children in our society:

We can expect those children to emancipate at age 18 without psychological permanence or a reasonable shot at lifetime self-sufficiency. If they are subsequently asked by researchers to indicate the ways that they can depend on their former foster parents . . . after foster care they are likely to answer as they did in my study—"I don't know, we never really talked about it."[97]

Moreover, permanence or continuity in care is only going to be good for children if the quality of caretaking is high. We have little information about the quality of care provided by long-term foster parents, by providers in "fost-adopt" programs, or by kinship homes, but the likelihood is that it is quite variable, and often seriously deficient.

Quality Parenting Concerns

1. Nonkin Foster Care and Fost-Adopt Programs

Many foster parents qualify for sainthood. They nurture children not "their own" without any expectation of the long-term benefits of permanent parenthood. They take on children who present all kinds of serious parenting challenges. They support efforts to reunite the children who are in their care with their birth parents while simultaneously laying the basis for a long-term foster or adoptive parenting relationship. Their fostering stipend from the state is generally intended to cover no more than the minimal costs of supporting a child, while the costs of the care they actually provide often go far beyond the minimal.

But there are reasons for concern that the quality of care provided by many foster parents, including some fost-adopt parents, is marginal at best. Those familiar with foster care today say that as the foster care population has increased in recent years, the population of qualified foster parents has *decreased*, forcing the state to reach out to marginal or even high-risk families to find places for all the children in need.

In addition, the state recruits in a way that raises concerns about quality. The goal in recent years has been to place children for foster care in the local community, with families that are seen as a good "match" racially and in other ways with their family of origin. This means that the state limits itself to a narrow segment of the population in reaching out to find foster parents. As compared to the typical pool of prospective adoptive parents, the foster parent pool is much worse off in socioeconomic terms. Many have incomes at or below the poverty level and live in neighborhoods characterized by drugs, violence, and poor schools.[98] In recent years states have often reached out to admittedly high-risk groups to find needed homes. In Massachusetts, stories in the press revealed in the mid 1990s that the Department of Social Services (DSS) had placed many children with foster parents who had serious criminal records involving acts of violence, including domestic violence and child abuse. DSS explained the practice as resulting from the policy favoring placement with kin, together with the general difficulty of finding qualified foster parents. DSS eventually admitted its error and agreed to change its selection criteria.[99] A few years later the press revealed that DSS was recruiting for foster parents from the welfare rolls, and that 7–10 percent of all foster parents were on welfare. DSS officials admitted that this practice caused quality concerns, but again claimed they had little choice given the difficulty of finding qualified foster homes.[100] Recently Massachusetts announced that it would raise foster parent licensing standards to demand that parents have "adequate" albeit undefined income apart from foster care stipends, that one parent in the home be literate, and that the parents have some access to transportation and have a telephone. These standards, criticized by some as too onerous, clearly went beyond those that foster care agencies in many other states applied, and apparently were not to be applied to kinship foster parents even in Massachusetts.[101]

For many in the foster parent pool, the financial stipend provided for fostering represents a significant amount of money. This stipend is typically considerably more generous than the welfare stipend for one child. The median monthly AFDC payment for one child in 1993 was $212, more than $100 per month less than the median foster home maintenance payment.[102] With each additional child the differential increases, since each foster child comes with a full foster stipend, while welfare payments for additional children increase only marginally. Thus in California in 1996 foster stipends for two children aged eight and sixteen totaled $859 per month, as compared to AFDC benefits, which came to $479. Greater disparities occur when more children are involved, and in states with lower welfare benefits, so that foster stipends can total several times what welfare stipends would.[103] Foster stipends are quite modest given the expenses of raising a child, including the special expenses often involved in raising the kind of children who come into foster care, and whose special needs may not be adequately addressed by medical services and subsidies provided by the state. But for people at the poverty level fostering may look like a relatively lucrative "job," even if they have no interest in the actual task of parenting. One lawyer I spoke to who worked with the Massachusetts Department of Social Services told of a case she was working on involving a foster parent whose six foster children brought her an annual income of $38,000. She had had three of the children for several years but had never adopted them, both because she was ambivalent about adoption and DSS was ambivalent about her fitness to adopt. DSS was now moving to take the children away. The lawyer said that the woman "seems to have thought of foster parenting as employment, but it was not a job she liked very much."[104] The risks inherent in this situation are obvious. Foster parents in it for the money will get money for themselves only to the extent that they fail to use their stipends for the benefit of their foster children; even if they provide their children with the basics, they are not likely to provide much in the way of emotional nurturing. Once a child is placed in a home, there is little supervision by the state to guarantee that the foster parents are doing a good or even adequate job. And even if the state did oversee foster families more actively, good parenting is hard to assess and impossible to mandate.

With federal welfare law reform, the problems are exacerbated. Traditional welfare payments have been cut back in ways that will make foster parent stipends even more tempting. Parents with dependent children now have a limited lifetime period to receive welfare stipends, no matter how needy they may be. Many states have initiated their own welfare cut-back programs, reducing the amount of money families receive, limiting the period of eligibility, and eliminating increases in welfare stipends for additional children.

No studies have attempted to assess the risks for children posed by a system that pays people to provide parenting, recruiting for the job from among those in dire financial need, and largely excluding from consideration those who can afford to parent children in need without significant state support. Obviously it's essential to make stipends available so that people who are genuinely interested in acting as substitute parents to children in need will be able to become foster parents without regard to their income. And it's appropriate for the state to provide support for children officially in its custody. But many people familiar with the impact of foster stipends in the current system are concerned about the risks involved.

Quality is similarly at issue in fost-adopt programs. Foster parents who adopt the children in their care generally qualify for adoption subsidies comparable in amount to fostering stipends. An additional plus for the parents will be freedom from any supervision by social workers. This of course puts the children who are adopted at additional risk if the parents are not appropriately qualified and motivated.

Fost-adopt children are generally denied the opportunity to be considered by the regular adoptive parent pool. This pool consists of prospective parents who have stepped forward on the basis of their desire to become adoptive parents. They are generally relatively privileged in socioeconomic terms, as compared with the foster parent pool, and live in neighborhoods with better schools and community facilities, which are relatively free from drugs, crime, and violence. Some members of this pool may apply and qualify for fost-adopt programs, but typically they are not recruited by the state system, and typically only limited numbers of them will adopt through it.

2. Kinship Care

The enormous increase in kinship care[105] in recent years accounts for virtually the entire increase in the total foster care population.[106] Nationwide, roughly one-third of out-of-home placements involve kinship foster care. In some of the larger states kinship care accounts for roughly half the children in out-of-home care, and in some large cities the percentage is even higher. If kinship care is a fine solution for children, we should perhaps not be so concerned with the increase in the total numbers in foster care. But the likelihood is that the quality of kinship care varies wildly.

Kinship care has grown for a number of reasons. The increasing emphasis on the importance of heritage and continuity with the past has contributed to the preference for kin. Kinship care has also expanded in response to pressures created by the increase in children needing care, the decrease in available nonkinship homes, and the preference for placing children with parents of the same race. Also, the economics of welfare and foster care have developed in ways that tend to promote kinship care. The law now requires that kin licensed as foster parents be paid the same stipends as other foster parents. Since, as discussed above, these stipends are significantly more generous than welfare stipends, both the kin foster parents and the original parents may see a financial advantage in kinship placement. It is notable that the 1996 federal welfare reform legislation, cutting back on welfare support, created a new federal push for kinship care, requiring states for the first time to consider giving relatives a preference.[107]

Studies don't tell us much about the quality of kinship care. They do tell us that this form of foster care is unusually long-lasting. Long-term foster care is usually interpreted as a system failure, given the generally agreed upon goal of providing children with early permanency, whether through returning home or being placed for adoption. But some would argue that long-term kinship foster care gives many children who have to be removed from their parents just what they need—a stable placement, with links to the extended family and the original parents. There is some evidence to buttress their claims. Children who leave kinship care to return home have lower reentry rates back into foster care than children originally placed in nonkin care do.

But there are many reasons for concern about the quality of the parenting some children receive in kinship foster care. In the first place, kinship foster care is by definition *not* permanent: as a legal matter foster parents have no permanent obligations to the children; they may choose not to foster the children until adulthood, even if fostering is needed. From the child's perspective, you cannot count on foster parents to be there in the future the way you can count on adoptive parents. Many kinship fostering arrangements prove in fact to be temporary, with the children moving on to other foster homes after a period of time.

Secondly, kinship foster parents are on average significantly poorer and older than nonkin foster parents, and they have significantly more health problems. The prototypical kinship care provider is the grandmother. Studies show that, despite their obvious need for support in parenting efforts, kinship foster parents receive far fewer services for their children from the foster care system than nonkin parents do.

Beyond this, there are risks inherent in kinship foster care which are the flip side of the benefits. Continuity with the past and ongoing relationships with the extended family, including the birth parents, are often the *opposite* of what the child needs. Many parents who abuse and neglect their children suffered similar forms of maltreatment as children. Many parents caught up in destructive patterns of substance abuse are the children of alcoholics and drug addicts. *Some* who abuse and neglect their children stand out as aberrations from their families, but this is the exception more than the rule. Maltreatment commonly occurs as part of a pattern of family dysfunction carried from one generation on to the next, in a community characterized by poverty, unemployment, drugs, violence, and despair. The extended kinship group has to be seen as a high-risk group for parenting purposes. As the CASA Report concludes:

> Without careful evaluation of kinship care arrangements, child welfare officials may lock children in a dysfunctional family poisoned by substance abuse and its common companions of violence and neglect.[108]

Even if the kinship providers are fit to parent, the birth parents' easy access to the child may be a problem, rather than the benefit that many claim. If birth parents have traumatized a child in the past, or if they are abusive in their current treatment, or if they see the child's foster payments as a convenient way to pay for their drug habit, the child will not benefit from the fact that they have ready access to the kinship provider's home, or indeed may live with the child and the fostering grandmother in an intergenerational home, as is often the case.[109]

A finely tuned system for selecting foster care parents might be able to separate the good from the bad parenting prospects, but no one familiar with our nation's current system would so characterize it. In fact, the system is shaped in ways that exacerbate the dangers of selecting large numbers of seriously unfit kinship parents. Formal and informal kinship preference policies tell social workers in most jurisdictions that they must recruit and select kin as foster parents without making a comparative judgment as to whether they will do as good a job as nonkin foster parents. Formal fitness criteria are often relaxed or waived for kinship candidates. And whatever criteria are supposed to govern, the reality is that under such preference policies social workers are unlikely to screen kin out unless there are obvious manifestations of gross unfitness.[110] Additional pressure to place children with kin without undue concern about their fitness as caretakers comes from the system's related biases in favor of local and same-race families. All this, together with the rising numbers of children who need homes, may leave social workers feeling they have no other choice as they assess kinship candidates.

Relatives may also feel pressured to take a child irrespective of their desire to parent. They may feel that the child has no other option, based on the social worker's sense that foster care by strangers is unavailable or unworthy. Only one-third of kinship foster parents offer on their own to take the child; one-half become involved only when asked by social workers.[111]

As with nonkin foster care, the stipends attached to fostering exacerbate the dangers inherent in the system for children. For extended family members at the poverty level, as many relatives of victims of maltreatment will be, these stipends may make it worthwhile to agree to foster whether or not they have any capacity or motivation to parent. Estimates show that total extended family income can drop 50–75 percent if children are returned home from foster kin,[112] and income would drop even further if they were placed elsewhere.

There has been even greater reluctance to voice concerns about the potentially corrupting influence of money in this context than in the nonkin foster context. One risks being considered not simply antipoor, but antifamily as well, and hostile to the black family in particular, since kinship care providers are disproportionately African-American. But again, in private conversations many familiar with the workings of kinship care testify not simply to the risks inherent in the system, but to evidence that the risks are regularly realized. And, as with nonkin foster care, welfare reform will most likely increase the risks.

Sabrina's story illustrates the risks of assuming that kin will necessarily care. Sabrina Green was found dead on November 8, 1997, at the age of nine years old. She was dead from untreated burns, gangrene and blows to her head which had fractured her skull. Her body was covered with sores, and the gangrene had spread through her right arm and hand, which was missing a thumb. In her final weeks of life she had been tied at night by the arms and legs to her bed to prevent her from stealing food, according to the half-sister who had been made her guardian, Yvette Green. Sabrina had been born to a cocaine-abusing mother who abandoned her at birth, and was not found for two months. Sabrina was sent home with her mother, who continued to abuse drugs until her death, when Sabrina was three. Sabrina spent the next five years with a family friend. When she died, Yvette Green, who had not seen her half-sister for years, petitioned to become her guardian, saying, according to the *New York Times* report, "that she wanted to keep her family together and that she would need the additional welfare and medical benefits that would come with legal custody." Ms. Green had ten children of her own, was living on welfare, and had been investigated by the child welfare agency twice previously for failing to take care of her children adequately. Several family members were dubious about her fitness to care for her own children or Sabrina, and at least one of her sisters said that she had a drug problem. But the child welfare agency never brought them to court and never objected to granting Ms. Green guardianship. The Family Court judge approved guardianship, based on the limited information before him. Family members, neighbors, acquaintances, and school officials all realized later that Sabrina was in trouble. But no one intervened to prevent Sabrina's torture and death.[113]

There can be no question but that in some cases the best possible solution for the child removed from home will be the loving relative, who already has a relationship with the child and can help maintain other healthy connections with the past, including with the birth parents. But we should be willing to face up to the fact that child maltreatment is only rarely aberrational. It ordinarily grows out of a family and community context. Keeping the child in that same context will often serve the child no better than keeping him or her with the maltreating parent.

3. Institutional and Group Homes

While most children in state care in our country are in foster homes, significant numbers are in institutional or group homes. A recent report found, for example, that 14 percent of California's children in out-of-home care were in group care.[114] Children in these settings are far less likely than those in foster care either to be reunified with their families or to move on to adoption. This is in significant part because many of the children placed in these settings have been harmed by prior abuse and neglect, are older, or for other reasons are now hard to place. But it is also true that the care they are likely to get in group or institutional homes will not be of the quality needed to overcome previous problems.

Institutions are not good places for children to grow up. Some contend that institutions may be the best option for certain children, because they have needs that are too extreme to be met in family settings. This no doubt is sadly true of all too many children today, but it argues for getting children out of destructive situations earlier in their lives so that they *can* be placed in families. Others contend that good institutions are better for children than growing up in destructive birth families.[115] This also is true, but it does not justify keeping children in institutions rather than placing them in loving adoptive families.

This country resolved many years ago that children who had to be removed from their birth families would generally be better off in some kind of family setting than in institutions. The thinking was based on the work of developmental psychologists who had demonstrated that children raised in institutions developed attachment and related bonding problems that plagued them throughout their lives. In the intervening years we have accumulated more evidence as to the difficulties of making institutions work as homes for children.

Worldwide the experience with institutions over the years has proved almost uniformly disastrous for children. Numerous studies demonstrate the harm children suffer when they are raised without the intensely loving attachments that characterize healthy family relationships. New evidence has surfaced in recent years as children have been adopted from orphanages abroad, and doctors and research scientists have begun to document the permanent damage many of them have suffered by virtue of their early deprivation.[116] Simultaneously, early brain research has given us dramatic new evidence of the permanent differences in brain formation that result from different levels of nurturing connection in the early months and years of human life.[117]

Our country has no exemplary history of success with designing public institutions that work for children. And nothing in what we know about today's institutional homes for children should give us comfort. The work is poorly paid, and working conditions are bad.

Not surprisingly, staff turnover is high, negating what opportunity there might be for staff to develop significant nurturing relationships with the children.[118]

At the same time, these institutions cost an enormous amount to run, with the costs per child much higher than foster care. A recent report on group care in California found the median cost per child per year to be almost $50,000, more than eleven times the standard rate for foster care.[119] Nationwide the average cost of care in group homes and residential treatment centers is $36,000 per year.[120] The prospects for massive *increases* in funding to maximize the chance that these kinds of institutions might actually work for children seem nonexistent.

Some group homes are no doubt better than the worst we provide children in the way of permanent homes and foster care. But we should not try to persuade ourselves that institutions can succeed in providing children with the kind of parenting they need.

THE IMPACT ON CHILDREN

Common sense and developmental psychology tell us most of what we need to know about the impact of abuse and neglect, whether it takes place in a child's original home, a foster home, or a group home. Human beings need to be lovingly attached to a nurturing parent figure from early on. This need is a primary motivating force for healthy development. Those denied early nurturing are at high risk in terms of their capacity for future relationships and functioning.[121] Child welfare experts have been sending consistent messages for decades about the destructive impact of abuse, neglect, and inadequate institutional care. Recent research expands our understanding but does not change the basic picture.

Early brain research has recently revealed that infants denied nurturing care never develop the complex web of connections in the brain that are essential to emotional and intellectual development.[122] But we have known for a long time that infants require nurturing care to develop normally. Brain scans of people physically or sexually abused as children show physical abnormalities that experts believe result from the abuse experience and produce future criminality. But lawyers for death row inmates have told us for years that they could trace their clients' conduct back to torturous experiences in early childhood.[123]

Psychiatrists and neurologists whose expertise is the study of convicted sociopaths, murderers, and other violent criminals tell us that they are, overwhelmingly, people who suffered childhood maltreatment and related neurological damage. They talk of a "new theory of violence," at the core of which is the idea that prolonged child abuse changes the anatomy of the brain in ways that produce criminal behavior.

Outcome studies show us that children subjected to abuse and neglect, or to foster and institutional care, do much less well in life than the norm. They do less well on various measures of human happiness and family relationships, and less well on such measures of worldly success as school grades, years of education, unemployment, homelessness, and involvement in crime, violence, prostitution, alcohol and drugs. Those coming from group or institutional homes generally have even worse outcomes than those coming from foster care.[124]

Roughly one-third of all maltreatment victims will continue the cycle into the next generation, subjecting their own children to abuse or neglect.[125] Another one-third will provide borderline caretaking.[126] The vast majority of all abusing parents were themselves abused as children.[127]

Outcome studies also show that many children damaged by their early experiences can be rescued; they can be nurtured in ways that will repair early damage caused by prenatal substance abuse or maltreatment in infancy, and enable them to go on to lead normal lives. *It is the compounding of early damage with continuing abuse and neglect that proves devastating to children.*[128] This evidence demonstrates the importance of intervening early in the lives of children who have been damaged and removing them to homes where they will receive the nurturing they need, unless they are able to get that nurturing in their homes of origin. Today's policies, however, keep victimized children in situations where they are at high risk for ongoing maltreatment. In the overwhelming majority of cases reported to CPS and of cases substantiated for maltreatment, the children are kept at home rather than removed.[129] Studies indicate that in one-third to one-half of the cases in which children subjected to maltreatment are kept at home, they will be maltreated again.[130] The great majority of children who are removed will be removed only to foster or institutional care, where the risks of maltreatment are higher than in the general population, and a significant percentage will be returned home. Of those returned home, roughly one-third will be removed again when their parents either continue to maltreat them or fail to satisfy conditions established as essential to improve their parenting.[131]

Research on the victims of maltreatment who manage to do well despite their early histories regularly reports that these children benefit from having had at least one major supportive presence in their early lives. It is sadly obvious that even those victims lucky enough to have such a parent figure in their lives will have a much harder time of it if kept at home or in institutional care than children who experience nurturing by substitute parents in adoptive homes where they are freed from the ongoing experience of abuse and neglect.

Child welfare experts have long known that children subjected to abuse or neglect generally do better in foster care than in their families of origin, and better still in adoptive homes, in terms of freedom from repeated maltreatment and other measures of well-being.[132] (Indeed, abuse is lower in adoptive families than the norm in the general population.[133]) The advantages of foster care over the homes of origin would clearly be more dramatic if foster care were better designed to give foster children certainty and predictability in their lives, as opposed to the current system in which so many children drift without any understanding of their future, and are subject to repeated attempts to reunify them with deeply troubled birth parents. Adoption studies consistently show that the earlier children are placed in adoptive homes the better they will do.[134]

We have long known that abuse, neglect, and institutional care produce lifelong damage. Studies fill in the details in some compelling ways, but leave us with the question—are we prepared to do anything to change children's lives?

4. UNDERINTERVENTION VS. OVERINTERVENTION

There is widespread agreement that we are in the midst of a child welfare crisis: too many children are victimized by abuse and neglect, too many are growing up in foster and institutional care, and the current child protective system is overwhelmed. But there is intense debate over what is fundamentally wrong with the system and how it should be reformed. Some argue that the central problem is underintervention, claiming that the state system does too little to protect children against abuse and neglect by their parents; they cite cases in which children have been tortured and killed while social workers filed reports on problems they had observed but failed to remove the children or terminate the parents' rights. Others argue that overintervention is the problem, citing cases in which CPS investigations are initiated on the basis of false charges; or social workers rush in to remove children from committed, caretaking parents on the basis of injuries caused by innocent accidents; or the disruption of being removed and later returned does more harm than good to children. The first camp pushes for greater state activism in supervising families, removing children, and placing them in adoptive homes. The second pushes for stricter limits on the state's coercive role and argues that we should transfer significant responsibility for protecting children from the state to the extended family and the local community and should rely yet more on parents' innate strengths and on their willingness to cooperate on a voluntary basis with support services.[1]

Our system is clearly guilty of both underintervention and overintervention. Child protection agencies throughout the nation are overburdened and underresourced, and endless anecdotes can be told by both sides of the debate to illustrate their points. But the important question is whether there is a systematic bias that needs to be corrected. There's no easy way to prove the case definitively one way or the other. Statistical reports on abuse and neglect convey only a limited sense of what is actually happening to children. Decisions as to whether we are intervening too much or too little depend on myriad judgments as to what kind of intervention might be useful, how we value family privacy and autonomy as compared to children's well-being, and many other factors. Also, the very terms of the debate fail to capture the range of choices at issue. The question is not simply whether to intervene more or less, but whether to intervene earlier or later, whether to intervene more or less coercively, whether to offer services on a purely voluntary basis or to mandate treatment, whether to remove children temporarily or permanently, whether to rely solely on the child protection system or to look also to the criminal justice system.

While there is no hard-science answer to the underintervention vs. overintervention question, it is important nonetheless to address it. Otherwise reform efforts risk simply tinkering with the system without solving essential problems. Increasing the pay of child welfare workers, decreasing their caseloads, increasing funds for CPS investigative or family preservation services, and other popular "reform" proposals, won't necessarily improve child welfare at all if the system is sending its workers instructions that are systematically biased in a problematic direction.

There is plenty of evidence, in my view, that underintervention is the systematic problem in the child welfare world. Organized society tends generally to intervene too little, and too late, and too ineffectively to protect children against maltreatment.

We don't do enough up front to prevent abuse and neglect. The most effective prevention program would be eliminating the social and economic conditions of poverty, unemployment, homelessness, and deprivation that produce dysfunctional families. Less radical prevention programs include early intervention to provide support services to families that can be identified as at risk for abuse and neglect. Many family support programs exist today, but most are designed to benefit families that are at least relatively capable of reaching out and taking advantage of the support offered. Families at the greatest risk for abuse and neglect are likely to be the most isolated from their communities and the least likely to reach out for support.

The home visiting movement is grounded on this insight. Home visiting programs send visitors into the home in part because this is a way to reach those who may not otherwise come out. These programs both provide support in the home and help link their clients with other support programs in the community. The home visitor movement has as its goal universal home visiting for all new mothers, with ongoing visits during the first several years of life. As chapter 7 describes, this movement holds enormous promise for children at risk of abuse and neglect. But we are far from realizing that promise.

Another form of prevention would involve the use of criminal law sanctions. We use the criminal law generally to prevent misconduct: our underlying assumptions are that criminal sanctions serve a preventive purpose by establishing or reenforcing moral guidelines, by threatening punishment for transgression, and by incapacitating serious offenders so that at least they can not offend again. As discussed in chapter 2, women's rights advocates have successfully pressed for the increased use of criminal sanctions against domestic violence involving adult victims, because they think this approach has been useful in protecting women from battering. But we have so far been enormously reluctant to use criminal sanctions as a way of preventing the abuse and neglect of children.[2] Rarely do we subject adults to arrest, prosecution, and the threat of imprisonment when they beat their children savagely and break their bones, although we would do so automatically were they to subject a stranger to the same treatment.

Women have argued vehemently that men who assault and batter their partners in the home should not be treated any differently than men who assault and batter strangers on the street. They have argued for recognition of marital rape as a crime, so that men cannot force sex upon their wives with impunity any more than they can force sex upon strangers. As political support has developed for the proposition that violence against women is a bad thing that should be prevented, society has moved systematically in the direction of criminalizing the conduct. This move has taken place in the absence of any definitive proof that criminal sanctions work as preventive measures in this area. But the absence of such proof has done little to dampen enthusiasm for criminalization. Questions have been raised only at the fringes and not at the core—only with respect to how best to go about criminalization, and not with respect to whether it would be better to abandon the push for criminalization altogether. This makes sense, so long as we agree that we care about preventing this kind of conduct, just as it makes sense to have criminal sanctions for assault and battery, rape and murder, involving strangers. We know these sanctions don't work perfectly to prevent stranger crime either. We have ongoing debates about the best way to go about designing criminal sanctions—about, for example, whether it helps to have mandatory minimum sentences, or capital punishment. We know that the best crime prevention programs would address the social conditions that breed crime. But we also know, or at least are prepared to act as if we know, with or without the benefit of sophisticated research, that criminal sanctions will help prevent some amount of serious crime.

There is every reason to think that criminal sanctions for child abuse and neglect would serve a similar preventive function. Richard Gelles makes an important point when he says that people subject members of their family to various forms of outrageous maltreatment *because they can*.[3] They know there's a risk of getting into serious trouble if they assault someone at work or on the street: if caught they risk losing their job or going to jail. Increasingly they have reason to be concerned if they assault their wife. But it's still relatively safe to assault their child, or to deny their child essential caretaking. Arrest and prosecution are incredibly rare events in the child abuse and neglect world. They are reserved primarily for cases in which maltreatment results in death, or involves horrible forms of torture and injury, and for cases of sexual abuse. Prosecution is more likely in sexual abuse than in physical abuse cases, more because of the political activism surrounding the sexual abuse issue in recent years than because of any considered judgment that physical abuse is less harmful to children.[4]

Instead of taking a preventive approach and intervening early and effectively our primary mode of intervention occurs after children have already suffered serious and repeated maltreatment. And our rules dictate that even at that point intervention should be minimal. The first goal is family preservation; children are removed to foster or institutional care only in a relative handful of cases. The next goal is family reunification; parental rights are terminated and the child freed for adoption only if it is decided, often after repeated efforts, that family reunification is impossible—and not necessarily even then. Adoption as a form of intervention is extremely rare.

The most common response to reported abuse and neglect is for CPS either to do nothing, or to engage in an investigation and nothing more. In 1993 CPS investigated only roughly one quarter of the cases of children reported as seriously harmed or injured.[5] In only one million cases are there any CPS findings of substantiated maltreatment permitting further intervention, even though National Incidence Study surveys reveal that some three million cases of serious maltreatment actually occur. The two million unsubstantiated cases will typically receive no services or other intervention; some 60 percent of unsubstantiated cases return to the CPS system as new reports with more serious allegations of maltreatment.[6] Even when cases are substantiated, CPS typically does little to protect the child. One review of New York cases found that more than half were closed the same day they were substantiated.[7] Substantiated cases that are kept open will be placed on the CPS caseload for monitoring purposes, but this monitoring will typically involve little more than occasional visits by a social worker. In roughly half the substantiated cases no treatment or other services will be provided.[8] When treatment services are provided, they are generally minimal, the most common being parenting education. CPS rarely insists in any serious way that parents take advantage of treatment opportunities. Even if treatment is formally required CPS is not likely to monitor and enforce compliance. Parents whose children have been removed may face a vague threat that they will not get the children back if they don't comply with CPS treatment plans, but little more. These parents will have a good chance of getting their children back regardless of whether they comply so long as they show signs of being fit to parent or, in many cases, so long as there is no new evidence they are unfit. Parents whose children have not been removed will often get to keep their children at home so long as they don't repeat their maltreatment in a way that CPS can discover and prove, without regard to whether they comply with treatment mandates.

Only in the most serious of the serious maltreatment cases is there any reasonable likelihood that children will be removed to foster care. One knowledgeable expert describes the cases in which children are removed as cases involving "such serious threats to children's safety that one cannot risk leaving children in the home, even if intensive services were to be provided."[9] Those familiar with the child welfare system regularly describe the children coming into care in recent years as more severely damaged and the families as even more fraught with problems than previously.[10]

The Association for Children of New Jersey (ACNJ) conducted a study in the early 1990s to assess the state's efforts to prevent children from being placed in foster care. *Their survey of a one-year sample of cases produced the "unexpected and alarming" finding that "there was almost no unnecessary placement"*: "Placement was considered only when the child was severely abused, when inadequate parenting became life-threatening, when young children were abandoned, or when parent-child conflict escalated to violence."

> In 21 percent of the cases, parental neglect was identified as the primary reason for placement; in an additional 17 percent of the case sample, neglect due to parental substance abuse was cited. In these cases, a combination of factors was involved. Parents failed to meet the basic needs of their children. Children were left hungry, dirty, and inadequately dressed. Necessary medical care—either routine care, such as well baby visits and immunizations, or specialized care for medically fragile children—was ignored. Living conditions were filthy, crowded and hazardous to the child. Living arrangements were chaotic, with many people in and out of the household, leaving the children vulnerable to abuse. Parental supervision was inadequate; young children were left alone or were left unprotected in risky situations.
>
> In 16 percent of the cases, physical abuse was the reason for placement. In many cases, the abuse was severe, often requiring the child to

be hospitalized. Several cases involved broken bones and serious burns, like the child who was routinely disciplined by being burned with a curling iron. Two were cases of shaken baby syndrome, in which infants were left permanently brain-injured and, in one case, blind. Two cases involved the death of a sibling due to parental abuse.

One-quarter of the cases were babies born to drug-involved mothers. Many were born premature, tested positive for syphilis or had serious medical problems. Most were placed directly from the hospital into foster care, some after being abandoned in the hospital by the parent. All but one of the children had older siblings, many of whom had also been born drug-exposed. In almost 90 percent of those cases, *all* older siblings were living apart from the parent, either with friends or relatives, in foster care or in adoptive homes. . . .

Abandonment was a pervasive theme in the lives of all these children. Children, often very young, were left alone at home. . . . Some were left behind by their parents in the hospital, a motel, a shelter or on the street. Some were left with relatives, neighbors, acquaintances, even strangers, by a parent who never came back. Some were abandoned indirectly by their parents' choice of drugs or alcohol or an abusive boyfriend over the child's safety and well-being. . . .

Whether or not there was really a family to preserve was a realistic question in many of the cases.

The ACNJ report found that parental substance abuse was a major factor, with devastating impact on children. But it noted that substance abuse was "never the sole reason for placement":

The cases documented extensive efforts by the DYFS to provide services to the parent at home so long as the parent could function to care for the child. The substance abuse that resulted in placement was severe and chronic, rendering the parent incapable of caring for the child.

Indeed, the report found that placement prevention services were generally good; the problem was that the array of available child welfare services were not capable of helping families that were as "seriously dysfunctional" as the families from which children were being removed. The report's conclusion was that family preservation had been taken too far:

[T]he state must . . . re-examine its policy of keeping families together and ask whether it has gone too far. Although the state has a strong mandate to support families, parents also have a responsibility to care for their children. Even the best service delivery system will not save families who ultimately do not accept that responsibility. Children cannot be sacrificed to a concept of family that may not exist.[11]

In virtually all removal cases, including the most serious, family preservation policies have required that intervention be minimized. Thus even in cases of vicious, ongoing torture, where proof is clearly made out, CPS authorities have been more likely to simply remove the children to foster care, and make reunification the official goal, than to move immediately to terminate parental rights. Parents who want their children back have generally been given the benefit of the doubt. The Massachusetts case involving "Baby Andy" illustrates the system at work. Andy was brought into the emergency room with a "ring burn" on his face, the apparent result of his face having been held in a pan of scalding water. Examination revealed evidence of numerous broken bones from prior abuse. Andy was removed to foster care, where loving care from age eight months to three and a half years helped him recover from the horrors of his early life. Andy's foster parents wanted to adopt him, but the Massachusetts court and the Department of Social Services agreed that he should instead go back "home," concluding that they had no choice given the absence of adequate evidence to prove his original parents' "present unfitness."[12]

Some states have created categories of egregious maltreatment in which CPS authorities are allowed to move immediately to terminate parental rights, but this has so far been the exception. The 1997 Adoption and Safe Families Act (ASFA) was passed in significant part out of recognition that child welfare workers felt they had to make family preservation efforts in every case, no matter how egregious.

Congressional hearings prior to ASFA's passage dramatically illustrated the problem, with experienced officials testifying to the frustration of having to comply with family preservation requirements in cases where families should clearly not be preserved.[13] Judge William D. Maddux, Supervising Judge in Cook County Circuit Court in Chicago, testified as follows:

In Illinois, for example, [child welfare authorities] slavishly follow that policy of reunification of the family. Family first, even in the case when it is obvious that the family will never be reunified, even in those cases they go through the routine of instituting services to see if the family can be put together.

In the case where you have got the mom who neglects her child, a single parent and she is on drugs, and she fails in two or three drug rehabilitation programs, so long as she continues to state that she wants her child, she wants to shape her life up, and she wants to get off of the drugs, people are all too willing to let her do that and time does go by. It may well be that enough time goes by that a child who is adoptable becomes unadoptable.[14]

Others testified to the horrors of forcing children to stay with or return to the parents that had tortured them. The Lieutenant Governor of Michigan, who had headed the state Adoption Commission charged with developing child welfare reform legislation, argued passionately that we should not be "victimizing children by sending them back to their abusers." She asserted that the torture cases were not rare but tragically common, referring to "the little ones who have been raped; the babies who have been shaken so hard the blood vessels burst in their skulls; the children who have been burned with cigarette butts or set on hot stoves or put in scalding water to 'make them behave.'"[15] She gave examples of reunification efforts at work:

A woman with four felony convictions and who was known by protective services to have abused, abandoned, terrorized and sold one of her children for one year's free rent and twelve hundred dollars cash was flown, on probation, round trip from another state, housed in a motel, provided meals and spending money for weekend visitation with her children. This continued for a period of thirteen months. These children were so traumatized by the visits that they experienced nightmares and bedwetting after the visits. In another case, services were provided for a parent who put her baby's face in scalding water because she was tired of her crying. The child's face was virtually melted and required countless surgeries to try to rebuild her face, but still "reasonable efforts" had to be made and reunification services were offered and visitation, though terrifying to the child, was ordered.[16]

Sister Josephine Murphy, administrator of a home for abused children, talked of being forced by the Maryland state system to send children who had come into her care to recover from horrific abuse at the hands of their parents, back to those same parents:

"Please don't send me home!" This is the cry we have heard more than once at St. Ann's Infant and Maternity Home. It is the cry of little Billy who at age three has suffered severe abuse over a long period of time. When he was just a year and a half old he was taken to the hospital for treatment of third degree burns to the heel and sole of his right foot. He also had a hematoma on the back of his head and bruises on his right jaw. In addition, X-rays revealed old skull fractures. The injuries were inconsistent with the explanation provided by his mother. Nonetheless he was returned home and came to St. Ann's another year and a half later after again going to the hospital and being seen for scrotal swelling and bruises. His buttocks were bruised and he complained of his stomach aching. He also had a rectal fissure and it took almost a year working with the doctors before he had normal bowel movements again. My question is—why was he returned home in the first place after the abuse he had suffered at age one and a half?

Pam who at 15 months of age suffered from venereal warts. She had been sexually abused by her mother's boyfriend and needed surgery because of it. Surgery was scheduled but before it took place she was discharged to her mother and right back to the same situation.

They are burned, oh yes, they are burned. That's what happened to Ben who came in with both hands so badly burned that we sent him to the hospital because the nurse on duty thought his hands were infected. He was hospitalized for six days while the hospital staff worked on his hands. When he came back to us we were told by the hospital that they were not water burns but that his hands had been held over an open fire. When his mother came the following week to visit him he took one look at her and raced off down the hall screaming. He and his brother both accused their mother of abuse, and the aunt admitted that there had been long-term sexual activity between the mother and the boys. Yet they were released to their aunt who had been around while all this was going on and done nothing.

Children today are beaten also, but no longer with a hair brush as in years gone by. The implement of abuse now is the electric cord because "loving" mothers and their boyfriends have found out that it inflicts much more pain and the pain lasts a lot longer. Tommy came in at age seven with his back all torn up in this manner. It took months to heal his "mommy sores" as he called them. As he prepared to go home he wanted to know why we were sending him back when we knew what was going to happen to him.[17]

CPS authorities are even more reluctant to intervene definitively in neglect cases, regardless of how severe and chronic the neglect. The "Keystone Kids" case that surfaced in Chicago in the mid-1990s illustrates the problem. An in-depth journalistic investigation produced a news report describing a judge new to the child welfare docket bucking the system to move children on to adoption who would in the normal course have been returned to their parents or kept in foster limbo. In February of 1994 the Chicago police found nineteen children in the kind of horrendous conditions that tend to get officially categorized as neglect:

> In February of 1994, when Chicago cops found 19 children jammed into a cold and squalid apartment on Keystone Avenue, one little girl looked up at a woman officer and pleaded for love. Conditions inside were horrific. On the floor, roaches scooted past rat droppings, and two hungry toddlers shared a bone with a terrier mutt. Bowls of rotting spaghetti sat by a flour sack crawling with bugs. One boy, crippled by cerebral palsy, had been burned and whipped. Child-protection workers seized the kids from their mothers—six women hanging out together, collecting $4,692 a month in welfare and food stamps.[18]

Experts on the workings of the system predicted that the children, temporarily removed to foster care, would be returned home. "This, they confided, was what the system calls a 'dirty house' case, in which parents convince a judge that they've learned better parenting and housekeeping skills." The report goes on to describe, how, over the course of the next few years, various welfare workers together with the judge explored ways to reunite the families. By this time twenty-eight children were involved, with new siblings discovered who had been out of the apartment that night, and others born later. Classic packages of social service treatment and support were offered: drug treatment, peer-support meetings, child-rearing classes, an educational program, and vocational training. "But the mothers' reactions suggested they didn't much care." The judge in this case took the unusual step of moving to terminate parental rights and to place the children in adoptive homes. Most children are not so lucky.

There is no evidence that the limited forms of intervention we typically use today work effectively to protect children from abuse and neglect, and good reason to believe that they do not. As noted in chapter 3 above, one-third to one-half of the children victimized by maltreatment are revictimized by their parents; the CPS method of intervention has failed them.[19]

Investigation alone—the typical response—may serve some deterrent and protective function, but not as effectively as doing something more. And in many cases investigation followed by inaction may be worse than doing nothing: perpetrators may feel vindicated and empowered, and victims may be exposed to retribution and have their feelings of isolation and helplessness confirmed and deepened.

There is no evidence that the treatment and other parent-support services which may be offered in the most serious abuse and neglect cases are helpful in reforming parents and protecting children.[20] The notion that parents who commit maltreatment can be rehabilitated is the lynchpin of the system. Yet the evidence is overwhelming that rehabilitation efforts don't work, at least in the serious cases in which they are likely to be provided. One of the most important and extensive studies of model family preservation programs, those that provided fairly intensive forms of support and services, found that the programs did not significantly change or improve the parents' functioning. It found that one third of the children involved were subject to repeated maltreatment during the period of support and treatment, and fully one half would likely be victimized after services had been concluded. The study concluded: "Treatment efforts in general are not very successful. Child abuse and neglect continue despite early, thoughtful, and often costly intervention."[21] A recent comprehensive study by the National Research Council and Institute of Medicine came to similarly devastating conclusions about the efficacy of all traditional social services prevention and treatment programs aimed at violence in families. Their analysis of the entire body of research indicated that there was no evidence that any of the social service interventions worked.[22] Experts believe that much of the problem is the result of concentrating our support and treatment services on families that are so seriously dysfunctional they are the least capable of benefitting.[23]

Temporarily removing the child and providing social services to the parents in an attempt to keep the family together has produced no better results for children. As discussed in chapter 3 above, close to one-third of all children who are reunited with their parents end up being removed again, and it is likely that many more are victims of maltreatment that goes unproven.

The most extreme forms of intervention work best for children. Children placed in foster homes do better than children whose families are kept together, and children placed in adoptive homes do better yet. They would do even better if we moved them on to adoption promptly, rather than subjecting them to the kind of damaging delays that routinely occur in today's system. But while adoption is extremely likely to be the intervention that best serves children who have been subjected to severe forms of abuse or neglect, only about 10 percent of the children who are removed from their parents are ever adopted.[24]

If we want to protect children from abuse and neglect, the case for intervening more aggressively both before and after such maltreatment occurs is strong.

THE ONGOING TRADITION

5. TRADITIONAL PROGRAMS
WEATHER THE STORM

FAMILY PRESERVATION IN ITS INFINITE VARIETY

Family preservation involves a huge range of laws and regulations, programs and policies, all of which make it a priority to keep children at risk for abuse and neglect with their families, or as closely linked to their families as is possible consistent with the goal of not placing children at too great risk. Family preservation includes, for example, the laws and constitutional interpretations that require states to make a very strong showing of the parents' unfitness before children can be removed to foster or institutional care, and an even stronger showing before parental rights can be finally terminated. State law generally requires proof of serious forms of abuse and neglect before state agencies are allowed to intervene in the family, and it rarely allows for the immediate termination of parental rights no matter how extreme the maltreatment, instead requiring that efforts be made to rehabilitate parents and reunify families. Federal constitutional law requires that states prove maltreatment by "clear and convincing evidence," a more demanding standard than the probability standard that typically governs civil court proceedings. Federal constitutional law gives adults fundamental rights to parent their children, while giving children no rights to *be parented* in a nurturing way.

Family preservation also includes the child welfare agency policies which mandate a preference for keeping children with their parents and for returning children in foster care to their homes of origin, rather than moving them on to adoption or maintaining them in the state's care. It includes the services which are traditionally provided—or are supposed to be provided—to families to enable them to improve their parenting so that they can keep their children. It includes kinship care policies, which are designed to keep children within at least the *extended* biological family and to maximize the chances of maintaining meaningful links with the biological parents.

Family preservation also includes the intensive family preservation services (IFPS) programs that are designed to provide social worker counseling, treatment, and other supportive services, on an intensive but short-term basis, to families described as being at risk of losing their children to foster or institutional care. The very definition is revealing: *the risk that is the focus is the risk of the family being broken up, not the risk of the child being harmed.* The period of time for services is usually four to twelve weeks. The Homebuilders program, on which many others are modeled, has a six-week period.[1] While many tend to equate IFPS with family preservation, the fact is that IFPS programs simply represent a characteristic part of a much larger whole.

Family preservation is more than simply a collection of policies and programs. It is a *mindset* that dominates the thinking of the people who make and implement child welfare policy from top to bottom, in the public agencies and the private foundations, in the courts and the legislatures.

The Storm

"Isn't family preservation dead?" asks a friend who is very knowledgeable about the child welfare system. One might easily get the sense that, if not completely dead, it is on its way out, a victim of attacks on many fronts in the last decade.

The newspapers have featured a succession of stories demonstrating the horrors that can happen when families are preserved in the face of evidence that children are at risk. In Chicago the papers told the story of the little boy returned to his mentally ill mother, only to be hanged by her shortly thereafter.[2] Loving foster parents, relatives, Cook County's Public Guardian, and the mother's own psychiatrist had testified to the dangers of returning Joseph Wallace to the mother who had been institutionalized for mental problems repeatedly since her own childhood, had threatened to kill Joseph, his infant brother and herself, had beaten her children in the past, and had repeatedly mutilated herself and tried to burn herself. The State division of Child Protection had warned that she might maim or kill him. But Joseph was returned by a judge who believed in family preservation and said he felt governed by state and federal law requirements, after a court hearing in which lawyers and social workers argued for the mother's parental rights. Two months after Joseph's return his mother tied an electric cord around the three-year-old boy's neck and to a door transom, gagged him, watched him wave good-bye, and then pulled the chair out from under his feet. A state investigative report later blamed lawyers, judges, and caseworkers for contributing to his death, finding that the evidence before the court that returned Joseph to his mother revealed the risk that she would harm him, whether intentionally or negligently, as well as the "absolute certainty" that if he lived to grow up it would be in the care of "a suicidal, anti-social pyromaniac." Joseph's death triggered loud protests against the family preservation bias in the system, demanding legislative reform that would place a higher priority on the best interest of the child.

In New York City the papers told the story of the torturous life and death suffered by Elisa Izquierdo because the courts and the social services system left her at the mercy of her mother.[3] Elisa was born in Brooklyn, New York, on February 11, 1989, with cocaine in her blood. About a month before her birth, child protection workers had found her half-sister and half-brother neglected and had taken them from their mother, a heavy user of crack/cocaine and alcohol. Elisa was placed at birth in the custody of her father, who cared for her lovingly during her early years. She was described by her school director as "a beautiful, radiant child." Her older siblings were returned to their mother after she had drug treatment, and Elisa was allowed to visit her. But the father stopped these visits when he discovered evidence of abuse and signs of emotional stress. When the father fell ill and died in 1994, Elisa was placed in her mother's custody, despite disturbing evidence about her mother's treatment of her. A relative of Elisa's father fought for her custody but gave up in face of the system's defense of the mother.

Elisa was repeatedly abused and tortured from the time she lived with her mother until her death on November 22, 1995, at the age of six. Reports were repeatedly made to child protective authorities during this time as to her suspected maltreatment, as later state investigations of her case revealed:

> After she died, the extent to which Elisa's situation had been noticed, but not intervened in effectively, became apparent: Relatives, neighbors, and school officials reported having been worried about Elisa's condition; some said they had reported their suspicions that Elisa was being abused to the state's child abuse hotline, to CWA [the CPS agency], and to the Family Court judge who awarded Mrs. Lopez custody of Elisa after her father's death. Hospitals, mental health, and social services agencies had multiple contacts with Mrs. Lopez in connection with Elisa and some of her other children, and one agency providing preventive services under contract to CWA had extensive contacts and submitted reports on the family to CWA.
>
> According to the New York State Department of Social Services, in its Child Fatality Report on this case, there were five reports to the State Central Register between January 1989 and March 1995 concerning Mrs. Lopez' children, the last one in March 1995 specifically about Elisa. The CWA caseworker responsible for investigating the March 1995 report, however, never completed the required investigation to determine if there was cause to believe that Elisa was at risk, and the case was still open—and months overdue for a determination—on the day she died.[4]

No action was ever taken to intervene. On November 22 Elisa was found by Emergency Medical Service workers, with "numerous bruises, wounds, and contusions on the body, face, and head." Pronounced dead on arrival at the hospital, she was officially found to have died of "child abuse syndrome with blunt impacts to head and subdural hemorrhage, attributed to homicide." Newspaper accounts at the time painted her life and death more vividly. They described

Elisa's siblings watching helplessly as she was forced to drink ammonia and eat her own feces, as she was sexually assaulted and beaten "until the white bones gleamed through her brown fingers." They described her body, when she was discovered lifeless, "so battered and sexually tormented that strangers wept over her fate." Elisa's story, and others similarly horrifying, has helped create popular outrage. And the press and public interest in these stories reflects a widely shared sense that family preservation has been pushed too far.

Some of these cases were taken up by public interest lawyers, interested in using the courts to force reform upon the system. Marisol became the named plaintiff in a major class action brought by Children's Rights, Inc., challenging New York City's child welfare system. The director of that organization writes:

> When Marisol was three and one-half years old, she was discharged from foster care and sent to live with her mother, who had placed the child in foster care at birth. Her mother had a history of drug abuse, for which she had been imprisoned. Nothing in her record indicated that she had been rehabilitated. In sending the child to live with her mother, the New York City child welfare system ignored reports that Marisol had returned from visits prior to discharge unfed and frightened by violence in the home, suggesting that her mother might still be abusing drugs. Instead, authorities applied the system's current operating principle that all children should be with their biological parents—without any kind of careful evaluation to determine whether this particular parent was able to care for her child, without providing any meaningful services to address the parent's problems, and without providing necessary supervision and oversight to ensure that the child was safe. Reports that Marisol was being abused by her mother went uninvestigated, and those concerned were given bland assurances that the child was thriving. But child welfare officials had no idea how she was doing. Fifteen months later, a housing inspector happened upon Marisol, locked in a closet in her mother's apartment, near death. She had been repeatedly abused over an extended period of time, eating black plastic garbage bags and her own feces to survive. After leaving the hospital, Marisol reentered foster care. Her permanency goal: return to mother. The service to be provided to enable her mother to resume custody: parenting classes.[5]

The case was settled at the end of 1998, pursuant to an agreement that an expert panel would monitor the City's progress toward a reformed system.

Various public figures have taken up the cause, calling for the reform of child welfare policies to limit family preservation priorities and place a greater emphasis on children's safety and well-being. Patrick Murphy, Public Guardian of Cook County, Illinois, has made it his business to advocate for abused and neglected children against both their parents and the child welfare system. His book, *Wasted*, is in his words about a "brutal" system which, although designed to help children, is instead helping to destroy them."[6] Politicians in many cities and states have initiated legal changes to limit what they see as the excesses of family preservation—changes which enable children to be freed more readily from parents responsible for particularly vicious or destructive maltreatment. On the federal level, President Clinton announced "Adoption 2002," calling for a significant increase in the number of children to be freed up from foster care for adoption. Congress passed the Adoption and Safe Families Act in 1997, telling states that they no longer needed to make "reasonable efforts" to preserve families in certain egregious cases of child maltreatment, and creating new incentives for states to free children up for adoption.

Not-for-profit organizations have called for a new child-centered paradigm, placing greater emphasis on adoption.[7] New organizations have been formed with the goal of promoting children's interests in growing up in nurturing families, and old organizations that saw themselves as committed to children's rights have been newly energized. These organizations mobilize advocacy efforts to free children from birth families which have been guilty of maltreatment, as well as to protect children's nurturing relationships with preadoptive families. They also promote legislative reform.[8]

Family preservation has also received some telling blows from the research community. Here the primary emphasis has been on intensive family preservation services (IFPS) programs.

IFPS advocates had developed their own research as part of the effort to sell the programs politically. Their claim was that this research demonstrated that family preservation worked. Anyone who took the trouble to unpack the research could see the problems inherent in this claim. First and most significant was the issue of how success was measured. IFPS programs defined their goal as family preservation: services were provided to families "at risk" of having a child removed, in the hope that with services the families could be preserved. But the underlying rationale was that preserving the family would serve another goal—the child's well-being. This *had* to be the underlying rationale, since IFPS programs were being sold politically as *child welfare* programs, not as general poverty programs. Nonetheless, the research focused solely on family preservation as the criterion for success, claiming that the programs were successful because in a high percentage of cases in which intensive services were provided, children were not removed. The blatantly obvious question was whether the children *should have been removed*—whether keeping them in their biological family after they had been maltreated placed them at undue risk for further maltreatment. This question was studiously avoided by the researchers. On a theoretical level there was no reason to think that IFPS programs *would* work to serve the child. Cases in which the removal of a child is being considered are generally cases of repeated, serious abuse or chronic neglect. Most of the families are plagued with a history of substance abuse combined with other serious problems of longstanding duration. While IFPS programs were conceived of with the idea of addressing short-term crises in a family's life, the programs were soon applied to the range of serious cases, including substance abuse cases, on the CPS caseload. There is no quick fix for the parenting problems in most of these families. Six weeks' worth of intensive social services may be gratefully received, especially if it involves concrete housing or welfare or housekeeping or child care services, but it is not likely in most cases to make a significant dent in the problems that put children at risk.

The second basic problem with the IFPS advocates' research claim had to do with the flawed methodology—in particular, the absence of controlled studies. The studies showed nothing more than that a high percentage of families identified as at risk of having children removed ended up intact after participating in IFPS programs. This was presented as proof that the intensive services were responsible for accomplishing the result. In fact there was no evidence that had IFPS programs not been in place, the number of children removed would have been any higher.

In the last decade, a significant body of research on IFPS programs has highlighted the obvious flaws in the advocates' early research and raised serious questions as to whether IFPS works either to prevent out-of-home placement or to promote children's welfare.[9] An early blow was dealt when The Edna McConnell Clark Foundation's own consultant, Peter Rossi, submitted his 1991 report to Clark concluding that the research claiming IFPS success was fundamentally flawed.[10] Then came the second wave of research—more sophisticated and dispassionate than that put out by the IFPS advocates. This new research demonstrates that *when IFPS program populations are compared to control group populations not receiving intensive services, a similarly high percentage of families are preserved in both groups.* There is broad agreement today in the research community that even if success is measured in the narrow terms of family preservation, rather than child welfare, claims for the success of IFPS have simply not been substantiated.

More important, the new research has clarified the centrality of the child's well-being to any assessment of IFPS, and it indicates that, measured in these terms, IFPS fails. As discussed in chapter 3, *roughly one-third to one-half of the children in families that are preserved or reunified after initial findings of maltreatment continue to be abused and neglected.*[11] There is no evidence children fare any better when their families receive the special support and treatment services of IFPS programs than when their families are relegated to the traditional CPS track.[12]

Recent research also calls into question the theoretical underpinnings of IFPS, the core notion that providing intensive services for six weeks or some other brief period of time will be sufficient to address the deeply entrenched problems that are typical of parents who subject their children to the severe forms of maltreatment that trigger CPS intervention today. Many have pointed to the absurdity of thinking that people caught in the toils of substance abuse, or other seriously dysfunctional patterns of behavior, will be able to turn their lives around overnight simply because social workers offer a helping hand for a month or two. They have pointed out that while short-term intensive services might be helpful to families with relatively minor problems to overcome, these are not the families that IFPS programs target.[13]

Future research may be able to detect that at least some IFPS programs succeed at preventing the removal of some children from families at risk for abuse and neglect. Indeed, it seems that IFPS programs would have some such impact. Social workers are likely to increase their efforts to preserve families the more that success is defined in terms of family preservation.[14] But there is obvious reason for concern that the more IFPS programs "succeed" in these terms, the more children will suffer. IFPS advocates regularly talk of children in these programs as "at risk of placement," yet placement is what many of these children desperately need. There is increasing recognition of this reality, and increasing recognition of the risks for children in the pressures that intensive family preservation programs create.[15]

Richard Gelles, Research Director of the Center for the Study of Youth Policy at the University of Pennsylvania School of Social Work, was once one of the most widely published and vocal defenders of family preservation. He is now one of its most eloquent and informed critics. His recent work, *The Book of David: How Preserving Families Can Cost Children's Lives*, assesses the entire body of IFPS research. Like others, he finds no evidence that IFPS programs are effective in reducing placements, and he calls it "nearly criminal" that children's safety and well-being have not been the focal points of research from the beginning.[16]

The Power of Tradition

The storm has had an impact. There is a new sense abroad that the excesses of family preservation have put children at undue risk.

But the critique, debate, and reform efforts within the child welfare system have been limited to date. Much of the critical attention has been directed at IFPS programs specifically, leaving the rest of the family preservation system—the laws and constitutional provisions that limit the state's ability to intervene in the family, the myriad child welfare policies that make family preservation and reunification a priority—relatively untouched. While IFPS may not be the panacea it claimed to be, it makes little sense to see the existence of IFPS as the key problem. Children will be no better off if we continue to preserve their families but *don't* offer these families services.

Laws and policies that seemed to require efforts to preserve the family even in egregious cases of abuse or torture have also been under attack. But no real challenge has been mounted to the impact that the family preservation system has on children's well-being in the many cases that get categorized as neglect. There is general recognition that substance abuse has caused a crisis in child welfare, but there is little consensus on what to do in substance abuse cases. It's telling that the 1997 Adoption and Safe Families Act (ASFA) failed to specifically address either neglect or substance abuse. And while ASFA signals a new priority for moving children into permanent homes, its loopholes and exceptions provide no guarantee that the status quo will actually change much. (See chapter 8.)

Nor has there yet been any fundamental change in the mindset of most of those who make and implement child welfare policy—the judges who interpret and apply laws, the social workers who make decisions whether or not to remove children, the bureaucrats who run federal and state child welfare agencies, the private foundation administrators who have provided essential funding for family preservation programs, the not-for-profit agency people involved in child welfare issues, and the lawyers who represent the parties in court, including those assigned to represent children's interests. These people have enormous power to determine whether new laws and policies intended to change the system actually have any significant impact. Most of them have been true believers in family preservation, and it appears that few have lost the faith. Many of them scorn criticism of family preservation as irrational "backlash."

As a result the great ship of family preservation sails on, its basic course not much changed to date, despite all the apparent turmoil. Indeed in recent years significant *new support* has been provided for family preservation programs, including the controversial IFPS variety. In 1993 Congress passed Family Preservation and Support Services legislation, providing approximately $1 billion over a five-year period for family preservation efforts, as well as general family support services.[17] In 1997 Congress continued this funding and also increased the level of funding by about $20 million per year, although this new funding is now restricted to "time-limited" family preservation, and states are required to use a "significant" portion of it for adoption promotion and support services.[18]

Support for family preservation in the form of kinship care has also been growing. As discussed in chapter 3, state and local child welfare policies require that social workers recruit kin for foster placements and mandate powerful preferences for kin over nonrelatives. The federal government endorsed kinship care explicitly in the 1993 Family Preservation Act noted above. Child welfare traditionalists fought successfully for a broad exception to the Adoption and Safe Families Act's general requirements that children be guaranteed an early permanent home, so that children placed with kin could be kept in long-term kinship care. The number of children in kinship homes has escalated dramatically in recent years. The 1996 federal welfare reform legislation added a new requirement that states "consider giving preference" to kin over nonkin when determining child placement.[19]

So family preservation in its traditional forms is far from dead. It has also appeared in some new forms that appear to be flourishing, as discussed in chapter 6.

COMMUNITY PRESERVATION: RACE MATCHING AND RELATED POLICIES

If children cannot be kept with their families of origin, traditional attitudes call for keeping them within their communities of origin, with communities defined primarily in racial and ethnic terms. Black children should be kept in the black community, and Native American children in their tribal communities. So goes the thinking.[20]

During the segregation era, laws and policies systematically prevented placing children for adoption across racial lines. The civil rights movement brought changes in the law and in attitudes in the 1960s. Courts ruled that the state could not constitutionally prevent the creation of interracial families. Social welfare agencies began to respond to the needs of the black children waiting in foster care because there were not enough black adoptive families. Increasing numbers of adoptive parents had been going abroad to adopt children from different ethnic and racial backgrounds. Increasing numbers began to express interest in similarly crossing racial and ethnic lines on the domestic front. For the first time, significant numbers of transracial adoptions took place in the United States, the great majority of them involving black, Latino, and Native American children placed with white parents. This was largely a function of the numbers—the children needing homes were disproportionately from minority racial groups, while the adults interested in adopting were overwhelmingly white.

In 1972 certain black and Native American leaders stepped forward to challenge transracial placement within the United States. The National Association of Black Social Workers (NABSW) denounced transracial adoption as racial genocide and issued a manifesto demanding that all black children be kept within the black community, whether in foster or adoptive homes. Native American leaders simultaneously attacked the practices which had resulted in the placement of many Indian children in white homes and called on Congress for legislation giving tribes the power to control the destiny of these children.

These appeals found a receptive audience. The establishment forces readily conceded that the black and the Native American communities had a right to hold onto "their own," and that black and Native American children truly "belonged" with their groups of origin. Social workers had always viewed transracial placements as potentially problematic. The Child Welfare League of America responded to the National Black Social Workers' manifesto by revising its standards of practice to place a higher priority on keeping children within their racial community. Child welfare agencies across the country established powerful preferences for placing children with families of the same race. In some states, new laws, regulations, and written policies mandated the preference for same-race placement, sometimes requiring in addition that children be held for a minimum period of time before they could be placed with families of another race. The unwritten policies were even more powerful than the written. These policies generally required foster and adoption workers to place children transracially only as a very last resort, if at all. They regularly resulted not only in long delays before children were adopted, but for many children in the permanent denial of the opportunity to find an adoptive family.

Congress responded to the Native American leaders by enacting the Indian Child Welfare Act (ICWA), which gave Indian tribes and families important new powers to hold onto Indian children. ICWA gave tribal courts exclusive jurisdiction over many cases involving Indian children, and gave tribes the authority to intervene in state courts to press tribal claims over children, even in cases in which Indian birth parents wanted to place their children outside the tribal community. It created powerful preferences for placing children with extended family, or within their own tribe, or within the Native American community. It also made it extraordinarily difficult to free maltreated children for adoption, requiring states to show parental unfitness "beyond a reasonable doubt."[21]

The new orthodoxy was quickly established, making the 1960s period of transracial placements seem a brief anomaly in the larger picture. Latino groups joined the fray, demanding that "their" children stay within their own ethnic community groups. The numbers and percentage of minority race children in foster care grew dramatically as these children poured into the system, and social workers, given the limited number of available same-race adoptive homes, felt constrained to keep them there. In 1980 Congress provided significant support for same-race placement by offering matching funds to states which provided subsidies for "hard-to-place" or "special needs" adoptions. Children of color could be designated as hard to place in significant part because same-race matching policies made them hard to place, even if they had no physical or emotional disability. This law meant that subsidies could be provided for the adoption of any black or other minority-race child if state law so chose. So even though the 1980 law made no mention of the goal of promoting same-race over transracial placement, it was designed to serve that purpose by providing services and subsidies for same-race adoptive parents. Even with the 1980 law, however, the numbers of minority-race children in foster and institutional care continued to build up. While less is known about ICWA's impact, it also seems to have resulted in an increase in the number of Indian children held in out-of-home care.[22]

The Storm

In the late 1980s through the 1990s challenges were mounted on many fronts to the notion that children should be kept at almost all costs within their racial, ethnic, or tribal community of origin. Media stories documented some of the horrors that resulted from insisting on this priority. They described children removed from the loving foster parents who had nurtured them to recovery after rocky starts in life, children removed solely because those parents were the wrong color and had nonetheless become so attached that they wanted to adopt. A popular TV news magazine reported on one such story which ended with the child being killed by the same-race family with whom he had been placed.[23] Foster parents took some of these cases to court and won on the basis of showings that state policy preventing transracial adoption violated the principle that child welfare policy should be guided by the best interest of the child, and also violated legal and constitutional provisions against racial discrimination.[24]

Social scientists published a succession of studies demonstrating that children placed with other-race parents did just as well in all measurable respects as children placed with same-race parents. Other studies confirmed earlier evidence that delay in and denial of adoptive placement was extremely harmful to children. Yet other studies demonstrated that this kind of delay and denial was an inherent part of the race-matching regime.[25] Legal scholars used these social science findings to help demonstrate that the kind of race-matching policies in place throughout the nation's child welfare systems violated state and federal civil rights laws, as well as constitutional guarantees against racial discrimination.[26] As some opponents of race-matching policies began to speak out, others who had felt silenced by the power of the orthodox view became more vocal, and opposition grew. Leading newspapers and journals published op-ed pieces together with their own editorials condemning race-matching policies.[27]

People who had been transracially adopted as children began to speak out in print for the value of this form of family.[28] One such adoptee founded an advocacy organization called The Transracial Adoption Group Worldwide, Inc., designed to promote transracial adoption.[29]

Critics took on the various arguments that had been made on behalf of the race-matching regime. NABSW and other advocates of same-race placement had argued that it served black children's interests. The critics contended that this argument was frivolous, noting that the entire body of social science evidence was consistent: there was not a shred of evidence that transracial placement injured children; there was overwhelming evidence that suffering long delays in placement, or being denied an adoptive home, caused them significant harm. NABSW and its allies claimed that the system discriminated against minority-race applicants; they argued that if more were done to recruit minority-race adoptive parents, there would be enough same-race families for all the waiting children. The critics pointed out that extensive affirmative action efforts had been made over the years to reduce selection criteria for minority-race applicants, to recruit them, and to subsidize same-race placements, and that these efforts had succeeded to a significant degree. Black adults were adopting at roughly the same rates as whites, despite the fact that they were disproportionately at the bottom of the socioeconomic ladder. The problem was that there so many black children in foster care, and waiting for adoption, that blacks would have to adopt at many times the rate of whites to provide homes for all of the waiting children. NABSW and its allies claimed that whites would not be interested in adopting the black children who actually are in need of placement. They claimed that whites were interested only in healthy black babies, rather than the older children and the children with disabilities who disproportionately populate the foster care system. But the critics pointed out that when whites are asked whether they are interested in adopting older black children with significant disabilities they say yes in very significant numbers. Whites who express interest in such children are regularly turned away by public adoption agencies. They regularly go abroad where they often adopt children from orphanages with significant disabilities and developmental problems, and where they typically adopt across a variety of lines of difference—racial, ethnic, religious, and national.

The critics contended that what lay behind same-race matching policies was a form of race separatism that had been rejected in other contexts and could not be justified as serving the interests of either black children or the larger black community:

> [R]ace matching policies only make sense when seen as part of a more general move for race separatism, a modern move reminiscent of the earlier trend which gave rise to the 1972 NABSW position. These poli-

cies make sense only in conjunction with a kind of racial fundamental-
ism which is newly popular. . . .

Arguments by the opponents of transracial adoption reveal the sepa-
ratist nature of their position. For instance, it is said that only black parents can teach black children the "coping skills" necessary to survive in
a racist society. Yet studies indicate that transracial adoptees actually
cope very well. What seems to lie at the heart of the "coping skill" claim
is concern that black children develop a particular mode of interacting
with whites, one that is arguably designed to advance the interests of
the larger black community.

Another classic argument made by the opponents of transracial
adoption is that it produces children with confused racial identities.
The evidence, however, shows that transracial adoptees develop a positive sense of self-esteem and are not at all confused about the fact that
they are black. Quite clearly, the real concern is that they may not be
sufficiently committed to the black, as distinct from the white, community.

These kinds of arguments could also be applied to oppose inte-
grated education and interracial marriage. If we think that black children can only develop appropriate coping skills and racial identities under the tutelage of black adults, then we should send them to schools
with all-black faculties. Furthermore, according to this logic, we should
also do our best to prevent marriage and procreation across racial lines
so as to protect black children from the problems involved in being
raised by a white parent and the confusion of racial roles in their own
mixed-race status and their parents' interracial relationship.[30]

Critics challenged the notion that NABSW's position should be
taken as representative of the "black community" position, noting
that polls of black people indicated no significant support for
NABSW's position or for the race-matching regime. They pointed
out that private decisions of many black adults indicate significant
and increasing support for interracial family relationships, with the
number of interracial marriages and mixed-race births escalating
significantly. They argued that same-race matching policies were
motivated and sustained by the commitment of certain adoption
professionals, more than by any "community" commitment. Richard Barth testified in Congress to his research findings:

My research and experience tell me that there is considerably more acceptance of interethnic and cross-racial placements among the general public than among the professional adoption community. Indeed, in California, African American children who are placed for adoption by their own biological parents are about three times more likely to be placed into homes with at least one white parent than are children placed by adoption agencies.[31]

NABSW and its allies had equated transracial adoption with racial genocide. The critics of the race-matching regime pointed out that such adoption would never pose the threat to a monolithic black community that interracial marriage and school integration posed. But more significantly, they challenged the idea that the black community would be in any way strengthened by keeping needy black children in inadequate foster and institutional care, preventing them from growing up in the kind of permanent families that are essential to human health and development.[32]

Liberal Democrat Senator Metzenbaum, who decided as he contemplated retirement to make the challenge to race-matching his swan song, introduced the bill that became known as the Multiethnic Placement Act, or MEPA. As enacted in 1994, MEPA prohibited child welfare agencies that receive federal funds—a category that includes virtually all the state foster and adoption agencies—from using race to delay or deny adoptive placement, but permitted agencies otherwise to make race a factor in their decisions.[33] Within a brief two years Congress was persuaded to strengthen the law, eliminating the language that allowed race as a permissible factor and creating powerful new penalties for any violations.[34] Both MEPA I and MEPA II drew significant support from across the political spectrum, from Gingrich Republicans to liberal Democrats, and from President Clinton and First Lady Hillary Rodham Clinton as well.

No comparable challenge has been mounted, at least as yet, to ICWA, and MEPA specifically excludes ICWA from its coverage. But there have been some rumblings of protest. One powerfully reasoned California court opinion held that ICWA could not be constitutionally interpreted to give Indian tribes control over children based solely on the basis of blood links as opposed to social relationship links with the tribes.[35] Some have promoted amendments to ICWA that would narrow Indian tribes' possessory claim to Indian children in ways consistent with this case, although so far they have made no progress.[36]

The Power of Tradition

The story surrounding the Multiethnic Placement Act dramatically illustrates the difficulty of accomplishing change in child welfare traditions. Senator Metzenbaum introduced and Congress passed MEPA I in 1994 with the goal of effecting very significant change in race-matching policies. A strong case had been made that they destroyed many children's prospects for life happiness and blatantly violated civil rights laws and constitutional provisions. Nonetheless, child welfare traditionalists lobbied fiercely behind the scenes first to prevent Senator Metzenbaum's proposed legislation from passing, and next to weaken its provisions. These forces included an impressive array: the Children's Defense Fund, one of the nation's most powerful children's rights organizations; the North American Council on Adoptable Children (NACAC), an organization which is supposed to represent the interests of children in foster care; Adoptive Families of America (AFA), one of the largest, nationally based, adoption support organizations; and a large number of other public and private organizations, including some funded by the U.S. Department of Health and Human Services.

MEPA I was enacted in a somewhat problematic form, given the sponsor's original goals. It not only included the provision making the use of race a permissible factor, but also a provision mandating that state plans provide for the recruitment of foster and adoptive families reflecting the ethnic and racial diversity of the children needing homes. Together with some other opponents of race-matching policies, I had argued that these provisions threatened to undermine the Act's goals. Noting the entrenched commitment to keeping children within their racial group, we warned that any leeway given to utilize race would be used to evade the new law's clear intent. Our advice was in the end ignored.

Within a short period after MEPA I's passage Senator Metzenbaum found himself seriously disillusioned with the Act's potential to accomplish its purposes. Frustrated with the resistance to

MEPA I, and newly impressed with the devotion of child welfare traditionalists to race matching, he began promoting action to repeal his own legislation and replace it with a new version designed to better accomplish its goals.

MEPA II eliminated the provision in MEPA I that allowed race as a permissible consideration. This provision had read:

> An agency or entity . . . may consider the cultural, ethnic, or racial background of the child and the capacity of the prospective foster or adoptive parents to meet the needs of a child of this background as one of a number of factors used to determine the best interests of a child.

MEPA II also eliminated related language indicating that some use of race might be permissible—language forbidding agencies to "*categorically deny*" foster or adoptive parenting opportunity, or delay or deny placement "*solely*" on the basis of race. MEPA II substituted language that tracked the language of other civil rights statutes, simply prohibiting discrimination. Agencies receiving funds from the federal government were told that they could not:

A. deny to any person the opportunity to become an adoptive or a foster parent, on the basis of the race, color, or national origin of the person, or of the child, involved; or

B. delay or deny the placement of a child for adoption or into foster care, on the basis of the race, color, or national origin of the adoptive or foster parent, or the child, involved.

The intent to remove race as a factor in placement decisions could hardly have been made more clear. The legislative history showed that the race-as-permissible-factor provision was removed precisely because it had been identified as deeply problematic. The simple antidiscrimination language substituted had been consistently interpreted in the context of other civil rights laws as forbidding *any* consideration of race as a factor in decision-making, with the increasingly limited exception accorded formal affirmative action plans.

MEPA II's remaining changes provided dramatic new fiscal penalties for noncompliance, sending the message that Congress was determined that this Act be taken seriously. Any single finding of violation was to trigger *automatic* reduction of the federal funds provided to each state for foster and adoption purposes. The reduction was to escalate for additional violations, up to a maximum of 5 percent of the total federal allocation. In addition to these administrative sanctions, MEPA provided aggrieved private parties with a right to seek enforcement of the Act's antidiscrimination provisions in court and, if successful, a right to have attorneys' fees paid by the defendant.

The United States Department of Health and Human Services issued a "Guidance" Memorandum on June 5, 1997, regarding MEPA's proper interpretation. It noted that in some states the Act's penalties could range up to more than $3.6 million in a given quarter and could increase to the $7–10 million range for continued noncompliance. It states clearly that states cannot take race routinely into account in making placement decisions, and that instead the appropriate "strict scrutiny" standard forbids the use of race or ethnicity "except in the very limited circumstances where such consideration would be necessary to achieve a compelling governmental interest. . . . Additionally, the consideration must be narrowly tailored to advance the child's interests, and must be made as an individualized determination for each child." The Guidance goes on to emphasize the extraordinarily unusual circumstances in which consideration of race might be permissible:

> For example, it is conceivable that an older child or adolescent might express an unwillingness to be placed with a family of a particular race. In some states older children and adolescents must consent to their adoption by a particular family. In such an individual situation, an agency is not required to dismiss the child's express unwillingness to consent in evaluating placements. While the adoption worker might wish to counsel the child, the child's ideas of what would make her or him most comfortable should not be dismissed, and the worker should consider the child's willingness to accept the family as an element that is critical to the success of the adoptive placement. At the same time, the worker should not dismiss as possible placements families of a particular race who are able to meet the needs of the child.
>
> Other circumstances in which race or ethnicity can be taken into account in a placement decision may also be encountered. . . . However, the primary message of the strict scrutiny standard in this context is

that only the most compelling reasons may serve to justify consideration of race and ethnicity as part of a placement decision. Such reasons
are likely to emerge only in unique and individual circumstances. Accordingly, occasions where race or ethnicity lawfully may be considered
in a placement decision will be correspondingly rare.[37]

Additional "Guidance" issued in 1998 warns against the use of "culture as a proxy for race, color, or national origin" and makes it clear
that "any routine use of 'cultural assessments' of children's needs or
prospective parent's capacities would be suspect if it had the effect of
circumventing the law's prohibition against the routine consideration of race, color, national origin."[38]

MEPA I and II in combination were clearly designed to achieve
massive change in the nation's public foster and adoption agencies'
policies. Race matching had been one of the most important factors
in agency decision-making.[39]

But MEPA appears so far to have had almost no impact. Nor is
there any evidence of the kind of enforcement activity that would
make significant change in the near future seem likely. The U.S. Department of Health and Human Services (HHS), responsible for administrative enforcement, has been awfully quiet since issuing its
tough-sounding Guidance. State officials responsible for bringing
their agencies into compliance with MEPA are similarly quiet. Listening to the sounds of child welfare activity around the country one
gets no sense that the revolutionary change called for by MEPA is in
the works. There is instead a deafening silence. All seems to be going
on more or less as usual. There have been some changes in the *written*
laws and policies that had demanded race matching: it is always
problematic to have written laws or regulations that are blatantly illegal. But the most common and most extreme race-matching policies
have always been *unwritten*. For there to be real change, federal and
state officials would have to send forth clear instructions to child welfare workers throughout the country that a new order prevails, and
that they are to change their practices accordingly. The 1997 and 1998
HHS Guidance, while a start, are not enough. Those in charge of enforcement and compliance, including lower level workers throughout the system, are for the most part believers in the tradition of
race matching.

While enforcement activity is limited, the MEPA resistance movement is quite active. Soon after MEPA II's passage, newsletters from various child welfare organizations promoted creative "interpretations" of its provisions. They argued that MEPA II could be read to allow some use of race, so long as race was not used to delay or deny placement, conveniently ignoring the fact that the main point of MEPA II was to eliminate MEPA I's provision allowing race as a permissible consideration. In leading child welfare journals articles appeared with titles such as, "Achieving Same-Race Placements for African-American Children," telling readers how to accomplish race matching despite MEPA.[40]

At child welfare organization conferences and meetings in recent years it has been hard to find any discussion of MEPA *implementation*. There is instead talk about the "problems" it poses. There is talk about the importance of interpreting MEPA so as not to prohibit what "good social work practice" clearly requires. There is talk about the only aspect of MEPA that even arguably supports race matching: the provision in the 1994 act that required that state plans "provide for the diligent recruitment of potential foster and adoptive families that reflect the ethnic and racial diversity of children in the State for whom foster and adoptive homes are needed."[41] Race-matching advocates have seized on this provision, which was unfortunately not repealed by the 1996 act, and often talk as if it was the essence of what MEPA was about. This kind of thinking has even found its way into one part of the federal HHS Guidance. Despite the strong strict-scrutiny language quoted above, the Guidance includes the following: "Active, diligent, and lawful recruitment of potential foster and adoptive parents of all backgrounds is both a legal requirement and an important tool for meeting the demands of good practice." What is this supposed to mean other than that "good practice" may demand race matching?

There is also a lot of talk at these conferences and meetings of "cultural competence." The phrase has been carefully chosen. Who can be against cultural competence? If you look and listen carefully it becomes clear that cultural competence is being used as a euphemistic cover, and that it is often understood in the field as a means of assessing and promoting race-matching policies. Thus a report evaluating "innovative permanency planning programs" uses cultural competence as one key criterion, rating programs according to their success at recruiting minority-race parents and placing children on a same-race basis.[42] When agency workers are encouraged to screen prospective adoptive parents for cultural competence, as they are increasingly, they are being given a tool for screening out prospective transracial adopters and are simultaneously being encouraged to use it.

Resistance to the MEPA mandate is the order of the day. It comes in an endless variety of forms. Most of them are invisible to those who aren't intimately familiar with the workings of the child welfare system. They are also incomprehensible to those who don't understand the profound commitment that many in the system have to the notion that children belong with their racial and ethnic group. What's easy for all to see is the superficial changes. Thus, in California, one of the three states in the nation which had a statute requiring race matching, MEPA's passage meant the statute was repealed. But this change merely scratched the surface. In California, as elsewhere, it was the unwritten policies on race matching that were the most significant. What is key is who runs the system and whether they are committed to the fundamental changes MEPA requires. MEPA I's passage inspired the creation of a privately funded task force in California to help design public policy changes in light of this legal development. The "Adoption and Race Work Group" issued its preliminary draft report in 1996, and its final report, adapted to include reference to MEPA II, in 1997.[43] Asked for my comments on the preliminary draft, I reported that it looked to me like a manifesto for resistance:

> From start to finish [the Report] reads like a justification for the present race-matching system, and an argument for continuing to implement essential features of that system in a way designed to satisfy the letter but not the spirit of [MEPA]. . . .
>
> The general thrust of the Report in terms of policy direction, together with its specific Recommendations, read to me like the advice prepared by clever lawyers whose goal it is to help the client avoid the clear spirit of the law. The general idea seems to be to tell those in a position to make and implement policy, that this is a bad law, based on a misunderstanding of the needs of black children, but that since it is less

than crystal clear, it will be possible to retool and reshape current policies and practices so that they look quite different but accomplish
much the same thing.[44]

This draft report became the final report, with no significant
changes in tone or substance. Although the final report referred to
the revisions made by MEPA II, it failed to reflect their real import.
According to the report, race could and should still be taken into account in placement decision-making so long as it was done on an
individual basis.

In Massachusetts, the Department of Social Services (DSS) has
long exercised an across-the-board preference for same-race matching. For many years media stories have documented the extremes to
which DSS has gone in order to keep children within their racial, ethnic, and other communities of origin. Children have been held in
foster care rather than being placed in waiting other-race families.
Children have been placed with parents previously found guilty of
serious felonies, including physical and sexual abuse, because of
DSS's apparent inability to find more appropriate parents within the
limited racial community it will consider.[45] While DSS regularly denied that it kept black children in foster care rather than place them
transracially, an internal DSS report helped give the lie to that
claim.[46] Together with a handful of other children's rights advocates,
I saw MEPA as providing an opportunity to achieve significant
change in DSS policy. At a meeting we set up in June of 1997 with the
DSS officials in charge, their commitment to maintaining the status
quo was apparent. They repeated their standard official position that
race was not used to delay placement, but admitted that no memo
had ever gone out to social workers telling them that this was the
policy. They saw nothing in MEPA requiring any action on their
part, in the absence of specific instructions by the U.S. Department
of Health and Human Services, and it was clear that to date HHS
had done little to push them. After the passage of MEPA I, HHS had
apparently required only that DSS revise their written regulations to
limit the use of race, telling social workers that they should consider
it simply as one factor in their decisions. When we pointed out that
MEPA II clearly prohibited such generalized consideration of race,
the DSS officials told us they planned to take no action to change

even their written regulations until specifically instructed by HHS. When we asked if there was any way in which we could be helpful to DSS in implementing MEPA, they only expressed interest in help in satisfying the recruitment provisions—the only part of MEPA arguably supportive of race-matching goals.

Similar stories could be told about other states' reactions to MEPA. Resistance in the form of evasion, avoidance, and nonaction, is commonplace.

Resistance also takes the form of promoting policies which serve the goal of keeping children within the racial community but can be justified in other terms. Kinship care has been promoted over the last couple of decades *both* because it keeps children within the extended family group *and* because, by doing so, it almost always keeps them within the racial group as well. Policies favoring foster placement in the same community as the child's family of origin have been promoted on the grounds that they minimize disruption for the children, especially in cases where they will eventually be reunited with their parents. But these policies also generally serve to keep children in their racial communities of origin, given neighborhood segregation patterns.

Child welfare traditionalists have been pushing enthusiastically in recent years to expand kinship care, as discussed above. They have also been pushing the goal of local placement with renewed emphasis. They have promoted forms of foster care which can work only when the birth and foster families live near each other, such as family-to-family care, in which foster families are supposed to help birth families develop the capacity to take care of their own children. Obviously those who support kinship care and local placement policies have a variety of motivations. But there is also no question but that for opponents of transracial placement, these policies function as convenient end-runs around the new MEPA mandate.

In September of 1998 Congress held an oversight hearing on the implementation of MEPA II.[47] The Chairman of the relevant committee, Clay Shaw, made clear his concern that MEPA was not being implemented adequately. The representative from the U.S. Department of HHS, Assistant Secretary for Children Olivia Golden, made the claim that MEPA was having an impact, and that HHS was appropriately enforcing the law's requirements. She admitted that HHS had taken no action to invoke the financial penalties for violation mandated by MEPA, but contended that this was because there had been no resistance to the act. Her claims were greeted skeptically by the Committee and were powerfully rebutted by most of the experts testifying, a list that included former Senator Metzenbaum. He testified to his tremendous sense of frustration at the absence of enforcement activity, saying: "The law is there but HHS is not." A representative from the U.S. General Accounting Office testified about GAO's assessment of MEPA implementation efforts in California, concluding that neither HHS nor the state had taken adequate action to implement the 1996 changes in law, and noting the ongoing need to address practices and deeply entrenched attitudes. An array of experts from different backgrounds testified that racial matching policies and practices were continuing, in old and new forms. The President of the Transracial Adoption Group, representing transracial adoptees, testified about the development of "cultural competence" tests to screen out white prospective adopters in violation of MEPA's goal.[48] Patrick Murphy, Public Guardian in Cook County, Illinois, testified that race-matching practices were ongoing, with social workers ignoring available white foster and adoptive homes and placing African-American children in "an overextended and at times inadequate black foster home network, without regard to the quality of care." He testified that MEPA I and II were "honored more in the breach than in the observance" and talked of specific cases in which state bureaucrats had fought the placement of children with apparently appropriate parents solely on race grounds. One case involved a six-year-old white girl who had been living in an outstanding black foster home for two years. The state workers had been trying to reunite her with her parents, who had tried to suffocate her as a newborn and shown only sporadic interest in visiting her in foster care. When the state eventually concluded that the parents could not be rehabilitated, it tried to remove the child from her foster parents to a different foster home. Murphy testified that the girl desperately wanted to remain with her foster parents, who wanted to adopt her and "were providing as good a foster home as I have seen in my 30 years of working in child welfare." He concluded that institutional racism was at work, with the agency determined to place the child in a family of the same race. He fought the case in court and got a ruling from the trial judge allowing the black foster parents to adopt the white child, but the state appealed. The case was still pending at the time of his testimony. Murphy went on to condemn what he saw as inadequate enforcement efforts by HHS, and he called for Congress to transfer HHS's responsibilities to another agency, in the interest of getting MEPA enforced:

> Based upon my own practical experience and upon the clear inferences of HHS's own pronouncements, it is obvious that if Congress is serious about eliminating the discrimination that prevents children from being placed in the best, [most] appropriate foster home as quickly as possible, then the obligation for enforcing the law must be taken away from HHS. HHS officials have preconceived notions that run directly counter to the law. These officials have and will continue to eschew their enforcement power to thwart the will of Congress.[49]

Randall Kennedy, Professor of Law at Harvard Law School, challenged the assumption at the heart of race-matching ideology—the assumption that children belong within their racial group:

> Race matching . . . harms the entire society morally and spiritually by reiterating the baneful notion, long entrenched in law and custom, that people from different races should not be permitted to disregard distinctions when creating families . . . . A preference for same-race placements buttresses the notion that in social affairs race matters and should matter in some fundamental, unbridgeable, permanent sense. It belies the belief that love and understanding can be boundless and instead instructs us that affections must be and should be bounded by the color line.

He went on to call for vigilant oversight by Congress of HHS's enforcement obligations, noting that, "as is widely known, influential persons and groups within the Department's bureaucracy are hostile to the aims and ethos of MEPA, particularly the amendments to it enacted in 1996."[50]

The resistance to MEPA brings to mind the resistance to *Brown vs. Board of Education*, the 1954 Supreme Court case ruling state segregation of educational institutions unconstitutional. But there is a major difference in the level of organizational support for change in the two situations. In the late 1950s and the 1960s there were major governmental and private institutions committed to fighting the battle to enforce *Brown* and dismantle segregation. The Civil Rights Division of the U.S. Department of Justice, and the NAACP Legal Defense and Educational Fund, together with other public and private organizations, played a major role in pushing for change. No such institutions are committed to enforcing the law governing racial barriers in adoption. While there may be generalized *popular* support for knocking down racial barriers to adoption, of the kind that helped make MEPA's passage possible, so far there is very little *organizational* support from the federal government or from state social service agencies or from private foundations and nonprofit groups involved in child welfare issues.[51] MEPA may someday have a significant impact, but for now race matching by the state is alive and well.

6. "NEW" PROGRAMS PROMOTE TRADITIONAL IDEAS

Some of the hottest new initiatives in the child welfare field demonstrate the continuing power of the ideas behind traditional approaches. "Family Group Decision Making" (FGDM), or Family Group Conferencing, is a concept that has been imported from New Zealand, where it was introduced quite recently. It is being promoted by a range of important child welfare organizations in the United States and experimented with in a number of jurisdictions. The Edna McConnell Clark Foundation, a leader in the Intensive Family Preservation Services movement, has ardently promoted "Community Partnership" programs; they are supported by other key child welfare players such as The Annie E. Casey Foundation. Both Family Group Decision Making and Community Partnership programs are being sold as new initiatives, conceptually distinct from family preservation. Politically it is of course useful to make this distinction, given the criticism to which family preservation has been subject in recent years. But the FGDM and Community Partnership concepts are in fact built on, and represent an expansion of, some of the same core ideas that are at the heart of family preservation: children belong with their families and communities of origin, and state efforts should be devoted to empowering those families and communities, rather than restricting their authority over children in the name of child protection.

At the same time, a new permanency movement is promoting a variety of permanency options other than traditional adoption: permanent foster care, traditional guardianship, and subsidized guardianship. These arrangements preserve ties between children and their families of origin, whether or not the birth parents will ever be capable of raising those children at home. The children therefore may get permanent *placements*, but they may not get the true *parents* and *homes* that adoption is designed to provide.

These new initiatives are a decidedly mixed bag. Obviously it is important to encourage members of a child's extended family and members of a child's local community to take responsibility for the child and to provide support to its family. And obviously there are many situations in which the best placement for a child will be a long-term placement with a loving relative who can maintain connections between the parents and child. But at the same time these new initiatives can be developed in ways which will put children at risk. And they represent a useful new escape route for child welfare traditionalists faced with what they see as the wrongheaded backlash against IFPS, race matching, and other forms of family and community preservation.

FAMILY GROUP DECISION MAKING

Family Group Decision Making is an approach in which child welfare authorities delegate to the child's extended family significant authority to decide how to resolve a case of child maltreatment. The basic idea is to empower the family to make decisions about the fate of its members. This empowerment is often justified in terms of autonomy and other "rights." Supporters of this approach also argue that family members are the most competent decision-makers because they are likely to care the most about all those involved and to have the greatest understanding of the situation.

The FGDM concept originated in the early 1990s in New Zealand in response to concern that indigenous Maori children who had been identified as victims of abuse and neglect were being removed from their families and placed with families who were not Maori. Family

Group Decision Making as it developed in New Zealand involves bringing the entire extended family group together in a group meeting. The child welfare authorities are responsible for getting the group together but not for facilitating the meeting itself. The family members meet in private and try to come to a decision as to what should be done, then report their proposed resolution to the authorities. The parents accused of maltreatment are ordinarily included in the meeting. The child who has been maltreated may or may not be present at the meeting, depending on age and other factors. Ordinarily no lawyer or other representative of the child from outside the family is at the meeting, although such a representative may be consulted before arriving at a resolution. A lawyer for the child is required to be part of the FGDM process only in cases in which court proceedings have taken place, and even then will ordinarily not be present during the private family meeting.

FGDM programs have been introduced in Canada, Australia and England, and in several jurisdictions in the United States, including in the states of Vermont and Oregon, in Santa Clara County in California, and in the cities of Chicago, Grand Rapids, and Topeka. Somewhat different models have developed in different jurisdictions. In what is sometimes called the Family Unity Model, parents are allowed to veto the participation of any family member, and professionals and support people are allowed to be present during the family discussion, to help facilitate the process whereby the family makes decisions and generates a plan.

The FGDM concept received an early boost from the U.S. Advisory Board on Child Abuse and Neglect, which in its 1993 report praised the New Zealand model as a promising reform initiative.[1] It has been enthusiastically embraced by important players in the child welfare world. The American Humane Association (AHA) has issued reports and sponsored conferences whose names signal the AHA's enthusiastic support for the FGDM concept: *The Practice and Promise of Family Group Decision Making*,[2] *Innovations for Children's Services for the 21st Century: Family Group Decision Making . . .* ,[3] and *Family Group Decision Making: Assessing the Promise and Implementing the Practice*.[4] The Children's Defense Fund has touted FGDM as a promising new development.[5] The American Bar Association Center on Children and the Law, with the support of The Edna McConnell Clark Foundation, published a major report in 1996 describing FGDM and the New Zealand model as a "particularly innovative approach to handling child abuse and neglect cases." This ABA Report and its author, however, caution that the approach should be adapted to the United States with care and should be pursued only on an experimental basis, in conjunction with scientifically designed research evaluations.[6]

FGDM advocates promote it in terms that seem irresistible. Who can be against reaching out to an abused child's extended family members, calling upon their understanding of their own family dynamics, appealing to their sense of concern and responsibility for the children in their own family group, and assessing whether they can be helpful in coming up with a good plan for the child's future? Who can be against enabling families to take care of their own?

Clearly it *does* make sense for child welfare authorities to reach out to involve extended family members in these ways. But this can be done, and often is done, within the present CPS system. More should no doubt be done on a systematic basis to canvas family members for information and advice. It might in addition often be useful to actually bring family members together in a group meeting.

But the FGDM concept at its core involves the delegation of decision-making authority to the family, or more specifically to the adult members of the family, with the goal of keeping children who have been subjected to abuse and neglect within the extended family, and maximizing the chances that they will be left with or returned to their birth parents. A related goal is to keep the children within the racial and ethnic community of origin.

Claims for the success of FGDM have been based almost entirely on demonstrations that state authorities have deferred to the plans developed by adult family members, and that those plans have reduced the number of foster and institutional placements, and reduced the number of transracial placements. At a recent conference in the United States devoted to promoting Family Group Decision Making a slide was projected onto the gigantic screen listing for the audience the four major advantages of the approach. One of the four was: "Helps to prevent transracial placement."[7] Reports on the New Zealand experience with FGDM talk enthusiastically of the fact that in almost every case the authorities go along with the plan developed by the family in its private meeting. The problem is that there is no evidence that this is a good thing from the viewpoint of the children at risk for maltreatment. There has been little attempt to monitor how the plans are implemented or even to assess whether agreed-to plans are being followed; cases tend to be closed once a decision is approved. Nor has there been any attempt to assess what impact FGDM programs have on abuse and neglect and on other measures of children's well being. In New Zealand and elsewhere, such research as exists has measured success in terms of whether the state accedes to the family's decision, and whether the families' plans reduce out-of-home placements and reduce transracial placements.[8] All this is of course reminiscent of the now-discredited early family preservation research put out by family preservation advocates, in which success was measured entirely in terms of whether the goal of family preservation was being served, rather than in terms of child welfare.

There is reason for concern that in fact FGDM programs may not further children's well-being. In the classic CPS process, children who have been subjected to abuse and neglect are represented by the CPS authorities, and if the case ends up going to court, they are usually represented additionally by a lawyer and sometimes by special child advocates as well. By contrast children are likely to go essentially *unrepresented* in the FGDM process, at least by anyone outside of the family. The key decision-making aspect of FGDM is supposed to take place in the private family group meeting. The adults responsible for maltreatment are generally at that meeting. Other adult family members are there. But the child is not likely to be present, or if present, as might be the case with an older child, is hardly in a position to advocate for his or her interests equally with the adults. The more serious the maltreatment, the greater the risk that the child will see it as dangerous to speak up against those who have been responsible for that maltreatment, for fear of being punished for this kind of betrayal. Nor is the child likely to have a lawyer or other special advocate during the FGDM process, since formal rights to be represented are associated with the court proceedings to remove a child and terminate parental rights that FGDM is designed to bypass. The child welfare authorities who convene the family group meeting, and who in some models may be present to facilitate the meeting, may see themselves as having some responsibility to represent the child's interest in making their decision as to whether to accede to the family plan. But since the FGDM process is one which defines success largely in terms of whether the family is allowed to make the decision, the model itself obviously discourages child welfare authorities from playing more than a minimal role.

There has been significant feminist opposition to using the FGDM process in cases involving adult women victimized by domestic violence. Concerns are expressed about the risk that male batterers will dominate the decision-making process, that women will not be able to adequately represent their own interests, and that plans developed through this process would accordingly put women's interests at risk. As a result FGDM programs often limit their jurisdiction to cases involving only child maltreatment, or exclude the perpetrator from the private family conference in cases of partner battering. It's hard to understand why infants and children subjected to maltreatment are in a *better* position than adult women to protect their interests in the FGDM process.

FGDM advocates have chosen the feel-good phrase *family empowerment* to describe the essence of what their movement is about. In fact it is about giving *parents* accused of maltreatment, together with other *adult* family members, even greater power than they now have over the fate of their children. It is about limiting the state's power to intervene to protect these children, and limiting the larger community's sense of responsibility for them.

It is important to support and empower families and to encourage extended family members to take responsibility for their youngest members. But when children have been subjected to severe forms of abuse and neglect, the state should not abdicate *its* responsibility.

COMMUNITY PARTNERSHIPS

The Community Partnership concept is to delegate to local community agencies responsibility for dealing with many of the child maltreatment cases that now become part of the CPS caseload.[9] Community Partnership advocates talk of doing more to involve the local community in efforts to support families and prevent child abuse

and neglect. They argue that CPS authorities now devote their resources primarily to investigation and, in the most serious cases, to
child removal and foster and institutional care, while doing little to
prevent maltreatment. They claim that a huge proportion of reported CPS cases are not serious enough to warrant state intervention, noting that roughly one-third of all cases investigated are not
substantiated and that slightly more than half of all maltreatment
cases fall in the neglect category. They want to divert most of the maltreatment cases that are now addressed by the official state intervention system to a voluntary, community-based services system. Many
parents who under the current system are reported to official authorities, and subject to the coercive power of the state for purposes of
treatment, monitoring, or child removal, would under the proposed
system be reported only to private community organizations, which
would offer treatment and other support services on a voluntary basis. The parents would not be stigmatized by CPS investigations; they
would not have their names filed in a child maltreatment registry;
they would not be *required* to accept services or to cooperate with
treatment regimens, or to improve their parenting practices.

Community Partnership advocates make many persuasive points.
They say that local community organizations are often in a better
position to work with families, given the suspicion in which CPS authorities are held. They say CPS does a terrible job, failing to provide
helpful services in cases where they are needed to protect children.
They talk of the advantages for children of intervening in ways that
prevent maltreatment from occurring in the first instance, rather
than waiting to intervene after the fact. And they talk of the importance of developing a sense of responsibility—at least in the immediate local community—for other people's children if prevention
efforts are to succeed. They are right about some of the problems
with the present system. But it's not clear that they have come up
with a solution that will be helpful for children.

Community Partnerships take an important conceptual step beyond family preservation along the noninterventionist continuum.
Family preservationists want to limit intervention in the form of removing a child and terminating parental rights after the CPS system
has identified the child as a victim of maltreatment. Community

Partnership advocates want to limit state intervention even in the form of recording the case, investigating, or monitoring when maltreatment is first suspected or reported.

The Community Partnership concept has to be understood as one of the major child welfare initiatives of the day. The fact that The Edna McConnell Clark Foundation has made this its current child welfare priority is itself enormously significant. The Clark Foundation has demonstrated in the past its willingness to commit significantly from its vast resources to effect programmatic change in the child welfare area. Clark has also demonstrated its ability to use its resources effectively. Clark was primarily responsible for initially promoting the Intensive Family Preservation Services (IFPS) concept and for propelling the extraordinarily successful IFPS movement over the years.

Several years ago the Clark Foundation set forth a sophisticated strategic plan for promoting its new Community Partnerships concept.[10] This plan envisioned an elaborate campaign for converting other key players in the child welfare area, for winning allies in academia and other quarters seen as important to mounting an effective public relations effort, and for advancing an ambitious agenda.

Clark has already made dramatic progress in implementing its strategic plan. Early on the Malcolm Wiener Center for Social Policy, at Harvard University's John F. Kennedy School of Government, decided to devote one of its prestigious "Executive Session" series to an effort to develop "New Paradigms For Child Protective Services." The Clark Foundation, together with The Annie E. Casey Foundation, an ally in efforts to promote family preservation, provided significant funding for the series and helped put together a group of national experts who met over the course of three years to develop the new proposals for child welfare reform. Not surprisingly the group focused on Community Partnerships as the core idea and produced in the end one "lead paper" which promotes it as the chosen "new paradigm." Called "Child Protection: Building Community Partnerships: Getting from Here to There," it is written by Frank Farrow, director of an organization which receives funding from the Clark Foundation. Its Executive Summary makes the claim that the Community Partnerships concept is *the solution for the cen-*

tral child welfare problems of the day. It sets forth a vision, and an agenda for action, which are essentially a modestly rewritten version of the program that Clark had been promoting in a variety of position papers.

There are many other signs of Clark's progress in implementing its agenda for changing minds and practices. The Executive Session group included representatives from public and private agencies key to policy reform in the child welfare area, such as the Children's Bureau of the Federal Administration on Children, Youth and Families, the Children's Defense Fund (CDF), and the National Committee to Prevent Child Abuse. Major child welfare conferences sponsored by organizations like CDF and The Child Welfare League of America have been getting out the word on the benefits of the Community Partnership approach through a variety of workshops and panels. The National Conference of State Legislatures issued a report, as part of an effort supported by the Clark Foundation, endorsing community partnerships.[11] Pilot projects have been sponsored in Cedar Rapids, Louisville, Jacksonville, and Los Angeles, and publications are regularly disseminated praising their achievements. Articles have been published in influential journals praising the concept and its implementation in various states and localities.[12]

Those promoting Community Partnerships have developed a powerful sales pitch. Who can be *against* empowering communities? Who can be against the idea of state agencies working on a cooperative basis with community agencies? Who can be against having community agencies provide families with the supportive services they need if CPS is not providing them? Who can be against neighbors helping neighbors? Who can be against preventing child maltreatment, rather than waiting until it happens to do something about it?

It's important to get beyond the sales pitch and focus on the real nature of the product being sold. The central idea is to divert the major portion of all cases now dealt with by the official state child protection system to an unofficial, local community system, which would offer families supportive services, but would have no coercive power over families to require cooperation, or to monitor children's treatment, or, of course, to remove children. The related idea seems to be to divert some of the funding that now goes to CPS agencies to the community agencies that would be taking over much of CPS's function.

Whether the Community Partnership concept is ultimately a good idea may depend on one's goals, and also on how it is implemented. Community Partnerships *might* help serve the goal of funneling new money into impoverished communities, an obviously worthy goal so long as it doesn't put children at risk. As with Family Preservation, the strategy may be to use the threat of child maltreatment to get the establishment to provide the kind of funding for impoverished groups that it is reluctant to provide. But it is not clear where the new money for community organizations is going to come from, except it seems that much of it is supposed to come from funds that would theoretically no longer be needed for traditional CPS agency functions. However, it is not at all clear that legislative and other bodies which now fund CPS agencies with the understanding that they serve to protect children against maltreatment will be willing to provide the same level of funding if the CPS jurisdiction is cut down, and much of the funding diverted to community organizations. The funding agencies might instead simply reduce child welfare-related funding levels, reasoning that the only *vital* child welfare needs are served by CPS.

Even if funding levels are maintained, with CPS jurisdiction significantly cut back and CPS funds proportionately diverted, there is reason for concern that children will be worse off than they are today.

The claim that Community Partnerships will serve the goal of children's well-being is premised on the notion that the CPS caseload is much larger than it "should be"—that it includes lots of minor cases, in which perfectly adequate parents need nothing more than a little support, as well as many cases based on false or mistaken charges. Community Partnership advocates have little to base this on other than the high percentage of neglect cases and the fact that many of the incidents of abuse reported to CPS are not substantiated. But, as discussed in chapter 3, in today's child welfare world neglect cases cannot be dismissed as minor. Many are extremely serious cases in which children are being denied the essentials of a nurturing upbringing; like abuse, neglect puts children at high risk for the kind of damage that leads to sadly limited life prospects—unemployment, homelessness, substance abuse, violence, and victimization. Neglect results in children dying at about the same rate as abuse. The fact that cases are "unsubstantiated" seldom means that the charges were false or mistaken; it is more likely to mean simply that there was not enough proof made out to satisfy the high standards required, or that the case was deemed insufficiently serious to warrant committing scarce agency resources, given the ever-increasing number of ever-more-serious maltreatment reports.

Papers produced for the Kennedy School Executive Session, devoted to exploring the Community Partnership concept, help explode the overintervention thesis on which the concept is premised. One of these papers demonstrates, for example, the degree to which serious substance abuse cases dominate the current CPS caseload. Another questions the ability to significantly reduce the CPS caseload without putting children at risk.[13]

Community Partnership advocates are somewhat fuzzy about how significantly they would cut the CPS caseload, but at times it seems that they think almost all cases could be dealt with better on a voluntary community service basis. Farrow's lead paper for the Executive Session indicates that 50 percent could be diverted immediately, and more later.[14] In Missouri, which has used this approach since 1994, approximately 80 percent of all reports of suspected maltreatment are directed to the voluntary "assessment" track. Taking together the five pilot areas using the Community Partnership concept as of 1998, 70 to 80 percent of the cases have been referred to the assessment track.[15] In any event it is obvious that the claims for this concept as the way to fix the seriously sick child protective system are based on an understanding that a major shift in responsibility would be made from the CPS to the community-based system.

If Community Partnerships operate to divert from CPS a large group of very serious abuse and neglect cases, it is hard to see why this would help protect children. Community Partnership advocates argue for the benefits of the supportive services that local agencies would provide, but CPS could also provide those services, either directly or through local agencies, without losing the power to take coercive action if needed to protect children. While under the Community Partnership concept local agencies could always report cases to CPS if they concluded this was necessary, the CPS apparently envisioned is a much smaller agency, with much more limited resources.

Community Partnership advocates talk glowingly about all the positive features of a voluntaristic community system. It's important to look at the flip side of the coin. They talk, for example, of the benefits of relying on community agencies which parents might be able to relate to in a more responsive, trusting manner than they do to the CPS authorities. But there's also a risk that neighbors and trusted community representatives will be unduly reluctant to intervene to protect children for fear of alienating their parents.

Community Partnership advocates argue against "stigmatizing" parents by accusing them of maltreatment, intervening in their families, and listing them on child abuse registers. But these kinds of measures can also function to protect children.

While child abuse registers may indeed stigmatize, the goal is to keep track of those who have been responsible for child maltreatment so that they can be prevented from repeating it in the future, either as parents or as employees with child care responsibilities. In investigating a child maltreatment case, where it is often hard to unravel the facts, it is helpful to have some place to go to see whether the alleged perpetrator has been involved previously in child abuse and neglect. Research indicates that children reported to a child abuse registry are three times more likely to die than other children.[16] It is obvious that we should do more to protect these children, but it is far from obvious that the way to protect them better is to stop reporting their cases to the child abuse registry.

While mandatory drug treatment may be more interventionist and, arguably, more stigmatizing than simply offering drug treatment on a voluntary basis, it is also likely to be more effective. (See chapter 9.) Abuse and neglect investigations, and child removal is obviously interventionist and stigmatizing, but it may be necessary to protect children from serious harm.

Community Partnership advocates talk as if "accountability" for child protection is an important feature of the system. They talk, for example, of community agencies entering into "contracts" with maltreating parents in which the parents commit to change. The parent would play a central role in designing the contract and its "enforcement" mechanism. This is, of course, in keeping with the underlying parent empowerment principle. One article describes in glowing terms how in one community experimenting with the community partnership concept, these contracts work "in keeping individual children safe":

> As part of a CPS worker's planning with a parent who has been the subject of an abuse or neglect report, the worker offers the parent the option of arranging follow-on contact with a person in the community whom the parent trusts—a minister, a relative, a friend. If this person is willing to become consistently involved in the plan of action, for example, by stopping by the house three times a week to ensure that the parent does not become isolated and over stressed, the CPS worker, the parent, and the third party sign a brief agreement to this effect.[17]

It is interesting to contrast the approach to accountability taken here with that taken by women's rights advocates in addressing violence against women. As discussed in chapter 2, their idea of accountability involves mandatory arrest, together with policies promoting prosecution, conviction, and the imposition of prison terms. How would they react if it were suggested that, instead, batterers should design their own contracts, in which they promised not to beat up their partners, and then choose someone to monitor their compliance?

Community Partnership advocates argue for putting responsibility in the "village" for raising the child. But they fail to address the realities of today's villages. Child abuse and neglect takes place disproportionately in the poorest, most dysfunctional communities in our society—in communities which are the least likely to have the healthy organizations which are seen as central to the Community Partnership concept.[18]

We do need to address the problems that Community Partnership advocates point to. We need to do more up front, such as the promising home visitation programs discussed in chapter 7, to try to prevent abuse and neglect from occurring. We also need to do better by the children identified as victims of severe forms of abuse and neglect. But the state should not abdicate responsibility by turning the problem over to community-based organizations, in the hope that they will somehow come up with the resources for needed support services, and that parents will voluntarily cooperate, take advantage of proffered help, and improve their parenting. Instead, the state should take more responsibility for children at risk. CPS should provide more treatment, support, and monitoring to ensure the well-being of the children who are kept at home, or reunified with their families. And we should do more to move children out of damaging situations—whether their original homes, foster homes, or institutions—and into permanent adoptive homes. (See chapter 8.)

THE NEW PERMANENCY MOVEMENT

The old permanency movement of the 1970s emphasized the importance to children's welfare of uninterrupted, committed parenting. The movement grew out of the experience of observing what happened to children who were kept for long periods of time in foster or institutional care, together with developments in attachment theory. The movement demanded an end to the practice of removing children from their birth parents only to place them for long periods in foster care, in which they were often moved from one home to another, and where every "home" was by definition temporary, and every "parent" had by definition limited responsibility. The movement's goals were to ensure that, to the degree possible, children were either kept in their birth families or moved promptly to adoptive families, so that they would be able to enjoy the benefits of continual, committed parenting.

These goals proved hard to accomplish. In the 1980s new emphasis was placed on preserving the family, but with the decade's drug epidemics and other social and economic problems came an increase in the number of maltreatment cases and, as a result, child removal rates. At the same time, the system's commitment to family preservation, and the resulting reluctance to terminate parental rights when children had to be removed from the home, meant that by the 1990s the number of children in out-of-home placement had enormously increased, rather than decreased. (See chapter 3.)

The new permanency movement grows out of much the same pressures and premises as the old. Too many children are growing up in out-of-home placement at too great a cost in terms of the damage they suffer, the expenses of financing foster and institutional care, and the price society can expect to pay in the future when children denied appropriate nurturing grow up to join the ranks of the homeless, the unemployed, the violent, and the victimized. Two decades of experience and research have produced new and stronger evidence of the importance of giving children a stable home and committed adults to parent them from early life on.

What is different today is that many seem reconciled to the difficulty of giving all children a traditional family, with parents who exercise the full rights and responsibilities of parenthood. Many advocate a form of permanency that involves neither full preservation of the birth family, nor placement in an adoptive family that legally replicates the traditional family. They call for keeping some children in permanent foster or guardianship homes, with ongoing ties to their birth families. This would eliminate the bouncing from home to home that characterizes much out-of-home care, and thus achieve permanency. But children would lose out on the benefits associated with having a true "home" and true "parents."

The new permanency advocates have proposed legal guardianship as one way of formalizing and ensuring the permanence of the custody arrangement. Guardians, like foster parents, are assigned custody by the state along with certain rights and responsibilities in raising the child, with the birth parent retaining some parental rights. Guardianships can be designed by law as permanent, or relatively permanent, with birth parents' rights to seek the child's return severely limited. But under today's law guardianship is typically *not* legally permanent: birth parents can always challenge the custody relationship, and if they ask for their child's return they will ordinarily be judged under a "current fitness" standard. During guardianship, the state typically delegates full decision-making authority to the guardians, rather than retaining certain authority as it does with foster parents. And typically the state does not take responsibility for monitoring the child's welfare as is characteristic of foster care. Traditionally guardians have not been paid. Accordingly the state and federal governments stand to save a lot of money by moving children out of foster care and into guardianship arrangements, which involve neither foster stipends nor the costs associated with maintaining these cases on the CPS rolls.

In recent years the new permanency advocates have been promoting *subsidized* guardianships. The idea is to give guardians essentially the same kind of financial stipend foster parents receive but to leave them free from the kind of supervision and monitoring associated with such care. Subsidies are seen as important incentives for those with limited resources to agree to become guardians. A number of states have experimented with subsidized guardianship programs, including, as of 1998, Alaska, Delaware, Illinois, Massachusetts, Nebraska, Oregon, and Washington. The federal government has encouraged experimentation with subsidized guardianships as an alternative to adoption by allowing the kind of federal matching funds to which states are entitled for special needs adoptions to be made available for subsidized legal guardianship in several of these states. Even with subsidies, permanent guardianships save the government money as compared to foster care. While the stipends are comparable, the administrative costs are much less.

Many of the alleged advantages of the new permanency options could be provided through adoption. Adoption can and increasingly does allow for various forms of "openness," which permit ongoing communication or other contact between the adopted child and the birth parents. Typically, adoptive parents are given full parental decision-making authority and so would have the power to decide whether to allow or encourage such contact. But an increasing number of states have amended their adoption laws to allow for *enforceable* openness agreements in certain cases, particularly when the child's interest in maintaining a relationship with the birth parents seems strong.

Adoption in all its current forms guarantees children one set of parents with the full rights and responsibilities of traditional parenthood. Even in the unusual case of enforceable openness agreements, adoptive parents have full parental decision-making responsibility, with birth parents given at most visitation rights. By contrast, the new permanency options leave children growing up with people who have been delegated by the state certain parental functions, but are not considered the legal equivalent of true parents. The birth parents retain parental rights in some sense, but since they have no custody or decision-making rights they cannot be seen as true parents either.

Permanent guardianship *may* be better for children than impermanent foster care, but this will depend on the circumstances. Permanency should not be seen as a panacea. Permanent homes will be good for children only to the degree that the permanent foster parents or guardians are chosen on the basis of their capacity to provide quality parenting, and to handle the complicated role of acting as parents while simultaneously acknowledging the rights of the "real" parents. The new permanency movement promotes the idea of keeping children—on a permanent basis—in the kind of kin and nonkin foster homes they are now placed in when they are removed from home. As discussed in chapter 3, the current system of selecting foster parents is deeply problematic, and quality is a serious concern. Near-absolute kinship preferences require social workers to select kin over nonkin without making an individualized assessment as to whether the kin home will be better for the child than the non-kin home. Racial matching systems operate—albeit unlawfully—to require workers to look only to the same-race prospective parent pool. Local placement policies require that children be placed in homes in their birth parents' neighborhood. The system has not recruited widely, looking for the best possible situation. It has used criteria that narrow the range of prospective parents to a relatively small group. This group looks problematic in terms of many of the criteria social workers have traditionally thought extremely relevant to parental fitness. Many kin and nonkin foster parents live on the economic margins, many are much older than the parenting norm, and many have significant health problems. State agencies regularly complain about the increasing difficulty of finding qualified foster parents for all the children in need. The financial stipends available for foster parenting, and for the new subsidized guardianships, may be essential to enable some of those who want to parent for all the right reasons to do so. But they also raise concerns that others will step forward who are motivated by the money and not the parenting opportunity.

Outcome studies tell us that most children graduating from foster and institutional care do quite badly in life, even though they do better than children kept in or returned to problematic biological homes. By contrast adopted children do very well. Indeed those adopted early do as well as children who grow up in untroubled biological homes. It seems extremely unlikely that simply eliminating the impermanence that has characterized out-of-home care will make the difference that needs to be made.

The new permanency options may represent the best compromise for some children. But they are being advocated as a major alternative to traditional permanency options. There is reason for concern that this has more to do with continuing the status quo and maintaining parental rights than with furthering children's interests.

The 1997 Adoption and Safe Families Act (ASFA), while endorsing adoption in its title, gives a major boost to the new permanency options. One of ASFA's most significant changes has to do with the "reasonable efforts" requirement. Agencies are no longer required to make reasonable efforts to preserve families in all cases, and they *are* required to make reasonable efforts to move children out of temporary care if they cannot be returned to their families. But while the 1980 federal reasonable efforts law contemplated that children who could not be kept with their families of origin would be adopted, ASFA makes the goal "permanency." The Act mandates a "permanency plan," a "permanency hearing," and "permanent placement." It requires, in cases in which the permanency plan is "adoption or placement in another permanent home," documentation of efforts made to "to find an adoptive family or other permanent living arrangement for the child, to place the child with an adoptive family, a fit and willing relative, a legal guardian, or in another planned permanent living arrangement, and to finalize the adoption or legal guardianship."

Another key change made by ASFA is to *require* states to file petitions for the termination of parental rights (TPR) in cases where children have been in foster care for certain periods of time, as well as in particularly egregious cases. However the Act's exceptions to the TPR requirements again demonstrate the degree to which it equates adoption with other permanency options, since the exceptions include all cases in which children are being cared for by relatives.

It is understandable why the new permanency options are so popular. They seem to answer the concern of those who have worried about foster limbo and foster bounce. They seem as if they might give children the best of all worlds—the permanency associated with adoptive homes, together with the continuation of connections with their birth families. They enable family preservation traditionalists to appease the demands of those clamoring for change, without actually having to give up all that much. The financial stipends and other services that go with kin and nonkin foster care and with subsidized guardianships funnel money to poor families at a time when welfare stipends are being cut back and cut off. At the same time, those concerned with limiting welfare budgets can take comfort from the fact that the move from foster care to legal guardianship promises to save money by reducing administrative costs.

It looks like everyone wins, except that it's not so clear that children win. How many will be placed in high-risk permanent homes? How many will in fact be living with the very parents from whom they were supposedly removed, as the mothers or fathers move in with the grandparents who are officially denominated the guardians? How will the CPS system that has given up any monitoring role know what is going on? And how many children would do better in permanent *adoptive* homes, with parents who have assumed full parenting rights and responsibilities? It's impossible to answer these questions in the abstract. But it seems likely that children would do better if adoption was established as the presumptive placement for all children who could not live with their parents of origin, leaving child welfare workers and the courts to choose another form of permanency only on the basis of an individualized determination that it would better serve a child's interests.

PROMISING NEW DIRECTIONS AND TRADITIONAL PITFALLS

7. INTERVENING EARLY WITH HOME VISITATION

There are some policy initiatives in the works today that represent a genuine challenge to the traditional child welfare way. These new programs and program proposals would have the larger community intervene earlier and more actively in the family both to support good parenting and to protect children against bad parenting. They call into question, at least implicitly, the degree to which our system has valued family autonomy and family preservation.

Universal home visiting programs for pregnant women and their children in the early months and years would provide families with the kind of supportive services that can help prevent abuse and neglect from happening, and the kind of surveillance that can trigger early intervention to remove children at risk if necessary. New adoption programs and policies, discussed in chapter 8, would intervene earlier and more readily than the traditional system has to remove children at risk for ongoing abuse or neglect and place them in permanent adoptive homes.

Home visitor and adoption programs are but some examples of the myriad kinds of programs that our society might promote were it to play a more active role in nurturing and protecting its young. But they are particularly worthy of attention. Both kinds of programs have generated significant political support. At the same time both are seen as highly controversial, precisely because they call for outside intervention in the privacy of the home.

In 1991 the U.S. Advisory Board on Child Abuse and Neglect issued its "Blueprint for an Effective Federal Policy on Child Abuse and Neglect."[1] The Board concluded that of the thirty-one recommendations it generated in its first report, issued the previous year, the single most important was its advocacy of home visitation for the prevention of maltreatment. The Board recommended that the federal government fund a series of pilot projects and assess the most effective way to implement a universal voluntary home visitation system. The 1991 report discussed a home visitation model that would be relatively intensive and long-term, noting with approval both David Olds's home visitation program in Elmira, New York, and the Hawaii Healthy Start Program.

While the federal government failed to take up this suggestion, private organizations combined forces with state governments to create a rapidly expanding home visitation movement. The National Committee to Prevent Child Abuse in partnership with Ronald McDonald House Charities launched Healthy Families America (HFA), which has as its goal the establishment of universally available home visitation for all new parents through the first three to five years of their children's lives. By January 1998, HFA was able to report that in its first six years it had established more than 270 programs reaching an estimated 18,000 families in 38 states and the District of Columbia.[2] Children's Trust Funds also promote home visitation in many states.[3]

This new home visitation movement built on earlier models. In the United States, home visiting had been an integral part of various family support and family preservation efforts, with social workers going into homes identified as particularly needy or at risk to help shore up fragile families, providing important services in the home, connecting isolated families to community resources, and monitoring troubled families to protect children at risk. Abroad, home visiting had been built into universal health care systems, with health professionals going into the homes of virtually all new parents for at least a couple of visits during the early infancy period to help get parenting efforts off to a good start.[4]

While building on old models, the home visitation movement has been promoting a program that is different in significant ways from anything that came before, and that has much more potential for addressing today's child maltreatment problem. This program is designed to reach out to new parents on a universal or near-universal basis, while at the same time providing relatively intensive services. It is designed to provide support services in a nonstigmatizing way, but at the same time it enables home visitors to perform a surveillance function, monitoring high-risk families to decide whether they need continuing intensive support, and whether they need more active intervention by the CPS system.

THE PROMISE

Home visitation in its new form shows promise because it addresses the internal dynamics of the maltreatment problem. It provides support and surveillance during the period of time when children are at greatest risk—during early childhood when maltreatment rates are highest, and when children are most vulnerable to immediate and long-lasting damage. As discussed in chapter 3, over 80 percent of maltreatment-related deaths take place in the first five years and 40 percent in the first year of life. It is infants and young children who are most physically vulnerable to abuse and neglect. They are also subject to the most devastating forms of mental and emotional damage from such maltreatment, as this is the period when they are developing most rapidly neurologically, and when trauma or the absence of appropriate nurturing is most likely to do the most serious and permanent harm.

Home visitation is also responsive to the needs of parents who are most likely to commit maltreatment. The classic profile of the parent at risk for committing maltreatment is the impoverished young single mother, who was deprived of nurturing parenting herself. Home visitation is designed to reach such high-risk parents: services are either targeted to reach the entire group of new parents, or to reach a group broad enough to include the higher risk parents. The frequency of visits after some initial period of time is calibrated to the apparent need for services as assessed by the home visitor, so that higher risk parents will typically receive more intensive visits over a longer period of time.

Home visitation services are designed to address issues that are predictors for maltreatment. Home visitors are trained to provide the kind of "parental" support that their young parent-clients may never have received, because parents who have not been nurtured are not likely to do a good job of nurturing their own children. Home visitors are trained to help parents pursue educational and employment opportunities, and avoid unwanted future pregnancies, because education and employment reduce the risk of maltreatment, while additional children increase the risk. Home visitors are trained to teach and to model parenting skills to parents who, with little idea from their own childhood of what good parenting looks like, are at high risk of perpetuating the cycle in which maltreatment is passed down from parent to child.

Child maltreatment occurs to an overwhelmingly disproportionate degree in families that are isolated—cut off from the kind of family and community support that helps make parenting work. Home visitation is designed to reach into the homes of families that are not likely to reach out for support, bringing helpful services to the parents where they live, and helping them come out of their homes to access existing community agencies.[5]

Child maltreatment occurs in part because the home is a private place where it can go unnoticed. The homes of children at greatest risk for abuse and neglect are likely to be intensely private. These are the children least likely to be seen by friends, neighbors, family members, pediatricians, child care workers, or anyone else who might play a role in deterring or reporting harmful conduct. Home visitation brings outsiders into the home during the key early childhood period when fragile families are free from even the limited surveillance provided by compulsory education. The very presence of such outsiders in the home is helpful in deterring maltreatment. And as health care or child welfare professionals, home visitors are mandated to report any maltreatment they observe to CPS authorities.

Early research results seem to confirm what common sense suggests as to home visitation's promise. A recent federal government study of all interventions designed to address family violence sees intensive home visitation as one of the few that shows any positive potential based on the research to date.[6]

Hawaii Healthy Start began in 1985 as a three-year demonstration program, then became a state program in 1988, administered by the Hawaii Department of Maternal and Child Health. A three-year study completed in 1996 by the National Committee to Prevent Child Abuse, Center on Child Abuse Prevention Research, found that Hawaii's Healthy Start program had a positive impact on program participants, as compared to a control group of nonparticipants. The study concluded that participation for a one-year period had a positive influence on parental attitudes, on parent-child interaction, and on the amount and severity of child maltreatment.[7]

David Olds has conducted the most significant research and now has reports on fifteen years of experience with home visitation in Elmira, New York. The Elmira program is an intensive, multifaceted program, providing new parents with services during the prenatal period through the first two years of life. Olds's carefully designed research indicates that the program has a dramatic impact on factors that are directly related to maltreatment rates. Low-weight, premature babies are at greater risk for maltreatment, and his program has significantly reduced the number of such babies born by reducing smoking among the mothers and otherwise improving their prenatal health care. His program has also reduced the number and frequency of repeat pregnancies and has succeeded in moving many parents off welfare and into productive educational and employment situations, other factors that are powerfully correlated with maltreatment rates. Olds's research also indicates that the Elmira program has a direct impact on the incidence and severity of maltreatment, reducing emergency room visits for injuries and reducing reported abuse and neglect. His fifteen-year follow-up study shows a reduction in child abuse and neglect rates and in criminal behavior on the part of low-income, single mothers.[8] And, finally, Olds's research found that home visits had an effect on the later behavior of the children of visited mothers, reducing their involvement in substance abuse, crime, and various other forms of risky and/or antisocial behavior.[9]

The Elmira program involved a white, rural population which was not significantly involved in the use or abuse of illicit drugs or alcohol. Olds started a program in Memphis, Tennessee, more recently, designed to determine whether the Elmira results would be replicated in a population with very different demographics, more typical of the areas with the highest child abuse and neglect rates. In the Memphis home visitation program, the overwhelming preponderance of the parents were poor, young, single African-American women, and the program was administered through a public health department. While Olds has results as of early 1999 only on the first two years of the program, they indicate so far that the program has had an impact on the women's subsequent pregnancy rates, and on their children's injury and hospitalization rates; these latter findings, together with other measures, led Olds to conclude that the program was having a beneficial effect on the mothers' parenting and had reduced abuse and neglect.[10]

Olds's research also provides some measure of the importance of the surveillance home visitors provide—their ability to protect children by their presence and to bring to the attention of child protective authorities maltreatment that would otherwise go undetected. His Elmira studies show that during the two-year home visitation period maltreatment rates are down, but that when visitation ends, rates go back up. Olds and others see the explanation for this phenomenon in the surveillance effect, noting that home visitors are likely to report high-risk situations when they have to terminate their visitation services and will no longer be in a position to protect the children.[11]

The research also suggests possible cost savings associated with home visitation—at least for programs directed at lower income populations. This is an important consideration given the concern many have expressed about the financial costs of providing intensive home visitation.[12] Olds has estimated that his prenatal and postpartum program cost about $3300 in 1980 dollars and $6700 in 1997 dollars for two and a half years of home visiting. He found that this investment from the standpoint of government spending was recovered for low income families during the first four years of the child's life. The cost savings were achieved largely from reductions in welfare and food stamp payments, and reductions in unintended subsequent pregnancies. He notes that it would take longer for the investment to be recovered today because the cost of such a program has increased more rapidly than the cost of welfare benefits.[13] Olds's calculations, however, seem to significantly underestimate the overall cost savings, since they omit long-term savings, including those associated with any reduction in child maltreatment.[14]

SOME PITFALLS

The intensive home visitation movement is still in its relative infancy. Home visitation programs seem to have enormous promise and could be developed in a form that challenges the reigning child welfare paradigm. But it's by no means clear that this will happen. Movement leaders express interest in only one aspect of home visitation's radical potential—the support, not surprisingly, as opposed to the surveillance aspect. Their vision of home visitation, if realized, would do little to protect the children at highest risk for the most serious forms of abuse and neglect. And even their vision of home visitation as a model family-support program may be diluted beyond recognition in deference to cost-cutting pressures. Certain characteristics seem key to home visitation's promise, and they will be difficult to maintain in a society committed to family autonomy and reluctant to commit resources to family support.[15]

Universality

It is important that home visitation services be provided on at least a very broad, if not a universal basis, so that they reach families that would significantly benefit from either support or surveillance, or both. There is a risk that the scope of home visitation programs will be unduly limited at both the high-risk and the low-risk end of the family spectrum.

1. The "voluntary only" limit

Home visitation advocates talk simultaneously about the importance of making services broadly available so that they reach the isolated, vulnerable families where children are most at risk, and the importance of making the parents' participation voluntary. The two principles are hard to reconcile. Existing home visitation programs struggle to enroll and engage families and experience high dropout rates. Research by one of the leading experts in the home visitation movement, Deborah Daro, indicates that the more troubled families are, the less likely they are to seek help.[16] She and others promote home visitation precisely because it reaches into the homes of those who can't or won't reach out. But the most dysfunctional families, in which children are most likely to suffer maltreatment, are also the most likely to refuse to participate in voluntary home visitation programs. Daro concedes this is true.[17] But she and virtually all others in the movement are adamant about the voluntary only limit.[18]

Arguments can be made that home visitation services won't work as well if they are forced upon families, that it is problematic to try to combine support and surveillance functions, and that the highest risk families can be dealt with by the mandated reporting and the CPS systems. But in the end these arguments are not very persuasive. Our compulsory education system requires children be provided with schooling for most of their childhood years, and few would argue that it's counterproductive to the educational mission. We regularly combine support and surveillance functions in our efforts to protect children. CPS workers are given the dual job of providing support services and of monitoring families. Teachers are required to combine their primary educational function with their mandatory reporting obligations under child abuse and neglect laws.

And the problem with leaving the highest risk families to be dealt with by the normal mandatory reporting and CPS systems, is that these are precisely the families for which those systems work least well. Children who live in the isolated families where the risk of maltreatment is greatest are children who may never be seen by mandated reporters, or by anyone else willing to take on the responsibility to seek out CPS intervention. The most dysfunctional families are the families for whom the surveillance aspect of home visitation is most important. If home visitors had the right to be present in such families on a regular, ongoing basis, they could not only help those parents capable of being helped, but could in addition protect those children at greatest risk against harm, both by virtue of their presence in the home, and their ability to trigger more interventionist action by CPS authorities.

However, a mandatory home visitation system, in which both the support and the surveillance functions were recognized as fully legitimate, would collide head on with our tradition of family privacy and family autonomy. Movement advocates seem either to have internalized these traditional values, or to have concluded that any proposal which conflicted significantly with these values would be politically doomed.

Mandatory home visitation does seem like a radical step in today's world. But compulsory education laws and childhood labor laws were once seen as radical interventions in the family. So were the abuse and neglect laws that took from parents the right they previously had to physically brutalize and to sexually violate their children. Mandatory home visitation would simply provide society with a realistic means of enforcing rights guaranteed in principle by those abuse and neglect laws—rights that are now universally accepted as fundamental.

2. The "high risk" limit

There is a debate within the home visitation field as to how broadly programs should reach on the lower risk end of the risk spectrum. HFA advocates press for making services universally available to all during the pregnancy and early childhood period. Some other home visitation proponents would target services to high risk parents, and programs have often been so limited to date: some target geographic areas where maltreatment rates are high, and others select only certain parents based on such risk factors as youth, the mother's status as a single parent, substance abuse, the mother's own victimization in childhood by abuse and neglect, her current victimization by domestic violence, the infant's low birthweight or prematurity, and low socioeconomic status.

But most home visitation advocates recognize the importance of at least reaching *broadly*, so as to provide services to the very large group of vulnerable families in which children are at significant risk. Child maltreatment is not a small problem. As one expert on child development puts it:

> What has served in the literature as the paradigmatic example of
> highest-risk early childhood and family life—a vulnerable and over-
> whelmed caregiver, and unsupportive community context, and per-
> haps, a constitutionally vulnerable infant—is rapidly becoming the
> norm for young children in poverty and their families.[19]

And the research indicates that home visitation support services can succeed in helping many vulnerable parents become the better parents that they want to be. The research also indicates that in terms of this support function, by contrast to the surveillance function, home visitation will likely work best with the *least* problematic families in the vulnerable parent group. Seriously dysfunctional families—those Deborah Daro refers to as "broken families"—are largely beyond being helped to health by home visitor support services.[20] As the recent report by the federal government assessing the research in this area concludes:

> The benefits of home visitation appear most promising for young, first-time mothers who delay additional pregnancies and thus reduce the social and financial stresses that burden households with large numbers of young children. . . . The intervention has not been demonstrated to have benefits for children whose parents abuse drugs or alcohol or those who are not prepared to engage in help-seeking behaviors.[21]

As the home visitation movement expands, pressures may mount to limit the scope to only relatively high risk families. Some will be motivated by cost concerns. Others will fear the incursions on family privacy represented by any form of home visitation system, whether voluntary or mandatory.

The obvious risk is that home visitation programs could be cut back so far that they would no longer reach the families most capable of benefitting from the support they provide. This would undermine one goal central to the home visitation movement, that of *preventing* the child maltreatment problem from developing. Home visitation programs are designed to take advantage of the motivating force of impending and early parenthood, so as to change the direction of the young parent's life, and as a result protect children from being damaged in the first instance. Limiting home visitation services to families that have already fallen into problematic parenting patterns means giving up on some of our most significant opportunities to protect children from harm.

Quality and Integrity

For home visitation to live up to its promise, programs need to be funded, administered, and staffed in ways that enable them to play a significant supportive and surveillance role. There is a risk that programs will be watered down and diverted from their initial course, as pressures mount from those concerned with cutting costs and from those concerned with protecting traditional values.

Central to the current home visitation model is the provision of services on an intensive, on-going basis. HFA promotes a model in which visits during early infancy are made on at least a weekly basis, with the frequency of visits during the next three to five years dependent on the demonstrated need for support and supervision. About one-third of HFA families are enrolled prenatally as well. Olds promotes an intensive, multifaceted program, providing visitors once a week for the first four weeks of pregnancy, once a month for the duration of pregnancy, and then, after birth, once a week for the first six weeks and once every other week until the child is two years of age.

This intensive model makes psychological sense. It's hard to imagine how home visitation programs could make much of a difference in the lives of the fragile, vulnerable families that are at significant risk for child maltreatment, *unless* they provide for regular visits on an on-going basis. Lives are not turned around that easily.

There is little evidence for the success of any home visitation programs that do not have this intensive character.[22] Nor has any success been demonstrated for the many family support and family preservation programs that use home visiting on an occasional basis, or on an intensive but short-term basis, after child maltreatment problems have surfaced.[23]

Given the financial costs entailed in making this intensive form of home visitation available universally, or at least very broadly, it seems likely that if the move to expand the reach of home visitation programs continues, the pressures to limit program services will mount.[24] The home visitation programs that exist in many countries abroad as part of the health care system can be looked to as models for a more limited kind of program. Providing only a few visits, typically during early infancy, these programs may help parents who are at no particular risk for committing maltreatment get off to a good start. But if the number of visits are limited without regard to the level of need that early visits reveal, they will do little or nothing to address our country's child maltreatment problem.

The success home visitation programs have demonstrated to date is likely associated with other features of the model that will be difficult to replicate and perpetuate. In the Elmira program, public health nurses were carefully selected and trained and were guided in their work as home visitors by a well thought through curriculum. Future home visitation programs' success in reducing the level of child maltreatment will depend on the quality of program design, and of staff selection and guidance. It will also depend on whether program goals continue to focus on reducing maltreatment, rather than simply providing support services.

As home visitation becomes institutionalized, the values of those who people the child welfare system are more likely to influence the design of programs. If those people remain committed to family privacy and family preservation as the overriding values, they are likely to emphasize support ever more at the expense of surveillance. They are likely to staff home visitation programs with people sympathetic to parents' rights and suspicious of state intervention.[25]

Home visitation could make a huge difference to our child maltreatment problem if we were prepared to take early child development in the first five years as seriously as we take childhood education in the elementary school years. We could create a truly universal home visitation system designed to ensure that children get the early nurturance they need to grow into sane and healthy adults. The goal seems at least as important as the goal of ensuring that children five and older receive adequate schooling.

A universal home visitation system could provide fragile but workable families with the support they need to make it. It could also help us identify the families that are so deeply troubled that the children are at imminent risk for abuse or neglect, where parents are plagued by substance abuse and other problems that make it impossible for them to function as parents. A universal home visitation system would enable us to monitor such families closely, removing children at risk, and assessing parents' compliance with treatment and other goals to help determine promptly whether children should be returned home or moved on to permanent adoptive homes.

But it's not at all clear that this is the direction in which we are moving. Home visitation advocates are not interested in its surveillance potential. The larger society is not interested in expensive new social programs, even when a good case can be made that they are cost-effective in the long run. There's a real risk that home visitation will develop in a way which simply makes it *look* as if we are protecting children. Sending visitors only into the homes that will allow them, and telling those workers that their job is to help the parents make it, may constitute a helpful expansion of current family support programs. It may help some fragile families with relatively minor problems make a success of their parenting lives. But it is unlikely to do anything to help children who are seriously at risk. Indeed there's a danger that this form of home visitation might do those children more harm than good by providing the illusion that they are being protected.

8. TAKING ADOPTION SERIOUSLY

There is a lot of positive talk about adoption today, and some action. One can easily get the sense that a revolution is in the works. The President has announced his Adoption 2002 initiative, calling for a doubling in the number of children adopted out of foster care. Congress has passed within the space of just a few years several pieces of legislation designed to promote adoption. New federal laws ban racial barriers to adoption, limit the excesses of family-preservation policies, encourage child welfare agencies to move more children at earlier stages into adoptive homes, and encourage potential adoptive parents by giving them tax credits for adoption expenses. State and local leaders have initiated reforms to place renewed emphasis on children's safety and welfare, and to make adoption a higher policy priority. And in the last few years the number of adoptions has been rising, with some states showing dramatic increases.[1]

Today's talk of adoption, and some new initiatives in the works, raise the hope that our society might be ready to make genuine changes in its child welfare system, taking adoption seriously for the first time as an option for children whose parents are not capable of parenting. But it will take a lot of work to turn that hope into reality.

Estimates indicate that as of 1998 roughly 110,000 children in fos-

ter care had been freed for adoption, or had an adoption plan—
about 20 percent of those in out-of-home care. Fifty-nine percent of
these children are African-American, 29 percent are white, 10 percent
are Hispanic, and 2 percent are of other races or ethnicities.[2] But the
need for adoption cannot be measured by these numbers. Many children are being kept in their families and in foster care, and shuffled
back and forth between the two, for whom adoption should be considered, but is not. The claim has been that adoption wouldn't be
good for them—that children are almost always best off with their
parents. The assumption has been that adoption wouldn't be possible anyway—that the homes just aren't there for the black children,
the damaged children, and the older children that dominate the foster care population.

Adoption Works

The evidence is clear that adoption works, and that it is the best of
the available alternatives for children who have been subjected to
abuse or neglect. This is true in terms of all the measures social scientists use to assess well-being, including measures of self-esteem and
outcome measures related to later education, employment, crime
and the like. It is also true in terms of abuse and neglect rates. Indeed,
adopted children are less likely to suffer child abuse than is the norm
in the general population of children raised by their biological
parents.[3]

Family preservationists' claim that adoption harms children by
depriving them of their family and roots relies on speculative theo-
ries that adoptees suffer from "genealogical bewilderment" and the
like. But empirical studies that assess how carefully selected samples
and control groups of children actually fare in life, based on all the
measures of human well-being that social scientists have devised, reveal no damage suffered by virtue of transferring children from their
biological parents to adoptive parents. Children adopted early in infancy do essentially as well, on measures of self-esteem, attachment,
and performance, as children in the general population. These studies confirm that what is central to children's welfare is that they be
placed in an appropriately nurturing permanent home as early in life
as possible.[4]

1. But can adoption work for today's foster care population?

Adoption skeptics say no. They say that the children in foster care are too damaged, and many of them too old, for adoption to work. They point to the numbers who are born impaired by drugs and alcohol, the numbers who suffer from physical and mental disabilities, the numbers who have been subjected to extreme forms of abuse and neglect, and the numbers who are in their teens, having first suffered harm in their original homes, followed by many years adrift in the foster care system, or moving back and forth from foster homes to their homes of origin. They argue that while adoption might work for healthy infants, it can't work for these children. They note that significant numbers of adoptions from foster care "disrupt," with the children sent back from their adoptive homes into the foster care system. They claim that the only solutions for this damaged, older population of children lie in renewed emphasis on family preservation, on long-term foster care or guardianship, and on group or institutional homes.[5]

But the evidence indicates that adoption can and does work for children who are damaged and for children who are older. These children do have extra-ordinary needs. Most of them are far more likely to find the extra-ordinary parenting they require to overcome their history and heal their injuries in the adoptive parent population than in the families that subjected them to abuse and neglect, or in temporary foster care, or in institutional care.

A significant percentage of today's foster care and group home population are infants, many of whom were born showing the effects of their mother's use of alcohol and drugs during pregnancy. Many were removed as a result of their parents' substance abuse and related maltreatment during the period soon after birth. Drug experts have been arguing for years that "crack babies" and other infants whose mothers used licit and illicit drugs during pregnancy have a variety of special needs requiring special care, but that with that care they can flourish. These experts have advocated vigorously against simply writing off this generation of children and have testified specifically to their adoptability.[6]

Studies of children who have suffered enormous emotional damage as a result of abuse and neglect, or wartime atrocities, show that adoption has the capacity to help many such children heal and recover, so that they can lead essentially normal lives.[7] Adoption critics point to the adoption disruption statistics, but given the damage that so many foster care children have suffered, the fact that only roughly 10 percent of the adoptions out of the foster care system disrupt should be seen as a mark of the success achieved in these adoptive relationships. Studies of special-needs adoptions generally show that these adoptive families form the same kind of loving, committed, and satisfying family relationships as those formed in other adoptive families.

It is true that some older children in foster care have developed meaningful ties with biological parents, but adoption need not destroy such ties. There is an increasing tendency toward openness in adoption which would allow children to gain the permanence and committed parenting of an adoptive family, while maintaining healthy links with their family of origin.

It is also true that adoption works better for children when they are placed in infancy and when they have not been horribly damaged by abuse and neglect, or by the inconsistency and uncertainty in parenting arrangements characteristic of foster care. Adoption studies regularly confirm that age at the time of placement is the key predictor for how well adopted children will do.[8] This is no surprise. And it is obviously no argument for giving up on adoption as a solution for the foster care population. Adoption will still work better for most foster children than any other option, although it is undoubtedly true that some children are so damaged by the maltreatment they suffered or by their experience in the child welfare system that they have to be relegated to institutional care.

These adoption studies *are* an argument for moving children out of their biological homes and on to adoptive homes as soon as it is reasonably clear that they are not likely to receive the kind of care from their parents that they need to thrive. Delay in adoption may not necessarily permanently destroy children. But abuse and neglect combined with foster drift injure children in ways that not only cause suffering but also damage their life prospects, diminishing the chances for them to flourish in the way that children adopted as infants typically do flourish. All too many foster children today *are* older and *have* suffered damage, and *do* as a result have diminished life prospects even in adoption. But these are realities that are in our power to change.

2. But can adoptive families be found for today's foster care population?

Adoption skeptics say no. They argue that potential adoptive parents are limited in number and interested only in healthy infants, and that the whites who make up most of the adoptive parent pool are not interested in the nonwhite children who make up most of the foster care pool.

The reality is that we have done more to drive prospective parents away from the foster care system than to draw them in. We could expand the existing parent pool by recruiting broadly; now we recruit on the most limited basis. We could socialize prospective parents in ways that would open their minds to the idea of parenting children born to other parents and other racial groups, and children who have physical and mental disabilities; for the most part we now do just the opposite.

Skeptics talk as if the number of adoptive parents and the nature of their interests were fixed in stone. In fact the "demand" for adoption is extremely malleable. What exists today is a reality that our social policies have created. History demonstrates our power to reshape this reality. Prior to the mid-nineteenth century there was no apparent interest in adoption, because there was no legal mechanism enabling adoption. It took legislative and administrative action setting up an adoption system before adoptive parents could step forward, but now that such a system has been created we have well over 100,000 adoptions per year, more than half of which are adoptions by nonrelatives. Prior to World War II there was no apparent interest in international adoption, but now that systems have been set up enabling prospective parents to adopt children from abroad, many thousands of foreign children per year come into the United States to be adopted by U.S. citizens—15,774 in fiscal year 1998.[9] Until a couple of decades ago, the only children considered adoptable were healthy infants. Now that efforts have been made to recruit parents for children with disabilities, there are waiting lists for Down's Syndrome children and for other children who used to be relegated to institutional care. Even children with extreme disabilities have been placed by child welfare agencies that have made the effort to reach out to locate and educate potential adopters. NACAC—the North American Council on Adoptable Children—says that *no child* in the foster care system should be considered unadoptable.

The potential pool of adoptive parents is enormous—it dwarfs the pool of waiting children. About 1.2 million women are infertile and 7.1 percent of married couples, or 2.1 million.[10] The infertile are potentially a significant resource for children in need of homes, but at present only a limited number of them adopt. It is even more rare for the fertile to think of adoption as a way to build, or add to, their family. About 1 percent of women age 18–44, or 500,000, are currently seeking to adopt. Only 0.2 percent, or 100,000, had applied to an adoption agency.[11] It is safe to assume that millions more would have pursued adoption had our social policies encouraged rather than discouraged them.

Ours is a society that glorifies reproduction, drives the infertile to pursue treatment at all costs, socializes them to think of adoption as a second-class form of parenting to be pursued only as a last resort, and regulates adoption in a way that makes it difficult, degrading, and expensive.[12] We could instead encourage not only the infertile but the fertile to think of adoption as a normal way to build their families. We now ask young couples when they are going to have their first baby. We could ask them when they are thinking of expanding their family, and whether they are thinking about adoption or procreation or both. We could encourage all adult members of our society to think that their responsibility as members of the national community includes caring for the youngest members of that community when care is needed.

Other countries and cultures provide evidence that our society's current attitudes are not genetically determined. Radical change is possible. In Africa and many other countries it is common for the larger community to assume responsibility for children whose parents cannot care for them. Churches and social welfare agencies have found that when they reach out to the African-American community, asking for people to step forward to provide foster and adoptive homes, they have had significant success in recruiting parents. African-Americans have recently been adopting at roughly the same rate as whites,[13] which is dramatic evidence of the impact of social-

ization and recruitment, since blacks are congregated disproportionately at the bottom of the socioeconomic ladder and would not be
expected to volunteer for adoptive parenthood at the same rates as
those more privileged.

Adoption skeptics say that whites are not interested in adopting
the children in the foster care system. But we have done little to recruit adoptive parents among the relatively privileged white middle
class. Instead we have told them that they may not be allowed to
adopt the children of color who make up roughly two-thirds of the
foster care group, and that they are guilty of racial genocide if they
try. We have told them that if they want to adopt the waiting white
children, they will be subject to more extensive parental fitness
screening and other bureaucratic manipulations than they would
face if they chose to adopt healthy infants through private agencies.

Race does matter to many adoptive parents in today's world. But
our state welfare agencies have been telling adoptive parents that race
should matter. When white parents have stepped forward to ask for
black children they have often been asked why they would want to do
such a thing. The written and unwritten policies discussed in chapter
5 have prevented whites from adopting transracially. Despite this
negative conditioning, whites continue to express interest in doing
so. When asked by one state welfare agency whether they would
be willing to adopt children of color from the foster care system,
roughly one-sixth of the waiting white prospective adopters an-
swered yes.[14] Many whites are adopting transracially in the private
adoption system, where state barriers don't stand in the way. Many
others adopt internationally, where most children are identifiable as
ethnically different from their parents, and many are black and
brown skinned. It is obvious that many whites would adopt from the
foster care system if only we would eliminate the racial barriers, as
the federal government's MEPA legislation now commands be done.
If we were to affirmatively socialize whites to believe that they *should*
consider adopting children of color we could expect to increase the
numbers of potential adopters exponentially.

Age and disability also matter to many potential adopters. But we
have made enormous progress in the last couple of decades in finding
homes for older children and for children with physical and mental
disabilities, simply because we have begun to recruit actively for

those homes. Our recruitment efforts so far have been extremely limited, reaching out to only a small portion of the potential parent pool. We have failed to recruit significantly beyond the community of color and beyond the working-class white community. We have failed thus to recruit among those who might be expected, on the basis of their relative privilege, to be in the best position to reach out to give to those most in need.

We could also change the current reality by changing the social policies that keep children in damaging homes and in foster care for years—policies that, in effect, *require* that children suffer the physical and mental damage that we bemoan as making placement difficult. If we take the mandate of the 1997 Adoption and Safe Families Act seriously, and move children more swiftly out of homes in which they suffer harm, we will begin to address the problem that many claim stands in the way of finding adoptive homes.

We Know Better Than We Do

At a recent meeting of experts convened by the federal government to review the research on child abuse and neglect and related treatment efforts, some of the country's most knowledgeable child welfare professionals discussed the merits of the various methods of intervention.[15] Some spoke of the research demonstrating the abject failure of family preservation programs to protect children from ongoing abuse and neglect. Others discussed the ambiguous results of the limited number of programs that provide treatment to children victimized by abuse and neglect. There was general agreement that providing some treatment was better than providing none, whether or not treatment seemed likely to achieve dramatic results for the children. No one wanted to discuss a central question that was posed, and then left hanging: why was everyone talking about providing treatment to children in the context in which we could least expect it to work, namely in the very families that had subjected them to damaging abuse and neglect?[16] Then one participant stated the obvious: *If we really wanted to help these children we all know what we would do—we would move them into adoptive homes.* The statement sat in the room like a grenade no one wanted to touch for fear it would explode. There were a few moments of silence. There was no disagreement. But then this roomful of experts who seemed genuinely committed to doing something better for children, and who seemed deeply skeptical of the benefits for children available in current child welfare programs, moved on. It appeared that there was no point in engaging the question of how to really help children, because all these knowledgeable people knew that family preservation was the order of the day and could not imagine a world in which it was not.

We know better than we do. We know that children require nurturing environments to thrive today and to have promising prospects for tomorrow. Common sense, confirmed by the research, tells us that children who are severely abused and neglected will do best if removed and placed permanently with families where they will receive the kind of nurturing likely to help them recover from their wounds. Common sense, confirmed by the research, tells us they would do better yet if we moved them when abuse and neglect were first manifest. This does not mean that in all cases of severe abuse and neglect we should immediately terminate the parents' rights and move children on to adoption. But it does mean that we should consider immediate termination of parental rights in many more cases and place a much higher priority on prompt adoptive placement.

We also know, or should know, that once we decide that children cannot be adequately nurtured in their homes of origin, they will be best off if we focus not simply on keeping them connected with their roots, but on taking care of them today in a way that will enable them to function tomorrow. Richard Barth, of the Jordan Institute for Families at the University of North Carolina School of Social Work, stands out as one of the few scholars willing to state the obvious: that for children to thrive it is important that we focus not just on their past but on their present and their future; that it matters if they are brought up by people who are capable of nurturing them, and in schools and communities where they can learn and be safe from violence. Barth argues that the current system places too much value on "family continuity," and not enough on a "life-course development approach," offering a "sufficient commitment of financial, social and interpersonal resources to help the child achieve and sustain self-sufficiency as an adult":

Biological parents clearly have a goal of productive development for their children. . . . Should the government—the responsible guardian for foster children—have any less?

. . . We should recognize that continuity with the past may have substantial disadvantages for children who come from homes so troubled that they could not be restored. These children often come from schools and neighborhoods that are almost unsalvageable. . . .

Keeping the children in the same school they were in may not be beneficial. . . .

Nor does neighborhood continuity offer great promise for many youth. The death rates in some American communities exceed that of Bangladesh. . . . Alternately, living in an advantaged neighborhood discourages teenagers from having children out of wedlock, encourages teenagers to finish high school, and increases teenagers' future earnings. . . . Although children should not be moved frivolously, nor should we strive to maintain them in the same neighborhood and school without more evidence that such continuity really can be expected to help foster children and youth beat the odds against them. . . .

What environments are we looking for instead? The socially rich environment is . . . one which includes people who are relatively "free from drain"—individuals who can afford to give and share with others. . . .

Placements that are most likely to provide physical, affective, cognitive, and environmental advantages through young adulthood should be favored over placements that do not, even if they require some discontinuities to achieve them. . . .

Unless we consistently encourage the self-sufficiency of children in foster care we cannot expect them to experience the well-being that our parents sought for us and that we seek for our own children.[17]

Barth notes the dominance of the family continuity perspective in current child welfare decision-making: "Every day, social workers make choices about permanently placing children in homes that have few or no characteristics that bolster the child's chance of succeeding," ruling out homes that would give the child a better chance for the future "because of concerns about maintaining psychological, cultural, racial, or community continuity." He argues for eliminating the mechanistic, absolutist preferences of the day, for a system that makes the child's lifetime welfare central, and takes account of the range of factors relevant to it.[18]

PROMISING INITIATIVES OF THE DAY
Federal Legislation

The federal government has passed a series of laws in the 1990s, each of which promotes adoption in very significant ways. Adoption tax credit legislation provides all adopters up to certain maximum income limits with a federal tax credit of $5000; those adopting special needs children receive a tax credit of $6000.[19] Legitimate costs of adoption can simply be deducted from taxes due, up to the applicable limits. The symbolic significance of this tax credit legislation may be more important than its immediate practical impact. As noted above, we have structured parenting choice in a way that drives people away from adoptive parenting and encourages them to pursue biological parenting at all costs. This structuring includes a set of financial incentives and disincentives. Employment benefit packages provide health benefits which cover pregnancy and childbirth, and often cover infertility treatment; a dozen states mandate insurance coverage for infertility treatment; and employment disability policies often provide extensive maternity leaves after birth. At the same time, while special needs adoptions are generally subsidized, other adoptions are regulated in a way that make them quite costly. In addition, employment benefit packages have typically not included benefits for adoption expenses; employment leave policies typically provide adopters with only limited parental leave. Federal tax policy, and typically state tax policy also, has provided tax deductions for the kind of medical expenses involved in pregnancy and childbirth, but no comparable deductions for the expenses involved in adoption. All this contributes to the stacked deck of parental choice. The new federal tax credit legislation represents an important step toward unstacking that deck, evening out some of the financial inequities between those who form their families through adoption and those who form them through reproduction.

The Multiethnic Placement Act (MEPA), as amended in 1996, is a truly revolutionary act in concept, eliminating race as a consideration in adoptive placement, when race has been used systematically by public child welfare agencies throughout the nation as one of the single most important factors determining whether and how to place children.

MEPA puts both private actors and the federal government in a position to enforce the act. Private actors aggrieved by a violation can go to court to seek injunctive and other relief, including attorneys' fees. The federal government has not only a right but an obligation to enforce the act: it is *required* to impose major financial penalties for any given violation of the act, with penalties escalating for successive violations.

MEPA has extraordinary practical significance for black and other racial minority group children suffering abuse and neglect at home, or languishing in foster care. In the past, the racial matching policies discussed in chapter 5 have functioned to bolster family preservation, keeping black children in inadequate biological homes, or locked in foster limbo. Social workers told that they should avoid transracial placement, and that there were not enough African-American adoptive families available, have felt greater than normal pressure to keep black children in troubled biological families, rather than condemning them to foster drift. Social workers have felt greater than normal pressure to reunify troubled black families, or to come up with permanent fostering solutions, rather than terminating parental rights. Even when parental rights have been terminated, child welfare workers have often held children in foster care rather than placing them across racial lines. One recent study of children freed for adoption found that of those under twelve years of age, virtually all white children have adoption as their official goal, whereas only one-quarter of nonwhite children do.[20] See generally discussion in chapter 5 above, of the degree to which racial matching policies have functioned as a barrier locking minority race children into foster care and preventing their adoption.

MEPA has extraordinary symbolic significance as well. It makes a powerful new statement about the state's proper role in the adoption process. For decades the general assumption has been that the state should play an increasingly intrusive role in forming adoptive families, screening for parental fitness and matching children with parents based on social workers' ideas of what families should look like. This has resulted in increasingly burdensome regulation surrounding adoption. MEPA represents a radical move in a different direction, with the federal government telling states that they have to back off—at least with respect to race—and permit people to form transracial families through adoption just as they can through marriage. In the United States and throughout the world it is bureaucratic barriers that have stood in the way of interested adults stepping forward to parent children in need. In eliminating what has been one of the most significant barriers to the placement of children in foster care, MEPA may set us down a road toward the elimination of other barriers that stand between the children who need parenting care and the adults who want to provide it.

ASFA, the Adoption and Safe Families Act of 1997, represents another radical shift in the nature of adoption regulation, which has typically taken a negative, restrictive form. Regulators have regarded adoption as involving risks to be protected against, rather than benefits to be sought after, and have accordingly focused on preventing adoption from happening inappropriately—on preventing, for example, children from being improperly separated from birth parents, or placed with unfit adoptive parents. ASFA shifts the regulatory focus so that it includes the benefits that adoption can provide, and the detriment to children if they are not adopted when they should be. It creates an affirmative obligation to move children on to adoptive or other permanent homes in cases where such action seems necessary to promote children's welfare.

ASFA grew out of a broadly shared sense that family preservation priorities had been taken too far and that adoption should be given greater priority. Congress recognized in passing ASFA that its 1980 Adoption Assistance and Child Welfare Act had been regularly read to require that "reasonable efforts" be made to preserve all families without regard to how destructive the parenting was or how unlikely the prospect of improvement in the future. ASFA changes the reasonable efforts mandate in several vitally important ways. It qualifies it generally by stating that "the child's health and safety shall be the paramount concern." It says that reasonable efforts to preserve a family are *not* required in cases in which the parent has subjected the child to "aggravated circumstances," as defined by state law, which may include but need not be limited to abandonment, torture, chronic abuse, and sexual abuse, and in cases in which the parent has committed murder or voluntary manslaughter of another child, or felony assault resulting in serious bodily injury to the child or another child, or if parental rights to a sibling have been terminated involuntarily. ASFA says that when a child is removed under these circumstances, and a court decides that reasonable efforts to reunify the family need not be made, then reasonable efforts *must be made* to move the child on to an adoptive or other permanent placement. ASFA tries to expedite permanency by requiring that permanency hearings be held within twelve months of when the child is "considered to have entered foster care" (which could be up to two months after the child's removal from home).

ASFA also requires that states file a petition to terminate parental rights under certain circumstances, namely, (1) if the child has been in foster care for fifteen of the most recent twenty-two months, or (2), in cases of removal, when courts have made findings that a child is an abandoned infant, or that the parent has committed murder or voluntary manslaughter of another child, or that the parent has committed felony assault resulting in serious bodily injury to the child or another child. And ASFA gives foster and preadoptive parents a right to be heard in court hearings involving their child.

ASFA gives adoption another boost by providing states with unprecedented "adoption incentive payments" in the amount of $4000 per adoption from foster care and $6000 per special needs adoption, for increases in the number of adoptions over previous years, with the total bonus payments limited by certain maximums, and with the program set to end in the year 2002.

State and Private Initiatives: Concurrent Planning and TPR Reform

State and private actors have instituted a number of promising reform programs designed to limit family preservation excesses and promote timely adoption placements.[21] "Concurrent planning" has been introduced in a number of different regions in the last two decades.[22] In these programs, children removed to state care who are identified as not likely to return to their homes of origin are placed simultaneously on two planning tracks: the family reunification track, providing services to enable the child to return home, and the adoption track, preparing for parental rights termination and adoption. If it turns out that indeed the child should not return home, the child can then move promptly and smoothly on to adoption. The child is often initially placed for foster care in a potential adoptive home, so that if in the end adoption seems the right plan the child need not experience the disruption of another move.

Concurrent planning has developed out of the "fost-adopt" practices that have been common in recent years, as an increasing number of children have been placed with foster parents who are open to or actively interested in adoption, and social work policies have come to give preferences in adoptive placement to foster parents who have developed bonds with their foster children. ASFA provides some new support for concurrent planning by simply recognizing its legitimacy, stating: "reasonable efforts to place a child for adoption or with a legal guardian may be made concurrently with reasonable efforts [to further family reunification]."

Concurrent planning means that even when reasonable efforts to preserve the family seem appropriate, children can spend all their foster care time in the same home that will be their adoptive home, if in the end the decision is made to terminate parental rights. They are spared the kind of bouncing around from one temporary "home" to another that has characterized much of foster care, and they are more likely to develop the kind of emotional attachments that are crucial to their future development. And their adoptions are likely to be finalized much earlier than they would be if adoption workers had to wait until family preservation efforts were declared bankrupt in order to begin the adoption planning process. It represents a radical change from the idea that was common a generation ago that child welfare workers should not begin any kind of adoption planning until they had tried and given up on family preservation efforts, and that, for related reasons, foster parents should not bond with their children or contemplate adoption but should recognize the necessarily temporary quality of the fostering relationship.

The American Bar Association has sponsored a reform initiative called the "Termination Barriers Project," designed to expedite parental rights termination and adoptive placement. Their model programs have demonstrated that by simply training judges, lawyers, caseworkers, and other service providers to work toward these goals, cases can be moved faster and children either reunified or placed in adoptive homes more promptly, all at a significant cost saving. This project is designed to work within the confines of a state's existing system, including its existing standards for terminating parental rights, without requiring any new resources or personnel, and without any changes in substantive law.[23] The ABA has also tried to nudge states in the direction of developing legislation to promote early termination of parental rights in appropriate cases.[24]

Many states have passed legislation, and created programs, designed to limit family preservation and promote adoption. In New York City the tragic life and death of Elisa Izquierdo resulted in the Mayor's declaring child safety a new priority. Nicholas Scoppetta, a highly respected former prosecutor whose childhood in foster care gave him an intense commitment to the issues, was brought in to head the new effort. Under his leadership the City issued a manifesto calling for a massive transformation of the child welfare system,[25] stating that children's safety and well-being were to be the agency's guiding principles, and promising a shift in the relative priorities accorded family preservation as compared to adoption. Colorado passed an expedited permanency bill in 1994 requiring that any child under six years of age be placed in a permanent home no later than twelve months after entering foster care. The expedited permanency legislation is being implemented in conjunction with concurrent planning. Comparative studies indicate that expedited permanency has resulted in a significant reduction in the period children in Colorado spend waiting in temporary out-of-home care.[26] A number of other states have made an effort to reform their TPR laws to limit periods spent in foster care, to expand the grounds for TPR, and to provide for expedited termination in certain egregious cases of abuse and neglect; some acted prior to ASFA's passage, and others acted in response to ASFA's requirement that states revamp their laws to comply with at least ASFA's minimum demands.[27]

A few states have taken action to remove racial barriers to adoption, both before and in the wake of MEPA. Texas took the legislative lead, first passing a statute in 1993 that prohibited the use of race to delay, deny, or otherwise discriminate in foster and adoptive placement and allowed no loophole for race as a permissible consideration. Then in 1996 Texas passed a law designed to deal with the resistance to change experienced in the interim. This law made adoption workers who refused to follow the new legal mandate subject to dismissal and threatened recalcitrant agencies with the loss of their licenses.[28]

SOME PITFALLS
Legal Loopholes and Rule-Swallowing Exceptions

Many of the new laws and policies, though, are written in ways that reflect political compromise with the forces of resistance, and that in turn provide those forces with inviting opportunities to express their resistance.

1. MEPA

As discussed in chapter 5 above, MEPA I prohibited the use of race to delay or deny adoptive placement, but allowed race as a permissible consideration. The MEPA I Guidance issued by HHS made it clear that race could only be used on an individualized basis and in a manner that would survive the kind of "strict scrutiny" review that the federal constitution requires for any race-conscious policy. This might seem to the uninitiated reader enough to prevent states from using race in the categorical way they had been using it. But the fact is that a similar rule of law had been established by state and federal courts twenty-five years earlier, and reaffirmed over the intervening years, and yet state child welfare agencies had felt free to continue their systematic race matching.[29] MEPA II was passed, eliminating the permission for states to use race as a consideration, out of recognition that the MEPA I loophole had been exploited to avoid the kind of fundamental changes in race-matching policies that Congress had envisioned.

MEPA I's other troublesome provision, requiring that state agencies recruit prospective foster and adoptive parents reflecting the ethnic and racial diversity of the children needing homes,[30] could be read *either* as simply a requirement for fair, nondiscriminatory methods of selecting prospective parents, *or* as a signal that race and ethnicity might be relevant in determining which children should be assigned to which parents. As discussed in detail in chapter 5, the latter reading was heavily promoted by those resistant to MEPA's goals.

The 1996 MEPA amendments failed to eliminate MEPA I's recruitment language, even though the obvious goal of MEPA II was to forbid any kind of systematic consideration of race. So we are left today, even after MEPA II, with a recruitment provision that can be used to undermine the Act's goals. Evidence to date indicates that it is in fact functioning that way, with race-matching advocates seizing on MEPA's recruitment provisions and treating them as if they were the central feature of the law.

The lesson of the powerful resistance MEPA has met in the field, and within the Department of Health and Human Services, the agency charged with enforcing it, is clear. Loopholes must be eliminated, and mandates spelled out in unambiguous language, leaving as little wiggle room as possible for those resistant to the spirit of the new changes. Beyond this, minds need to be changed within the child welfare world from top to bottom. Minds also need to be changed outside the child welfare world. Experience with the enforcement of civil rights legislation during the decades following *Brown vs. Board of Education* demonstrated that legal change can make a difference even in the face of resistance, if public and private organizations are committed to enforce the law, as the Civil Rights Division of the U.S. Department of Justice, the NAACP Legal Defense Fund, and other agencies and organizations were committed to enforcing the civil rights principles embodied in *Brown* and in the federal Civil Rights Act of 1964. The individuals and organizations already committed to the enforcement of MEPA principles need more powerful organizational allies to push change forward.

2. ASFA

ASFA is filled with loopholes and exceptions which could potentially undermine Congress's apparent intent. It's understandable that Congress would have wanted to leave the states plenty of room to decide how to administer their child protection systems. This has traditionally been an area for state and not federal regulation. But ASFA may have left too much room for those in the child welfare system who are committed to family preservation to resist and evade ASFA's apparent purpose.

On one level ASFA reads as if it is intended to create a new regime, one in which states are required by federal law, at least if they want to keep their all-important federal funding, to move to terminate parental rights in cases of egregious parental misconduct or serious dysfunction, and in cases in which children have been in foster care for fifteen of the most recent twenty-two months. *But these tough-sounding TPR provisions apply only if the state chooses not to preserve the family. ASFA allows the state not to make reasonable efforts to preserve families in certain cases, but it does not forbid the state from making such efforts in all cases.* States have leeway under ASFA *not* to make reasonable efforts to preserve or reunify families in certain egregious cases specified in the law, and in "aggravated circumstances" that states can spell out in their own laws, but for this leeway to mean anything, state legislation would have to permit this also; state child welfare workers would have to decide not to pursue reasonable efforts and state judges would have to make findings that this was appropriate. If states want to make efforts to preserve families in *all* cases, including those egregious cases listed in ASFA, they can. The provisions requiring states to file TPR petitions in certain egregious cases, and when a child has been in foster care for fifteen out of twenty-two months, apply only if the state has already intervened, removed the child, and presented the case to a court so that the court can make the requisite findings triggering the requirement to file the TPR petition.

In addition, the Act lists three exceptions which threaten to swallow entirely its TPR mandate:

The kinship exception. The TPR requirements do not apply if the child is being cared for by a relative. Again it's understandable that Congress would have created *some* kinship exception. Kin will sometimes provide the best placement for a child, and will sometimes have legitimate reasons for not wanting to formally adopt the child, even if there is no reasonable likelihood that the child will or should ever return home. Making kin the permanent guardians, rather than the adoptive parents, will sometimes be the best solution. But ASFA makes no attempt to limit the state's discretion here. There is no requirement, for example, that the state make a finding, or make a showing to the court, that it is preferable from the child's viewpoint to keep the child in foster care with a relative than to place the child in a permanent adoptive home. One-third of all foster children today are in kinship care; in many urban areas at least one-half are (see discussion in chapter 3). For all these children, ASFA's tough-sounding TPR provisions are essentially inapplicable. States *can* consider adoption as an alternative for these children, but ASFA does not require that they do so even when the kinship care is marginal, and adoption would be far preferable from the child's perspective. States *can* encourage kin foster parents to consider adoption, but ASFA does not require that they do so. Given the popularity of kinship care among child welfare professionals, and given their traditional reluctance to terminate parental rights, one has to wonder whether ASFA will have any real impact in encouraging states even to consider terminating the parental rights of those whose children are in kinship care. Instead the act may simply motivate workers to expand the use of kinship foster care, so as to avoid having to deal with the new TPR requirements.

The bureaucratic failure exception. The TPR requirements also do not apply if the state has not provided the child's family in a timely manner "such services as the State deems necessary for the safe return of the child to the child's home," in cases in which reasonable efforts to preserve or reunify the family are required. Again it's understandable why this provision is here. It seems unfair to take children away from parents who might be able to function as adequate parents if only they received certain services from the state. But there's a risk that this exception will swallow the new TPR rule. The problem is that the state typically does *not* provide adequate and timely reunification services. Child welfare agencies are notoriously underfunded and overburdened. Appropriate services are often unavailable or, if available, they are costly and agencies have not been given the funds to pay for them. We have had experience for two decades with laws and policies which, like this bureaucratic failure exception, use children as hostages to try to gouge family support services out of state legislatures and state welfare agencies. States have been told for two decades that if they don't provide the requisite services, then they may not be able to remove children from the families where they are suffering abuse and neglect, or terminate parental rights so that children can be adopted. It turns out that punishing children for the sins of the state doesn't have much of an impact on the sinning state's conduct. States still fail on a systematic and widespread basis to provide the services that they are supposed to provide.

The best interests of the child exception. Even if the other two exceptions don't apply, the state can escape ASFA's TPR requirements by "documenting in the case plan (which shall be available for court review)" a "compelling reason" for determining that TPR would not be in the best interests of the child. Again this exception is understandable, and this one is at least *defined* in a way that implies some limits. But it's not clear they will be meaningful. Social workers can easily *document* a compelling reason in the sense that they can lay out their claim for the importance of not terminating the parents' rights. Nothing in the Act's language requires meaningful court review or court findings that a compelling reason actually exists. So the exception lies there ready to be exploited by workers opposed to TPR, in all cases for which no more obviously appropriate exception is available.

This exception's reference to the child's best interests may also increase the risk that the other two exceptions, in which no such language appears, will be interpreted as *not* requiring consideration of the child's best interests.

Programmatic Limits

1. The Safety and Permanency Mantras of the Day

Children's *well-being* is—or ought to be—the central concern. We want children growing up in homes in which they can be happy and thrive. We don't want them simply to survive. It is essential not only that they be free from destructive abuse, but that they receive affirmative nurturing. It is essential not only that they be spared damaging disruption and get permanent homes, but that they get the kind of permanent homes likely to provide true parenting. If *well-being* is the issue then we have to worry about abuse *and* neglect. We have to worry about the children growing up in households where because of substance abuse or other reasons the parents are simply not functioning as parents much of the time, whether or not they beat the children or sexually exploit them. If *well-being* is the issue we have to focus on the quality of the permanent home we provide. And we have to recognize that adoption generally gives children a form of committed, nurturing parenting that is often absent in other permanency arrangements.

However, safety and permanency are the accepted mantras of the day. Child welfare traditionalists have been willing to concede that we owe children this much. And those interested in changing the system to make it more child-oriented have settled too readily on this common ground. ASFA—today's most significant challenge to the family preservation tradition—illustrates the kind of compromise that conflicting forces in today's child welfare field have been able to reach. It is a compromise that stops far short of giving children what they need.

Those who initially promoted ASFA's passage talked a lot about children's well-being. But as the legislative language went through the fires of debate and deal-making, well-being lost out to safety. It is the "Adoption and *Safe* Families Act," and safety appears throughout its various provisions, defining the Act's central goals. The Act starts by redefining the reasonable efforts mandate to make the child's "health and safety" the paramount concern, and goes on to define family reunification as enabling the child "to safely" return home. The Act's specific provisions permitting states not to make efforts to preserve the family in certain cases, and mandating states to file TPR petitions in a closely related set of cases, are limited to cases involving abandonment, prior TPR, and the various forms of egregious maltreatment set forth above (torture, chronic abuse, sexual abuse, murder, voluntary manslaughter, and felony assault resulting in serious bodily injury).

The emphasis is on *abuse*, with no mention of neglect, even severe or chronic neglect. States are relieved from making reasonable family preservation efforts when the parent has subjected the child to "aggravated circumstances" as defined in state law, but the state is not encouraged by the statutory language to define those circumstances to include severe forms of neglect. ASFA says only that the state law definition may include but need not be limited to "abandonment, torture, chronic abuse, and sexual abuse."

There is no mention of what should be done for children whose parents are incapacitated by substance abuse and unable to provide the most basic physical and emotional care. But since ASFA says nothing, presumably the states are still required to make reasonable efforts to preserve these families, unless they take the affirmative step of defining "aggravated circumstances" to include severe and chronic neglect and emotional abuse. ASFA mentions drugs only in the context of requiring a study of the drug problem.[31] This passed the buck in a major way.

Despite its name, the Adoption and Safe Families Act seriously compromises the adoption goal by making "permanency" its focus and treating adoption as only one of various acceptable permanency options. Thus the Act requires "permanency" plans and efforts to make "permanent" placements, and seems in one place to equate placement for adoption with placement with a permanent legal guardian, and in another to equate adoption with all other permanent arrangements. While the Act's title and the adoption bonuses it offers might be seen as modest signals that adoption should be considered the preferred permanency option, all other things being equal, all other things are never equal, and modest signals can be overlooked by those who are not already motivated to go in the direction they point. Giving children permanency in their homes of origin or in their kinship or other foster homes may not give them the kind of homes they need.[32]

2. Expedited Termination of Parental Rights

Expediting the termination of parental rights in cases where it is unlikely that the children will or should be returned home makes obvious sense for the children, minimizing the risk of further damage, and maximizing the chances for them to attach and flourish in new adoptive families. When parents subject their children to deliberate torture or to other forms of severe intentional harm, immediate TPR seems appropriate. It seems similarly appropriate when parents are so caught up in their drug or alcohol addiction that they are unable to function as parents and are unable or unwilling to engage in treatment.

While there is a lot of talk about expedited TPR today, reform initiatives are quite limited. Few propose immediate termination, even in the most egregious cases. The general assumption is that efforts to preserve families should still be made but should not be as prolonged. As noted above, ASFA goes only so far as to *allow* states *not* to make reasonable efforts in egregious cases, but does not *prevent* them from doing so, or require that TPR take place. A study done for the ABA found that state law often did not permit expedited TPR, even in the most egregious cases, requiring instead that extensive efforts be made to rehabilitate the parents before the children could be freed for adoption.[33]

The ABA study found further that none of the states that did permit expedited TPR included an adequate set of grounds in their TPR statutes. Finding no model law in existence, the ABA report set out a list of grounds that states should include in amended TPR legislation:

1. Despite diligent and appropriate or reasonable efforts by the child protection agency, the parent has failed to make the necessary improvements for the child's safe return.

2. There exists a long-standing pattern of abandonment or extreme parental disinterest.

3. There is a projected long-term parental incapacity to care for the specific child based upon mental or emotional illness, mental retardation, or physical incapacity.

4. There is a drug or alcohol related incapacity or unwillingness to care for the child, with a past history of repeated, unsuccessful efforts at treatment.

5. There has been prior abuse or neglect of the child, a sibling, or other children in the household, with diligent but unsuccessful agency efforts to rehabilitate the parent.

6. The neglect or abuse of the child was so extreme that returning the child home presents an unacceptable risk.

7. As a result of the prior abuse or neglect, the child has developed a deep aversion or pathological fear of the parent.

8. The parent is sentenced to prolonged imprisonment, and will be unavailable during an extended period of the child's minority.[34]

This list provides an extremely modest starting point for state legislative reform. While some states, perhaps most notably California, have taken action in recent years to establish new grounds for TPR, most states have a long way to go to meet even the ABA report's standard. Few states have begun to seriously address the problems of substance abuse and chronic neglect. Few have begun to adequately define the cases in which expedited termination is appropriate, and the procedures to make this meaningful, so that children who should not be kept in or returned to their homes of origin can be moved promptly on to adoptive homes.

The ABA Termination Barriers Project noted above works within the parameters of existing state law, trying simply to streamline the bureaucratic process so that children are not subject to unnecessary months and years of delay waiting to be adopted. While it has shown success in expediting parental rights termination, it can only do so for children the state is willing to identify as appropriate candidates for adoption. And although delays are reduced for these children, they still wait for periods ranging from one year and seven months to three years and two months, depending on the county involved.[35]

3. Concurrent Planning

Concurrent planning programs similarly facilitate earlier placement than the traditional system, but stop far short of the kind of fundamental reform needed. They are generally targeted to only a limited subset of foster care cases—those of relatively young children who are highly unlikely to return home because of the extreme nature of the abuse and neglect they suffered, and their parents' insufficient capacities for future nurturing, as judged by today's child welfare standards. This leaves out many serious cases in which, though it is unlikely the children will ever return home, no steps will be taken to prepare the way for adoption until and unless the usual "reasonable efforts" have failed. At the same time it's questionable whether we should be doing concurrent planning at all in the most egregious subset of cases. Many of them should be considered good candidates for immediate TPR and adoptive placement, instead. But proponents argue that concurrent planning is appropriate in cases in which:

- "Parent has killed or seriously harmed *another* child through abuse or neglect and no significant change has occurred in the interim;"
- "Parent has repeatedly and with premeditation harmed or tortured *this* child;"
- "Parents' only visible support system and only visible means of financial support is found in illegal drugs, prostitution, and street life.

· "Child will be abused or neglected by parents or parents' compan-
ions, or will be essentially abandoned in foster care while parents continue their illegal lifestyle."[36]

Clearly it makes sense in cases like these not to hold the child for years
before beginning to plan for adoptive placement. But does it make
sense to pursue family reunification at all, and to keep the adoption
plan on hold pending the outcome?

Concurrent planning's potential is also limited by the narrowness
of today's system of selecting adoptive parents. The system typically
looks to the foster parent as the preferred adoptive parent, assuming
that the family reunification goal is not achieved. There is an advantage in selecting the foster parent, in that it allows the child to stay in
the same home rather than suffering an additional disruption. But,
as discussed in chapter 3, foster parents are typically recruited on a
narrow basis, with strong preferences given to those from the same
community and to kin. These preferences may or may not make
sense in the context of short-term foster care, depending on the circumstances of the case and whether social workers assess these factors in an absolutist way rather than weighing them against other
important factors. But these preferences are generally much less appropriate for foster care which transforms into permanent adoption.
It makes sense to try to keep a child in his neighborhood and his
community if he will shortly return home, whereas if he is not likely
to return home, it may be well worth it to go through the kind of
disruption involved in relocating, in order to find parents who will
provide the best nurturing environment for all his remaining childhood. For concurrent planning to truly serve children's interests, we
need to radically revise the system by which we recruit and assess
the fost-adopt parents, reaching out to include the broad group of
middle-class, relatively privileged people who are more typically involved in adoption than in foster care. We may not want to favor that
group, but it seems odd, and unfair to the children in need of homes,
to exclude from consideration the very people who are now volun-
teering to parent in the adoption world, and who have the resources
generally thought helpful in facilitating parenting. It seems particularly irrational given the regularly repeated complaints about the

difficulty of finding qualified foster parents, and related claims made as to the need to increase fostering stipends to attract more foster parents to the dwindling pool. As discussed in chapter 3, there are lots of reasons to worry about the overall quality of the current foster parent group. Concurrent planning will not work as it should for children unless those in charge are willing to radically rethink the recruitment of parents for these programs.

Bureaucratic Resistance and Legal Evasion

Bureaucratic change comes hard. Legislatures have limited tools with which to force change upon resistant bureaucrats. Congress's classic tool has been the threat to withhold funds from state child welfare systems. But this is a threat that has rarely been realized, for understandable reasons. Withholding money from the systems which provide children with protective services in their homes, as well as with foster care and adoption services, is a hard thing to do in the name of protecting children, even if the goal is to force child welfare agencies to act in a more protective manner. The greatest threat to the new proadoption movement has to do with the thinking of the people who run and staff the child welfare system, and the people who design and implement new child welfare programs. As discussed in chapters 5 and 6, these people are overwhelmingly committed to the family preservation tradition and have demonstrated an impressive ability to resist demands for change.

MEPA's history to date represents dramatic evidence of the problem. Despite the Act's call for fundamental change in the nation's child placement policies, and its severe mandatory financial penalties, so far little real change has occurred.

ASFA is another law that was obviously intended to bring about fundamental change. For all the loopholes and limitations, there is no mistaking ASFA's basic demand that a shift be made from the traditional emphasis on family preservation to a new system in which child safety and adoption are given much greater priority. ASFA may function as one among a number of forces that will transform the thinking of the nation's child welfare professionals and policymakers. But until and unless that happens, there's no reason to believe that ASFA itself will have much impact on the workings of the child welfare system.

Those resistant to ASFA's mandate can simply take advantage of the loopholes and limitations written into the letter of the law to defy its spirit. They can also easily do end runs around the law, promoting programs which allow them to avoid its provisions altogether.

Two of the hottest new programs of the day, described in chapter 6, seem designed to limit CPS authorities' decision-making power in abuse and neglect cases and to limit the number of cases which will result in children being removed to CPS jurisdiction. The Family Group Decision Making movement wants CPS to delegate much of its current authority to extended family members; its goals are to maximize the child's chances of staying within the extended family, and eventually if not immediately being returned to the family of origin. FGDM programs would limit the number of children formally removed to foster care, and therefore covered by ASFA.

The Community Partnership movement, touted by some influential players as the major solution for today's child welfare problems, would similarly bypass ASFA's requirements. Community Partnership advocates want most of today's CPS cases diverted from CPS to a voluntaristic community-based system, which would allocate needed services to families. A major goal is to enable children victimized by abuse and neglect to stay with their families. To the degree Community Partnership programs are successful, child removal would be avoided, and ASFA would again simply not apply.

RADICAL REVOLUTION OR MODEST REVISIONISM?

Taking adoption seriously would involve a revolution in thinking and practice. It's a revolution that is needed if we care about children's well-being, rather than simply their survival. ASFA demonstrates that it's at least possible today to get agreement on matters related to child survival; in cases of murder and torture the Act says that states don't have to attempt to preserve families. This is progress, astoundingly enough, but it's limited progress. Too many children have been kept with or returned to their birth parents when the risks of their being tortured and killed were very high. But these cases represent only a small part of the child welfare problem. The overwhelming part has to do with children who are surviving, but in no way thriving. It has to do with children who are growing up, but not being brought up. It has to do with the neglect and drug cases which ASFA fails to mention, where the parents are effectively absent. And it has to do with the placement of children already traumatized by abuse and neglect in substitute homes which stop far short of providing the kind of quality care and committed parenting that these children so desperately need.

Taking adoption seriously means being willing to remove children even if physical safety is *not* at issue. It means being willing to take action *immediately* upon removal to terminate parental rights and place children in adoptive homes, in cases where there's no real chance children will or should grow up with their original parents. It means looking to the *entire community* in recruiting foster and adoptive parents, rather than insisting that children remain in the communities into which they were born. We may be moving in this direction, but so far we have taken only the most modest first steps.

CONFRONTING THE
CHALLENGING ISSUES

9. SUBSTANCE ABUSE

The widespread use and abuse of drugs and alcohol are wreaking havoc on a generation of children in ways that will come back to haunt us all if we don't do something about it. Reform proposals that fail to address the issue are simply beside the point.

The dramatic escalation in the size of the foster care population, and the severity of today's abuse and neglect cases, is generally attributed to the increase in drug use, particularly in crack/cocaine, during recent decades. The overwhelming preponderance—some 70 to 80 percent—of the CPS caseload consists of drug- and alcohol-related cases. As described in chapter 3, a significant percentage of all pregnant women abuse drugs, alcohol, and tobacco during pregnancy. A significant percentage of all children born reveal at birth the impact of exposure to these harmful substances during pregnancy. A significant percentage of all children are born to and raised by parents whose abuse of alcohol and illicit drugs destroys their capacity to nurture. Many women who give birth to drug-exposed infants are repeat offenders, giving birth to a succession of children who suffer the combined impact of having been exposed to drugs and alcohol during pregnancy and of then receiving the negligent, erratic, sometimes violent treatment that characterizes parents who are abusing drugs and alcohol. The children victimized by their parents' substance abuse will often go on to repeat the cycle. Disproportionate numbers will grow up to abuse alcohol and illicit drugs, to live lives characterized by deprivation and violence, and to subject the next generation to abuse and neglect.

THE TRADITIONAL SYSTEM'S RESPONSE

Typically the system has intervened only marginally. The great majority of the children born showing evidence of drug exposure go home to the parents who abused drugs during pregnancy, and who, in the absence of intervention, can be expected to continue their abuse. CPS has generally provided these families little or nothing in the way of surveillance, monitoring, or services until and unless abuse or neglect is identified and documented. When that occurs and CPS intervenes to investigate, typically only the most egregious cases will trigger any action, whether family preservation services or child removal. If services are offered they may or may not include the treatment for substance abuse so obviously needed.[1] And if such services are offered the abusing parents will only sometimes be subject to any meaningful requirement, backed by the realistic threat of losing their children or other sanction, to accept the services, to stick with the treatment regimen, or to stay clean of the offending drugs or alcohol. Even when court orders to enter treatment are issued, compliance with treatment requirements is low.[2]

Drug-exposed infants will typically stay at home for significant periods of time, at high risk for abuse and neglect. Many will eventually be removed to state care, but only after documented postnatal abuse and neglect, and related damage, have occurred.[3]

Children removed from their parents for drug-related reasons are likely to stay in the state's care, or bounce back and forth between the state and the family of origin, for very long periods of time. The state is reluctant to terminate parental rights in these cases, yet family reunification is very unlikely to be successful. Substance abuse is a long-term problem. Treatment resources are limited and often not well-designed to address the special needs of women with young children. Most addicts can be expected to resist treatment in any event. Of those who pursue treatment, few will stay with it. Of those who do stay with treatment for a period of time, most will relapse on a repeated basis. Those who eventually free themselves from their drug habit will have generally spent many years on a bumpy rehabilitation road. The current system asks children to wait while we see if their parents make it to the end of that road. The National Center on Addiction and Substance Abuse (CASA), in its recent report on the impact of substance abuse on child welfare, states the problem bluntly:

> There is an irreconcilable clash between the rapidly ticking clock of cognitive and physical development for the abused and neglected child and the slow motion clock of recovery for the parent addicted to alcohol or drugs.[4]

The U.S. General Accounting Office's recent report on the problem substance abuse poses for the child welfare system expresses this same concern. The report describes a case which illustrates how waiting out the drug-abusing parent's recovery process puts the child's life on hold:

> This case involved one of six children. He and most of his siblings were known to have been prenatally exposed to cocaine. As a result of neglect related to his mother's crack-cocaine and alcohol abuse, he entered foster care shortly after birth. . . . His mother successfully complied with most of the requirements in the case plan for reunification —including visitation, a parenting class, and family therapy. However, about 2 years after this child entered foster care, his mother was dropped from a drug treatment program for lack of attendance. About that time, the permanency goal was changed from family reunification to long-term foster care. Over the next few years, the mother entered treatment several additional times but failed to complete any of these programs. About 3 months prior to the birth of his youngest sibling, the mother entered a 12-month residential treatment program, which she successfully completed. Because of her success in treatment, the child who was the focus of this case was returned to his mother for several trial visits after spending about 7 years in foster care. However, the mother subsequently failed several drug tests, indicating she had relapsed. At the time we reviewed the case, this child was still in foster care after almost 8 years.[5]

Some early intervention programs have been designed to provide drug treatment and parenting education during pregnancy and early infancy. Not surprisingly, these programs grew primarily out of a concern to prevent family break-up and promote family preservation. In the 1980s the drug crisis had produced the "boarder baby" phenomenon: thousands of babies were growing up in hospital wards, either because they had been abandoned by their parents, or because authorities were unwilling to allow them to go home to parents whose drug habits put the children at risk. The federal government came to the rescue with the Abandoned Infants Assistance Act of 1988 (AIA), funding demonstration programs and the National Abandoned Infants Assistance Resource Center. The federal goal was to promote family preservation, by encouraging these babies' parents to take them home, and offering home-visiting services. The home visitors were to support the family generally and to encourage the parents to pursue drug treatment. So this program was designed to "rescue" drug-exposed babies by insisting that they be sent home with drug-involved parents, rather than placing them in foster and adoptive homes.

In late 1997 I learned something of what these programs involved when I attended a training conference in New Haven, Connecticut, at which two home visitors from an AIA demonstration project conducted a workshop based on their experience working with a pregnant mother I'll call Sandra and her young children. Their project was designed to work with women using cocaine during pregnancy or after birth. They had been assigned early in Sandra's pregnancy to visit her at home on a regular basis, to help her to address parenting issues involving her existing children and her future child, and to try to get her off cocaine and into treatment. She had been using cocaine for ten years, with occasional ineffective encounters with treatment during that time. She was now living with a boyfriend, not the father of her children, whom the home visitors suspected was also on drugs, although Sandra denied that he had any problem. The home visitors had met with Sandra two or three times a week, over a period of many months. They showed a video of meetings they had with her at various points during this period. They discussed their awareness that during these months she continued to use cocaine, while refusing to admit her use to them until close to the time of the baby's birth. They told us how they had found drug paraphernalia hidden throughout the various rooms of her house once when they had helped her clean and do her laundry in response to a lice infestation. They showed us a scene on the video where she appeared quite obviously drug impaired. They came to realize she was very savvy about how the system worked. She knew they would not report her to CPS unless they saw evidence of obvious maltreatment of the children. Since the home visitors saw this as a family that was "functioning at times" they saw no reason to report her to CPS for abuse or neglect. Sandra also knew that CPS would not intervene based on her continuing cocaine use during pregnancy unless the child was born showing the signs of drug exposure. So as the end of the pregnancy period approached she began talking to the home visitors openly about her drug problem and her plan to try to get off cocaine prior to the birth so that the baby's drug test would be negative. They encouraged her to consider going into a special one-year residential program for mothers and infants after the baby was born, in order to finally kick her habit. She said that no, she couldn't stand being in a residential program for a year, which they interpreted as indicative of her continuing inability or unwillingness to commit herself to rehabilitation. She turned out to be unable to get clean for the birth, and the baby's drug test was positive. At that point CPS threatened to remove the child unless Sandra agreed to go into the residential treatment program with her baby. In response to this threat she went in, but she lasted only twenty-four hours. When she left, CPS placed the baby in "foster care," but the foster father was Sandra's boyfriend, so the baby was in fact sent home to live with Sandra and the boyfriend, together with the other children, as if no "removal" had occurred. Two weeks later the boyfriend tested positive for drugs. CPS initiated proceedings to remove the baby from the home at this point, but several months later the baby remained at home.

This program is on the interventionist end of the CPS spectrum of responses to the drug-abusing parent. It does much more to protect children against harmful exposure during pregnancy than is done generally. It does much more to protect drug-exposed newborns, and any other children in the home, than is done generally. Sandra was encouraged to reduce, and, if possible, to eliminate her drug use. The home visitors were in a position to observe her children during the pregnancy period, and as mandated CPS reporters they had an obligation to report any abuse or neglect. Sandra's baby was tested at birth, and the positive test results triggered a requirement that she enter a treatment program, which, as a residential program for mothers and infants, was specifically designed to meet her needs. Her failure to stay in the treatment program and her boyfriend's drug use triggered action to remove the baby to foster care. These protective measures are not a regular part of our system for responding to the drug-abusing parent.

But even these relatively interventionist measures don't seem adequate. For me and some others listening this was a deeply problematic story. The state seemed engaged in classic enabling conduct. It had its social workers in the home, carefully observing Sandra exposing her fetus to drugs which could cause significant damage, during the entire pregnancy period. While they encouraged her to consider treatment, they at the same time acted in a way that seemed to mean that there was nothing terribly wrong with taking drugs during pregnancy. If there was, why wouldn't these home visitors and the CPS authorities insist that she stop? The system was sending her a pretty clear signal that all that really mattered was that she stay off of drugs during the period immediately before the baby was born. And, as it turned out, since the baby was sent home anyway, despite the positive drug test, the system didn't even seem to care much about that.

THE HARM TO CHILDREN

Parents' use of drugs and alcohol represents an enormous threat to children's well-being. Many try to minimize the threat today, out of understandable and important political concerns. Some worry that poor black mothers involved in drugs are being unfairly targeted for punitive action. Others worry that if babies are stigmatized as drug-damaged they will be denied vital opportunities for treatment services, education, and adoption. Their concerns point to the importance of getting the facts right. But a careful look at the facts set forth in chapter 3 shows that overwhelming numbers of children are being very seriously damaged by their parents' drug and alcohol abuse.

Substance abuse during pregnancy puts children at high risk for various forms of damage. Sending children exposed to harmful substances during pregnancy home with parents who are abusing illicit drugs and alcohol increases the risk of harm exponentially. As discussed in chapter 3, professionals with extensive experience describe many of these drug-abusing parents as essentially *incapable* of parenting. In addition, substance abuse tends to be associated with other factors that predict for abuse and neglect. Those who abuse drugs and alcohol are disproportionately likely to have been victims of abuse and neglect themselves as children, to be victims of domestic violence as adults, and to be single, unemployed, and isolated, living without appropriate support from extended family, friends, or community.[6] Ira Chasnoff, one of the nation's leading experts on the impact of substance abuse on child welfare, writes as follows:

> [T]he lifestyle of substance-abusing parents is filled with factors that tend to interfere with attempts at parenting, effective child rearing, and participation in the education of their children. . . .
>
> Addicted women frequently have poor family and social support networks, have few positive relationships with other women, and often are dependent on an unreliable, abusive male, thereby increasing their vulnerability to physical and sexual abuse. Children of substance abusing women are at greater risk for neglect and sexual, physical and psychological abuse. These difficulties are magnified in children living in poverty, because their mothers frequently lack the social and economic supports that could help lessen some of the social isolation as well as the biological impact of prenatal drug exposure.[7]

The overall picture is not pretty. Children exposed to drugs and alcohol are likely to be particularly difficult and demanding. They are at risk for long-term damage, and in need therefore of special support and nurturing to help them compensate for injuries suffered. They are going home to parents who are uniquely ill-suited to cope with the special demands and needs these children present.

Some argue that the harm from cocaine abuse during pregnancy has been exaggerated.[8] They are right in drawing attention to the harm caused by licit drugs like alcohol and tobacco. They are right that the discrete harm caused by cocaine use during pregnancy is hard to isolate given all the other risks that crack babies are subjected to. But they are wrong to the degree that they imply that cocaine abuse during pregnancy poses no problem, or that crack babies can be expected to develop normally if we send them home to live with parents who abuse alcohol or illicit drugs.

As discussed in chapter 3, there are lots of reason for concern that cocaine abuse during pregnancy may cause lifelong damage. It is true that studies that have followed these children into early school years have not found the devastating damage predicted when crack first hit our nation's consciousness. But these studies are comparing the crack babies to "control groups" consisting of other children growing up in similar socioeconomic circumstances, most of whom have been subjected to their own damaging experiences both during pregnancy and after birth. It is not at all surprising that social scientists and medical experts have found it difficult to isolate the particular impact of prenatal exposure to cocaine from the impact of prenatal exposure to other illicit drugs, to alcohol and tobacco, and to lead paint, or from the impact of children's exposure to domestic violence, abuse, and neglect, and other horrors with which so many poor kids in our society are familiar. It is also not surprising that research has found it hard to separate the effects of prenatal drug exposure from the influence of being raised by a drug- or alcohol-abusing parent. The fact that kids exposed prenatally to cocaine are not functioning worse in obvious ways than kids who are doing badly by virtue of the damage they have suffered from things other than prenatal cocaine exposure should not make us sanguine about the impact of cocaine.[9]

Drug experts remain worried that prenatal exposure to cocaine puts babies at risk for significant long-term damage. The research discussed in chapter 3 indicates that cocaine abuse puts children at risk for neurological damage, and controlled studies indicate an impact on language development and performance in early education settings. Experts who work with and study these children talk about seeing subtle but disturbing signs of neurological damage in them as they grow up.

Those who minimize the crack baby problem misstate the issue by focusing on the discrete impact of prenatal cocaine use. Prenatal cocaine use is simply not a discrete and separable problem. It is associated with the abuse of other substances, so that we can assume most children identified as "crack babies" have in fact been bombarded by a variety of damaging substances in utero. Prenatal cocaine exposure also affects infants' behavior in ways that make them difficult to parent, exacerbating the already high risk of their being maltreated by drug-abusing parents. A recent review of the research describes the compound problems these babies face:

> Most of [the cocaine using mothers], especially the crack addicts, are desperately poor. Most use other illicit drugs, tobacco, and alcohol. If they are crack addicts, the effect of smoking itself has to be considered. If they trade sex for drugs, they may transmit syphilis or AIDS to the child. The father is probably absent and the child's nutrition and medical care inadequate. With an addicted mother who is depressed, demoralized, and concerned mainly about her next fix, the healthiest infant might become a problem child.[10]

In reacting against the extremely negative claims made about the prospects for crack babies, and other babies born drug-exposed, drug and adoption experts have provided an important service. It *is* important to recognize that prenatal cocaine use doesn't necessarily have devastating lifelong consequences.

Recent studies have made an important contribution by demonstrating that a mother's use of cocaine during pregnancy was ultimately not as important for the child's development as whether she continued to abuse drugs and alcohol afterward.[11] Barry Zuckerman is one of the leading drug and parenting experts who has helped to debunk some of the claims in earlier years that crack babies were doomed. His work stresses the fact that home environment may be more important than prenatal damage to the prospects of these children. But he goes on to say:

> Unfortunately, drug- and alcohol-abusing mothers are likely to be dysfunctional caretakers. Thus, their infants may experience a double jeopardy: they suffer biologic vulnerability due to prenatal substance exposure, which may be exacerbated by caretaking dysfunction such as neglect or abuse.[12]

Another expert writes:

[Many substance-abusing mothers] are from families with an intergen-erational legacy of chemical dependence and physical, sexual, and/or emotional abuse. Their histories of chaotic family life interact with stressful living situations and difficult behavioral characteristics of drug-exposed newborns to create scenarios in which inadequate parent-ing or child neglect and abuse are likely.[13]

Recent studies have also made an important contribution by demonstrating that babies exposed to cocaine, alcohol, and other damaging substances during pregnancy can be helped to function within relatively normal parameters if they receive special support services and nurturing during the formative months and years of in-fancy and early childhood. The experts have testified persuasively to the fact that adoption will make a very significant difference in these children's lives.[14] Studies comparing children exposed to drugs in utero who were adopted at a young age with those who were raised at home show the adopted children functioning much better than those not adopted.[15] The experts have also testified to the adoptabil-ity of these children, noting that professionals throughout the coun-try report that there are families who are interested in adopting them, and noting the successful adjustment of those who have already been adopted.[16]

The recent research makes an impressive case for not simply giv-ing up on this group of children as hopelessly damaged. It demon-strates how much difference a nurturing environment can make and stresses the importance of intervening early to provide special sup-portive services and treatment for these children. It confirms that the developmental and behavioral problems many of the children suffer may be attributed to severe environmental deprivation and to the fact that they are being parented by addicts at least as much as to any prenatal damage.

But current policies ignore the clear implications of this recent re-search. We are systematically refusing to place these babies in early infancy with the kind of adoptive parents who could be expected to provide the special support and parenting they need. Instead we gen-erally send them home to situations in which they cannot be ex-pected to get what they need. We wait until documented abuse and neglect in the severe forms that trigger removal in today's child welfare world have occurred, before we consider moving them to another home. When we do move them we typically place them in kinship or local foster care, or in institutional homes, which again can rarely be expected to provide the superior care they need.[17]

THE FUTURE: PITFALLS AND PROMISE

A variety of different reform proposals argue for changes in policy that would move us in radically different directions in addressing the substance abuse problem. Some argue for reducing the state's coercive role in these kinds of cases, and some for increasing it. Many of the major reform initiatives of the day simply sweep the drug problem under the rug, preferring not to confront the politically challenging issues involved, but failing as a result even to address what is clearly the central child welfare issue of the day.

Avoiding the Issue

The failure of the 1997 Adoption and Safe Families Act to address the substance abuse problem is an extraordinary omission in a law enacted in this era, given the broad understanding of the centrality of the drug problem to today's child welfare situation. It seems obvious that the lobbying forces involved did not simply forget the drug problem, but settled on omission as a political compromise.

The problem is that this compromise is one which threatens to simply continue the status quo. As noted above, ASFA focuses on egregious abuse in listing the kinds of cases in which reasonable efforts to preserve families need not be made and parental rights termination petitions must be filed. But only a small percentage of all CPS cases involve documented murder, torture, or other forms of egregious abuse, or involve previous TPR decisions involving siblings. The vast majority of the drug cases that crowd the child welfare system fall officially into the categories of neglect and other physical abuse that ASFA seems to marginalize.[18] So there is a good likelihood that even states doing their best to understand ASFA will see it as calling for no real change in the vast majority of drug cases.

ASFA's various loopholes and exceptions also lend themselves to the perpetuation of current practice in drug cases. When children who have been removed from their parents are placed with kin, as they so commonly are, TPR requirements are inapplicable, and kin will be looked to as long-term guardians. Yet there is little reason to think that they will be capable, as a general matter, of providing the special care these children need. Strong preference policies tend to preclude individualized consideration of kin. Studies indicate that by virtue of their age, disability, and poverty, many of the relatives who are chosen have limited resources to provide the kind of special support services and intensely involved parenting that children damaged by drugs need. If the children are placed in nonrelative foster care, and the state does not make appropriate drug treatment services available to the parents on a timely basis, then the bureaucratic failure exception kicks in to excuse the state from terminating parental rights. This exception will likely be applicable in many cases. There is a dearth of the kind of programs that many think are essential for treating women with children: residential programs that welcome infants and children and have services for them as well as their mothers, programs that include child care and a spectrum of services to cope with a wide range of problems including unemployment, domestic violence, and homelessness.

ASFA does not, of course, *prevent* states from developing wise policies to address the drug problem. But by avoiding the issue, and providing loopholes and exceptions that are broadly applicable, ASFA not only neglected to give the states guidance, but sent a dangerous signal that business as usual on the all-important drug front might be appropriate.

Cutting Back on State Intervention

Leaders of the important Community Partnership movement tend to sweep the drug problem under the rug. They talk as if all CPS cases other than a tiny subset of atypical egregious abuse cases are relatively minor, and they advocate removing all these "minor" cases from the coercive CPS system. At the Executive Session on New Paradigms for Child Protective Services conducted at Harvard's John F. Kennedy School of Government, an impressive paper was circulated documenting the degree to which drug cases dominated the current CPS caseload.[19] Some participants talked about the serious nature of these drug cases and the limited prospects for rehabilitative treatment offered on a purely voluntary basis. But the important implications of this background paper, and these concerns about the limited effectiveness of voluntary treatment programs, were ignored in the only summary paper produced at the end of the Executive Session process. That paper argues, as the Community Partnership movement's leaders have generally, for diverting most of the CPS caseload, including by definition most of the drug cases, from CPS to a voluntary, community-based system.[20]

Community Partnership advocates would presumably argue that once we got these cases out of the CPS system, we would be able to provide more in the way of treatment services. However, as discussed in chapter 6, they don't make a persuasive case as to why more resources will be made available to voluntary community organizations than have been made available to the CPS agencies assigned the job of reducing child maltreatment. Moreover, it seems most unlikely that eliminating the element of coercive power inherent in the current system will be helpful in persuading parents caught up in substance abuse to get into treatment and off of drugs and alcohol. Indeed the available evidence indicates just the opposite. There is no magic bullet for dealing with addiction. But drug treatment experts believe that making addicts aware that there are real-world consequences associated with substance abuse and related misconduct is an important part of the rehabilitative process. And such research as exists indicates that coercive pressure is in fact useful.[21]

Expanding State Intervention through Sanctions, Mandatory Treatment, and the Use of Child Removal, TPR, and Adoption

1. Current Initiatives

There has been a lot of noise surrounding the idea of increased state intervention. Proponents express outrage that babies are being born damaged by drugs and call for action ranging from criminal prosecution of the mothers, to civil commitment to prevent drug use during pregnancy, to removal of the children at birth. Opponents express equal outrage at these proposals, condemning them as classist, racist, and sexist attacks on impoverished black mothers.

To date there has been more noise than action, and most of it has focused on illicit drugs to the exclusion of alcohol. Prosecutions have been brought against a number of pregnant women for using drugs during pregnancy, based on the theory that these women are knowingly passing harmful drugs on to their unborn children.[22] However, as of the end of 1998, convictions had been upheld as lawful by the highest court of only one state.[23] Legislators have not designed criminal laws to specifically address the problem, and courts have generally concluded as they no doubt will continue to conclude, that for prosecutors to try to use existing criminal laws designed for other purposes to punish drug-abusing mothers violates fundamental fairness.

Some have advocated civil commitment as a way of stopping drug abuse during pregnancy, assuming that the mother is unwilling to enter treatment or otherwise stop using drugs voluntarily. Minnesota passed a law in 1989 providing for civil commitment for women who refused recommended voluntary services or failed at recommended treatment, but the state had made only the most limited use of this law as of several years after its passage.[24]

Far more common have been programs that enable or encourage some level of CPS involvement when babies are born showing the effects of their mothers' drug use during pregnancy. Many areas have instituted drug testing if drug use is suspected based on the baby's symptoms. Many require that infants with positive drug test results be reported to CPS authorities. Such reports sometimes trigger a CPS investigation to assess whether any follow-up action is necessary, such as providing services, including drug treatment for the mother, or deciding whether or not child removal is warranted, based on all the circumstances of the case.[25]

Some have advocated more extensive use of such testing, reporting, and CPS intervention methods. Some propose universal testing of newborns, in place of today's limited testing which tends to focus on the poor people who use public hospitals. Some propose testing and reporting to CPS not just for illicit drugs, but also for alcohol. Some propose making it mandatory both for positive test results to be reported to CPS, and for CPS to provide services and continue to monitor the case when they receive such a report.[26]

Some states have enacted legislation making an extensive history of chronic use of drugs or alcohol and resistance to treatment grounds for expedited TPR in cases in which parents have been found guilty of abuse or neglect.[27]

An experimental New York program being instituted in certain New York City courts in the late 1990s threatens drug-abusing parents charged with child neglect with the removal of their children, requires that they enter treatment, and conditions reunification on their demonstrated compliance with treatment requirements. The parents are given a three-month grace period for adjustment to treatment, during which relapses are tolerated, but after that failure to live up to treatment requirements can trigger parental rights termination. The program is designed to ensure that by the end of a one-year period children are either returned to parents who have freed themselves from their drug habits, or can move on to a permanent substitute home.

Related family drug court programs have been instituted in Reno, Nevada, Pensacola, Florida, and San Diego, California.[28] These family drug court programs build on the apparent success of the criminal drug court model, applying it to substance-abusing parents who have maltreated their children. They provide immediate access to treatment. They use close monitoring of compliance with the treatment regimen, combined with sanctions for failure to comply, including sanctions for positive drug tests, to motivate parents. Sanctions may include incarceration or fines. While these programs don't tie child custody to compliance as directly as the New York program does, they are designed to enable children to be moved more expeditiously to permanency, either by returning them to their parents when progress towards rehabilitation is demonstrated, or else by freeing them up for adoption or other permanent placement on the basis of the showing that the programs help provide that the parents are not able or willing to comply with treatment regimens. To date such court programs lead a relatively lonely existence on the interventionist fringe.

2. A Modest Proposal

We could intervene to provide support *and* to demand accountability during pregnancy and early childhood. We could accomplish this through a mandatory home visitation program, and through the threat and the use of coercive state action, including the early removal of children when necessary to protect them against the risk of abuse and neglect.

Under the proposed system, a universal home visitation system of the kind discussed in chapter 7 would reach out to all pregnant women, sending trained health aides into the home during the prenatal period to provide advice and support on appropriate prenatal care and early parenting issues. These visitors would be in a good position to identify drug or alcohol abuse problems, to advise the women of the risks involved for their unborn children, and to assist in obtaining appropriate treatment. They would also be able to alert CPS and other appropriate authorities to substance abuse problems during pregnancy and early childhood, and to help monitor compliance with any treatment requirements imposed by courts in connection with CPS intervention. In the absence of such a universal system, existing home visitor programs could be used to send health aides into homes identified before or after birth as at high risk for substance abuse and related child maltreatment.

A universal screening and neonatal testing program would identify infants exposed during pregnancy to illicit drugs or alcohol. A mandatory reporting system would trigger immediate CPS involvement and investigation in cases in which significant abuse during pregnancy or impact on the newborn was suspected. Confirmation that mothers had abused drugs or alcohol during pregnancy in ways likely to endanger the healthy development of the fetus would trigger additional CPS intervention, and the possibility of child removal at birth, mandatory treatment, and monitoring for compliance with treatment requirements. CPS would have no obligation to make additional findings of parental unfitness, or to send infants home with their parents to see if patterns of child abuse and neglect in fact developed.

In cases in which the parents had a serious history of substance abuse, or a history of child abuse or neglect, and there was no good reason to believe that they were now committed to and capable of succeeding in rehabilitative efforts, CPS could move immediately to terminate parental rights, placing the child in the meantime in a pre-adoptive home.

In other cases CPS would give the parents the option of enrolling in a family drug court program along the lines of the New York program described above. The drug-exposed infants might or might not be removed at birth, depending on how strong the parents' likelihood of successful rehabilitation appeared. But in any event, parents would be required to immediately enter treatment and would be given priority access to the most appropriate programs available. They would be carefully monitored for ongoing drug use, and for compliance with the treatment regimen, and they would be required to waive any confidentiality rights in connection with treatment, so that treatment programs' cooperation with the court program could be assured.

In cases in which infants were removed at birth, they would be placed on a fast track for adoption. They would be assigned to a concurrent planning program, so that in the event that they could not be returned to their parents, they could immediately move on to adoption. Their birth parents would be required to enter into treatment, and to live up to the requirements of the treatment regimen after a brief period of adjustment—no more than three months—allowed for relapse. Within one year of the child's removal a decision would be made as to whether the parent was entitled to full parental status, based on a record of compliance with treatment requirements and a period of clean tests, together with an assessment of parental fitness. Failure to demonstrate meaningful compliance with treatment program requirements in the course of that year would trigger immediate action to terminate parental rights.

In cases in which CPS decided to allow infants to go home with their parents, the parents would be held similarly accountable to treatment requirements, and the parenting relationship would be monitored by home visitors. Failure to demonstrate adequate parenting and meaningful rehabilitation would trigger immediate removal of the child, who would be placed on a fast track for permanency as described above, and parental rights would be terminated within a year of the child's birth if the parents failed to comply with treatment requirements.

In other cases CPS might first discover a parental substance abuse problem during a traditional child abuse and neglect investigation. A decision that parental use of drugs or alcohol is causally related to child maltreatment would trigger CPS intervention comparable to that described above. Depending on the parent's prior history of substance abuse and child maltreatment, CPS would either move to terminate parental rights immediately, or would place the family in the drug court program. In the latter case, CPS would either remove the child, or monitor the child's situation at home, with return of the child and restoration of full parental status conditioned upon the parent's demonstrated rehabilitation. Failure to demonstrate meaningful rehabilitation after a brief period of adjustment would ordinarily trigger TPR action within one year of the child maltreatment finding.

Drug programs would be required to give priority access to persons referred by CPS authorities. However, parents would be held accountable for their actions and for any continued substance abuse without regard to whether they were in fact offered appropriate drug treatment services.

Consideration could be given to revising criminal and civil commitment laws and policies to give CPS and other authorities additional methods of preventing damaging substance abuse during pregnancy. Commitment to residential treatment programs could be used as a last resort for pregnant women who adamantly refuse treatment and continue their use of drugs or alcohol. Criminal penalties for repeated abuse of drugs and alcohol during pregnancy in a way known to put the fetus at significant risk, might succeed in deterring those undeterred by the threat of child removal, and might encourage those apparently unable to free themselves from substance abuse to at least avoid successive pregnancies by using birth control.

3. The Pros and Cons

This modest proposal builds on the existing family court drug program in New York, and drug court programs elsewhere in the country. It also builds on proposals made by the ABA in its publication on TPR standards, and on legislation enacted in a few states.[29] It will nonetheless strike many as outrageously draconian. But we need to question whether our current regime, with its relative tolerance for parental substance abuse, is truly any more benign. This regime allows parents to continue drug habits which are destructive not only for their children but for themselves. Many of these parents will in the end lose their children in any event. But in the meantime the state has played an enabling role, watching as pregnant women abuse drugs and alcohol, watching as they take their infants home, and then again watching as parents continue to abuse drugs and alcohol, waiting until significant damage is actually done and documented. When the state finally acts to remove children it continues to participate in the pattern of child maltreatment, holding the children for long periods of time in inadequate temporary homes, and often returning them home to be victimized yet again.

There are obvious advantages for children and parents in a more interventionist regime. The modest proposal I've described is designed to prevent harm to the fetus and to the young child from ever occurring. If children were nonetheless born damaged, they would be protected against the risk of being abused and neglected by parents dominated by their drug and alcohol habits. Many of these children would move immediately into preadoptive homes and receive the kind of intensive nurturing and special services they need. For parents the advantages have to do with the increased opportunities for achieving rehabilitation. Demands for accountability and the threat of meaningful sanctions for continued substance abuse seem at least more likely to encourage rehabilitation than today's regime.[30] Many substance abuse experts talk of the importance of addicts recognizing that continued substance abuse brings negative consequences. Many talk of the threat of losing parental rights as perhaps the most powerful motivator for addicted parents, and the period following birth as a unique window of opportunity for rehabilitative efforts.

But there are risks and dangers inherent in this interventionist approach that are worthy of concern. One is the risk of diversion from more useful approaches. Authorities might see punitive approaches as cheaper and easier than efforts to expand drug treatment services. But we can limit this risk as the modest proposal does by only using penal sanctions and civil commitment as a last resort, making child removal the focus of coercive intervention, and linking the threat of child removal to efforts to encourage parents to pursue drug treatment and rehabilitation. This strategy will not *guarantee* an increase in appropriate drug treatment resources, but it seems at least as likely to *encourage* such an increase as the current regime.

One oft-cited concern with the interventionist approach is that it will simply drive those with substance abuse problems away from the possibility of help, thereby ultimately putting their children at even greater risk of harm. This argument would not have much bite if there were a truly universal home visiting system in place, since home visitors would be in a position to observe what was going on during pregnancy and early childhood. Nor would it have much bite if there were a universal neonatal drug testing system, since few will choose to give birth outside of a medical setting in order to avoid such testing.

But in the absence of such systems, there might be some risk that pregnant addicts would be scared away from prenatal care, and addicted parents scared away from trying drug treatment, if they saw their parental rights threatened. The modest proposal minimizes this risk by using the threat of child removal as a means of inducing compliance with drug treatment requirements, and by giving most parents whose children are removed the opportunity to regain them through demonstrated rehabilitation.

But even if some risk remains, this is the kind of risk we live with whenever we use coercive state intervention to prevent child maltreatment. We risk having parents keep their children away from school when we tell teachers that they must report suspected child abuse. We risk discouraging abusive parents from taking their grievously injured children to the emergency room when we tell parents that they can be punished for child abuse. This kind of risk exists in other areas of state intervention as well. We risk discouraging women victims of domestic violence from seeking help when we subject their abusive mates to arrest, prosecution, and conviction. In all these contexts we recognize the risk but generally conclude that it is outweighed by the benefits of deterrence and protection. The same conclusion is warranted for pregnant women and parents whose substance abuse threatens their children's welfare.

Many will see the threat to remove children and to terminate parental rights in the absence of a showing that parents have freed themselves from substance abuse as brutal given the realities of drug and alcohol dependence. There is no question of the difficulty most addicts have achieving freedom from their drugs. The experts regularly describe substance abuse as a chronic condition, and the road to rehabilitation, even for those who manage to make it, as characterized by repeated relapses, often over a period of many years. The question is what to *do* about these realities. It does seem harsh to take from people who are typically the victims not only of their drugs but of difficult, and often tragic, life circumstances, the children who may be their only joy and hope. But it is also harsh to condemn children to lives ravaged by their parents' substance abuse during pregnancy, by maltreatment during their early months at home, and by the years spent on hold waiting for their parents to overcome their problems. And for the parents, the threat of losing their children may constitute a form of "tough love," propelling them into the treatment they so desperately need.

Family preservationists regularly claim that, while growing up with parents who are abusing drugs and alcohol is far from perfect, it is better than the alternative. They argue that substance abuse is not necessarily inconsistent with good-enough parenting, and that children will benefit from maintaining the loving connection with their parents, as compared to bouncing around for years in impersonal institutional situations. Everything is, of course, a question of degree, and there are obviously some people who can manage to function as parents despite ongoing abuse of drugs and alcohol. But it is unrealistic to think that many of those who have a serious substance abuse problem, and who are unable to sustain treatment, can function very well, and even more unrealistic to think that many can function well enough to meet the special needs of drug-exposed infants. Indeed research indicates that treatment may have no impact on the quality of parenting provided even by those limited numbers of addicts willing to stay in treatment for significant periods of time.[31] Those who make the better-than-the-alternative argument regularly ignore the adoption alternative. The fact is that if we were willing to move children promptly on to adoptive homes as the modest proposal recommends, the evidence indicates clearly that they would be much better off.

A regularly expressed concern about current interventionist initiatives has to do with their impact on racial minority groups and on the poor. Critics note that neonatal drug testing is concentrated in the public hospitals that serve the poor and minority groups, and that prosecutions for fetal abuse have targeted black women overwhelmingly. They argue that the current focus on illicit drugs like cocaine and heroin, rather than on alcohol and tobacco, is discriminatory given the different patterns of abuse in the black and white communities, and given the damaging effects that alcohol and tobacco have on fetal health and development.

The critics are right in part. It is irrational from the viewpoint of fetal health to draw the line between licit and illicit drugs, when both kinds of drugs have similarly harmful effects. The modest proposal calls for universal drug testing to assess the impact of the abuse of alcohol and illicit drugs on babies born to rich and middle-class whites, as well as to poor minority group members. It calls for child removal and TPR policies that address alcohol abuse and illicit drug abuse equally. The proposal does not focus on tobacco because it does not affect parents' capacity to care for their children (though intensified government action to discourage smoking during pregnancy would make sense).

However, it is politically easier to condemn parental conduct involving the violation of already existing criminal laws governing drugs. Efforts to impose sanctions for parental use of alcohol will likely meet enormous political resistance, and the resistance will not be limited to groups protecting traditional family autonomy interests. Women's groups will join in, claiming that any attempt to control their use of alcohol during pregnancy interferes with their procreative freedom rights.

If it proves politically impossible to treat alcohol abuse equally with illicit drug abuse, we should not retreat from any action at all out of concern that dealing with the latter alone is discriminatory. After all, it is poor and black children who are suffering in disproportionate numbers the impact of fetal abuse and child maltreatment. They should be seen as having rights to be protected against this form of discrimination. Moreover there are good reasons to conclude that illicit drug abuse poses a greater threat to children than licit drug abuse: parents involved in an illegal lifestyle are likely to be even more isolated from the kind of mainstream activities and connections that can protect children. Also, since today's addict is so often involved in the abuse of drugs *and* alcohol, policies directed at illicit drugs will sweep in much of the worst of the alcohol problem.

Women's rights advocates have argued that interventionist policies discriminate additionally against women. They say that focusing on substance abuse during pregnancy unfairly ignores risks that male addicts pose to children, arguing that men may physically abuse their pregnant mates in ways that do fetal damage, and that sperm damaged by drug use may produce genetic defects in progeny. Obviously CPS authorities should not focus on pregnant women to the exclusion of the risks to children posed by male addicts, but it is absurd to ignore the harm that can be done to a fetus by a mother's substance abuse.

Many women's rights advocates are concerned that attempts to control substance abuse during pregnancy represent unconstitutional and unconscionable invasions of the woman's right to control her body. They rely on federal court abortion cases giving women the right to terminate pregnancy, arguing that this right must include the lesser right to take substances during pregnancy which may harm the fetus but will almost always stop short of killing it. These arguments misconceive the nature of the abortion cases. Courts in these cases have shown deference not simply to rights of bodily integrity but to the right to choose whether or not to carry a child in pregnancy, and the related right to choose whether or not to undertake the burdens of parenting. They have held that these rights taken together outweigh any fetal right to live, at least prior to fetal viability. But if women don't exercise their right to abort, and do go forward with their pregnancies, nothing in the abortion rights cases provides them with the right to damage the fetus they are carrying in ways that may have lifelong consequences. One of the U.S. Supreme Court's most recent pronouncements in this area holds that the state has the right to assert the fetal interest from the beginning of the pregnancy, not simply from the point of viability,[32] and indicates that the woman's rights must always be balanced against the state's rights to protect the fetus. This case opens the way to state regulation protecting the fetus during the previability period when drugs and alcohol can do such significant damage. And it creates a balancing test which would favor a state's attempt to regulate based on its concerns with the painful and lifelong problems posed for individuals and for the entire society when babies are born damaged by substance abuse during pregnancy. While the future of abortion rights is unpredictable, and depends to a great degree on who is appointed to fill future vacancies on the Court, this case indicates that at least today's Court would probably uphold reasonable state regulation designed to protect the healthy development of fetuses that are destined to be born. And so long as women retain the right to use contraception and the right to abort, it seems fair to impose some level of parental responsibility on them during the period of pregnancy for fetuses they have elected to carry to birth, just as we impose responsibility on parents after birth.

A final concern has to do with limitations in drug treatment resources. Critics of current intervention efforts regularly argue that it is unfair to penalize parents with substance abuse problems when there are not nearly enough treatment slots for the nation's addicted population. They point to the particular unfairness of penalizing women addicts, when many drug treatment programs refuse to admit pregnant women, and when few programs have been designed with the needs of women and parents in mind. This argument is a familiar part of the general family preservation pitch: it's not fair to parents to break up their families because of child maltreatment when we don't provide the kind of support that might prevent the maltreatment. It is an argument that has won the day for the past several decades. It is an argument that needs to be confronted head on and rejected outright. Society has *not* been fair to many of the people who are caught up in substance abuse. They were deprived of the basics of nurture in their own childhoods and denied decent life opportunities thereafter. We do not do enough to provide drug treatment generally, much less appropriately tailored drug treatment for pregnant women and for parents. We do not do enough to combine treatment with the provision of child care, employment opportunity, and other services that are desperately needed to make rehabilitation work. All this is reason to take action to do better to address the problems at the heart of substance abuse. But none of it is reason to condemn the children who suffer as a result of substance abuse to continued suffering. None of it is reason to continue the cycle by ensuring that another generation of children grow up in situations that will lead them to abuse drugs and alcohol in order to cope with life's pain. We send addicts to prison for assault and robbery and a variety of more minor crimes when adult victims are involved, without regard to whether they had appropriate access to rehabilitative treatment services before they committed their crimes. There is no reason to focus so singlemindedly on the question of whether the drug addict has been given a fair chance for rehabilitation simply because children rather than adults are the ones injured.

We should, of course, seek to expand treatment opportunities. But as noted above, there is no reason to think that moving in the direction of more intervention is inconsistent with this goal. It might in fact provide a new impetus for increased treatment resources.

And there's no reason to think that simply increasing treatment opportunities, without an interventionist program, would provide the protection children need. Claims that treatment limitations are responsible for preventing parents with substance abuse problems from getting help are highly dubious. *Most don't pursue treatment even when it is available*, either on their own or when mandated by CPS or court authorities. *And most who do pursue treatment initially eventually drop out.* CPS workers and drug treatment programs regularly cite the problems they have getting addicted parents to pursue recommended treatment even when programs are available.[33] The CASA Report found that child welfare professionals "overwhelmingly" named lack of motivation as the primary barrier to getting parents into substance abuse treatment.[34] Early results from DATOS, the current federal research designed to assess drug treatment success, confirm earlier research showing that the major problems treatment programs face have to do with recruitment and retention.[35] Relapse rates are high even when drug treatment services are initially sought after.[36] Even programs that have been specifically designed to serve parents with children, and that offer extensive child care, employment counseling, and other services thought helpful to this population, have enormous difficulty attracting and retaining clients.[37] Claims for treatment success are typically based on statistics limited to those addicts who have in fact pursued treatment and stayed in treatment for sustained periods of time. The problem is that the overwhelming majority do not do so.[38] Simply making treatment available has not worked very well. There is a strong likelihood that using coercive pressure to induce addicts to pursue treatment, as the proposal suggests, will work better.

Obviously it is important to fund more model programs for substance-abusing parents. It's important to provide the wide range of services needed to help motivate them to get off drugs, to stick with treatment regimens, and to improve their parenting practices. It's important to educate them as to how best to meet their children's special needs. But we can't assume that most substance abusers are going to get the ideal form of treatment services, or that they will take advantage of them even if offered.

If we want the children born to substance abusers to have a future, we have to be prepared to use legal pressure to make successful participation in substance abuse treatment, and ongoing abstinence, a condition for the parents' being granted custody. We have to be prepared to move these children into preadoptive homes immediately upon removal, and to terminate parental rights upon a showing that the parents are unable or unwilling to comply with treatment requirements and to abstain from drugs. Making treatment available is not sufficient. Nor is the imposition of vague legal pressure to pursue treatment. Nor should participation in treatment, or progress in reducing the level of problematic drug use, be considered sufficient basis for giving the substance-abusing parent custody. The presumption should be that the person who continues to abuse illicit drugs or alcohol is a person who is unfit to parent. Demonstrated rehabilitation should be a prerequisite to that person's obtaining custody, and children should not wait while parents work out their problems. If parents cannot show that they are on the road to rehabilitation within the first few months after the state has intervened, then parental rights should be terminated and adoption promptly finalized. This would give children damaged by their parents' abuse of drugs and alcohol, whether before or after birth or both, their best chance at recovery, and their best opportunity for a meaningful and productive life. It would probably also constitute their parents' best chance at recovery from their own problematic histories.

10. RACE, POVERTY, AND HISTORIC INJUSTICE

THE CONNECTION WITH CHILD MALTREATMENT

There is no denying the strong connection between socioeconomic status and child maltreatment. For political reasons many have found it important at various points in history to minimize this connection, but today it is widely acknowledged.[1] This does not mean, obviously, that all poor people are destined to abuse or neglect their children. Most do not. And it is of course true that child abuse and neglect occur among all racial groups and on all economic levels. But statistics confirm what the psychological literature and our own experience and common sense suggest: to an overwhelming degree the people who treat their children badly are people who have been treated badly by their own parents and by the larger society. They are people who fall disproportionately into groups that are at the bottom of the socioeconomic ladder. Children from families earning less than $15,000 per year are more than twenty-two times more likely to suffer maltreatment involving demonstrable harm than children from families earning more than $30,000, and they are more than forty-four times more likely to be neglected.[2] More than 90 percent of child maltreatment occurs in families with incomes below the median, and the highest maltreatment rates are concentrated in the poorest of the poor families.[3] Children from poor families, and from racial minority groups who are of course disproportionately poor, are much more likely to be removed from their families to foster and institutional care. The percentage of African-American children in foster care at any one time is roughly five times their percentage in the general population.[4]

Many say this is simply demonstrative of "discrimination" by the child welfare system. They say that we are removing children from parents solely on the basis of the parents' economic situation. It's no doubt true that children are occasionally removed simply because a parent cannot afford any form of child care, or because a parent loses her home. But these are exceptions to the general rule today, which holds that so long as the parent is guilty of nothing more than poverty, or homelessness, or other victimization by societal injustice, they will not be found in violation of the abuse and neglect laws. Children are not typically removed on the basis of minor neglect charges. Nor is poverty correlated simply with minor forms of abuse and neglect. It is especially strongly related to *serious* neglect and *severe violence* toward children.[5] It is poverty together with other factors that results in child maltreatment:

> [R]esearchers suggest that dynamics over and above poverty (such as disorganization and social isolation) differentiate neglecting families from others. . . . The effects of poverty appear to interact with other risk factors such as unrealistic expectations, depression, isolation, substance abuse, and domestic violence to increase the likelihood of maltreatment.[6]

Many argue that CPS workers apply biased standards to poor and other-race families in making maltreatment findings and removal decisions, and that the system is otherwise discriminatory. Discrimination does happen. Poor people's problems—their substance abuse during pregnancy, their abuse and neglect of their children—are much more likely to come to the attention of authorities, and poor people may not be able to defend themselves adequately against maltreatment charges. But the evidence is overwhelming that differences exist in *actual* as opposed to simply *reported* maltreatment rates, that correlate with differences in the well-being of the children's parents.[7]

The issue is how to respond to this reality. Warring factions in the child welfare world today tend to agree on the powerful connection between poverty on the one hand, and child maltreatment on the other, but they tell conflicting stories about how various child welfare policies have functioned to exploit the weak and vulnerable. They also have different prescriptions as to how we should reform child welfare policies for the future.

EXPLOITATION STORIES OF THE TWENTIETH CENTURY

Family preservation advocates tell a story of exploitation in which black and poor *families* are the primary victims. They describe these families as victims of racism, of an unfair economic system, and of other forms of historic injustice. They condemn the state's reluctance to intervene in supportive ways to provide the kind of services that might enable vulnerable families to survive and to care adequately for children. They condemn also the state's willingness to intervene in coercive ways after child maltreatment has been identified, removing children and terminating parental rights. They tend to equate parents' interests with their children's interests, arguing that both are similarly victimized when families are broken up, with children injured by the loss of family, community, and racial group ties.

Family preservation critics tell a story of exploitation in which *children* are the primary victims, suffering active abuse and extreme forms of neglect during childhood, and at risk for a lifetime of trouble and torment. They condemn the state for being too reluctant to respond to serious child maltreatment with coercive measures, to remove children from harm's way, and to terminate parental rights so that children can be moved on to safe, nurturing families. They see children exploited for the benefit of their parents, their communities, and their racial groups, when child maltreatment triggers the provision of adult welfare services rather than child protective services.

There is some truth in both these stories. Family preservation advocates are right in describing the people responsible for child maltreatment as victims themselves. Many are the products not simply of societal injustice, but of childhoods in which they were themselves abused and neglected. If we want truly to solve the child maltreatment problem we need to get at the root causes, which would mean to begin seriously to address issues of racism and economic inequality. It is no real solution to wait until some children have been identified as injured and then remove them to live with other families.

And although we can hope to help some children with this kind of limited, coercive intervention, we have to recognize that there will be costs and risks involved. Coercive intervention will predictably have more impact on poor and minority race parents than on more privileged parents. There are good reasons to limit state intervention in the family generally, and to worry in particular about intervening disproportionately in the families of the least powerful groups in the society. There are good reasons to worry about transferring children in large numbers from relatively victimized groups to more privileged groups.

Coercive intervention can also be done badly. The state does not have a very good record as a parent. Children raised in foster care or institutional care don't fare very well, even though they generally fare better than children raised by parents who maltreat them. Coercive intervention works best for children when the state gets out of the parenting business as quickly as possible, using its parens patriae power to transfer children from a harmful biological home to a new adoptive home, with a transfer of full parenting rights to the new adoptive parents. But the state has rarely been willing to make this transfer, tending instead to keep children in its less than ideal forms of substitute homes, or to return the children to their parents.

Foster care and adoption have also sometimes been exploited in ways that seriously threaten children's welfare. Many foreign countries are suspicious of international adoption because in their own countries children are treated like indentured servants when they are removed from their homes to be placed in substitute homes. In this country's early history with child removal and adoption, more than 150,000 children were shipped west on "orphan trains" to be handed over to farm families, with little or no investigation of the families' parental fitness or even interest, and with apparently mixed results; in some instances the children were considered free labor rather than family members.[8] Orphaned or abandoned children were, until the late 1800s, often placed in grim institutions or sent to work for their board as apprentices or servants.

Coercive intervention can also be done in ways that threaten the existence of minority group cultures, and that victimize parents who are innocent of any wrongdoing and fully capable of parenting. The Australian government recently apologized for having systematically used child removal and adoption in ways that were extremely destructive of indigenous groups within the country.[9] In Argentina and El Salvador some children were apparently treated as the spoils of civil war, stolen by members of the armed forces from mothers who belonged to the dissident groups, then illegally adopted.[10] In this country's past, Native American children were taken from their parents to be put into boarding schools where they were required to surrender their names and their native language as part of the process of forced assimilation in the majority culture.[11]

But the story told by family preservation critics has its own compelling truth. We make family preservation the primary goal even after serious abuse and neglect have been identified, with little regard to whether this serves children's interests. We pretend that at that point the parents' interests and children's interests can be equated, when we know better. We talk about a "child welfare" system, but use the system to promote more general poverty program goals. We use child abuse and neglect as a means of gouging limited resources out of a stingy society, and then direct those resources to "family preservation" or general social services, rather than using them to protect the children suffering from that abuse and neglect.

This strategy may have been modestly successful if judged in terms of the general welfare services goal. Significant funding has been devoted to family preservation services, which translates into some supportive social services, including some concrete assistance with vital needs in such areas as housing, employment, child care, and drug treatment. Significant funding has been devoted to poor and black parents who take on responsibility for fostering or adopting children. Judged in the same terms the strategy has some promise for the future. Foster and special-needs adoption stipends are generous by comparison to welfare stipends, and are not subject to the stringent time limits on the length of support imposed by welfare reform. Extended families may be able to eke out a meager existence through kinship care stipends that would not have been possible otherwise.

But this kind of modest success comes at a high price for children.

From their perspective, support services triggered by serious abuse and neglect come too late. Programs designed to keep them in the homes in which they have suffered maltreatment put them at too great a risk. Exploiting child abuse and neglect to obtain needed welfare services ends up exploiting the children who suffer that abuse and neglect.

OUTLINES OF A NEW STORY

We should give families the kind of general upfront support they need to nurture children. We should create a more just society in which all members have a real opportunity to participate in the good life. This would be the most effective child maltreatment program we could devise.

But what if we don't do this? And even if we should work toward this for the future, what about today? If coercive state intervention measures look promising as a means of protecting children, should we institute them knowing that they will have a disproportionate impact on poor and minority group parents? Should we be prepared to use those measures in cases where support services that might have enabled an impoverished black or Latino mother to make it have not been made available to her?

Sadly we can predict that profound social and economic reform is not on the horizon, and we can also predict that our society will continue to scrimp on the support services that it makes available to poor people, including those at risk for child maltreatment.

For decades we have responded to this dilemma by limiting coercive action and effectively sacrificing children. This is an easy giveaway for politicians. They avoid taking action that can be condemned as harsh and discriminatory. They stand up for traditional American values by protecting family autonomy. They are thus able to appeal to left and right simultaneously. At the same time, they are not themselves at risk of maltreatment, and the children who are have no vote.

We need to develop a different response. We should press for increased family support services, but should not condition child protection on their availability. We should instead use coercive measures as needed to shield children from abuse and neglect and give them the opportunity to grow up in nurturing homes. We might discover that this works better than the old system to create pressure for increased social services. But whether or not increased support services are forthcoming, and even if state intervention appears likely to have a disproportionate impact on poor and minority group parents, we need to act. Children, like their parents, come in black and brown skins, and suffer the ravages of poverty. We should not refuse to protect them from child maltreatment simply out of fear that this will have a discriminatory impact on their parents.

Highlights of the new child welfare story should include universal home visitation or some comparable program designed to provide families with support and children with protection during the vital periods of pregnancy and early infancy. This is a time when parents are most likely to be susceptible to positive change. It is also a time when they pose the greatest threat to their children, through substance abuse during pregnancy and maltreatment during the needy and vulnerable period of infancy and early childhood. Early childhood is a time when the fragile families most at risk for child abuse and neglect are most isolated from the kinds of social institutions and networks that function to protect children: the children are not yet required to go to school, and their contact with physicians or any other outsiders depends entirely on their parents. Universal home visitation sounds expensive, but there is reason to think that it would be cost-effective, at least with respect to those groups which are at relatively higher risk for child maltreatment. Social policies that produce repeat generations of damaged children who go on to live diminished and destructive lives are the truly expensive policies, even if we counted only the financial costs of the welfare services, the child protection services, the drug treatment programs, the crime control programs, and the prison programs, that these lives entail.

But merely proffering home visitation services will not be a panacea, any more than proffering family preservation services has been. Voluntary home visitation programs can help prevent fragile families from falling into the destructive patterns that produce child abuse and neglect. But they are extremely unlikely to help to health those families already deeply in trouble, those parents already caught up in alcohol and illicit drug abuse, those already abusing and neglecting their children. What's needed to protect children in these families is mandatory home visitation. Health aides or other professionals could be sent into the home on a mandatory basis as part of a new, truly universal, home visitation system, covering children from the prenatal period through the preschool period, comparable to our mandatory educational system for older children. Or they could be sent only into the homes of parents identified by the CPS system as at high risk for serious abuse and neglect, based on their past substance abuse during pregnancy, or postnatal abuse or neglect. The goal would be to provide parents with support, but also with surveillance, monitoring children to be sure they were safe from maltreatment, and monitoring the parents' compliance with any requirements established by courts as conditions for keeping their children.

Other highlights of the new story should include greater willingness to use child removal, parental rights termination, and adoption, when serious abuse or neglect is identified. We also need more individualized assessment of potential foster and adoptive homes, and more work recruiting more broadly for such homes. We need real monitoring and real services for families in those cases when preservation or reunification efforts make sense. We need follow-up services for longer periods of time when children once subjected to maltreatment are living at home again.

Skeptics will say that the kind of program suggested is hopelessly impractical. The levels of child abuse and neglect, and of related substance abuse, are too overwhelming. If the CPS systems of the nation are already overwhelmed by the three million reports they receive, and the one million cases they substantiate, if they can't provide a decent level of service to even those one million cases, how can it make sense to talk about providing more services to more cases? If child welfare agencies can't even place the 110,000 children now awaiting adoption, and if those they do place wait intolerable periods of time for placement, how can we expect these agencies to move hugely increased numbers promptly into adoption?

These are serious concerns. They are the kinds of concerns that motivate many to think that the answer lies in increasing our efforts to keep children in their families and communities of origin, either through traditional family preservation programs or new ones such as Family Group Decision Making and Community Partnerships. If the system is overwhelmed, there is something to be said for taking the relatively minor cases out at the front end, so that the more serious cases have a chance of getting serious attention.

But the problem is that the system is overwhelmed with a range of what are mostly very serious cases; there's no reason to think that once families have fallen into destructive, abusive patterns all that many of them will be helped by the kind of support services that family preservation provides at its best, particularly if they are offered on a purely voluntary basis.

In the long term the only good solution is the one that reduces the scope of the problem, that deals with the causes of substance abuse and child maltreatment. In the relatively short term the only good solution is a major revamping of the child welfare system, reorienting it so that we take adoption seriously as an option for children for the first time in our nation's history.

We do need to remove large numbers of cases from the CPS caseload if CPS agencies are to be able to function without enormously increased resources. We need CPS to do more, not less, on the cases it has. But CPS agencies are now devoting their resources to the many cases in which children remain in foster or institutional care for extended periods, or bounce back and forth between foster homes and their original homes. We could reduce the burden on CPS by moving many more of these cases on to adoption at much earlier stages.

Skeptics will ask where the adoptive homes are to be found. It won't do children much good to cut back on family preservation and remove more children from their homes, if we end up relegating yet more children to foster homes and institutions. Out-of-home care is far from ideal, and it might well get worse if the number of children went up dramatically.

But the assumption that adoptive homes are unavailable is grounded in another assumption: that the child welfare system won't change the way it functions. It's true that in the current system it is hard to find enough appropriate adoptive homes even for those children currently freed up for adoption. But this is because we have a system that holds children too long in their homes of origin and in out-of-home care until they have suffered the kind of damage that makes it hard for them to adjust and to bond in a new family, and to function normally and happily in school and work and life. It is also because we have a system that looks to a very narrow segment of the larger community for potential adoptive homes.

We can't know in concrete numbers how many adoptive homes would be available in a revamped system. It all depends on how we change it. The potential adoptive pool is a highly malleable concept. More than two million married couples are infertile, and most of them desperately want to be parents. Millions more are fertile, and most of them want to be parents too. Relatively few in the fertile or infertile groups think seriously about adoption as a way of becoming a parent, in significant part because social policies discourage them from thinking this way. Most of those who do think about adopting are interested in adopting healthy infants. But we don't do much to encourage many of them to think about adopting older children with disabilities. And we could do a lot to free up more children when they are younger and more capable of overcoming any early damage suffered.

We need to revamp our child welfare policies so that we remove children and make it possible for them to be adopted much earlier. We need to limit the period during which reunification can be tried and limit the number of reunification attempts that can be made. We need to use concurrent planning to place children immediately into preadoptive homes, so that they can begin to recover and to bond, and so that they won't have to suffer additional disruption and damage if the decision is made to terminate parental rights.

We need to reach out to the entire community for adoptive homes. We should of course include kin and friends from the child's neighborhood if they are interested in parenting the child. But we shouldn't exercise automatic preferences, based on presumptions that blood or race relationships are key to parenting capacity. We should not exclude from consideration all those who don't come from a particular child's kinship group, or racial group, or local community. If we were willing to look to the entire community, we would find a large group capable of providing good parenting. If we were willing to encourage them to think about taking responsibility for these children, we would be well on the way to finding the adoptive homes we need.

All this would take a huge change in the cultural mindset of those within the child welfare system, most of whom still believe that children belong in some essential way in their families and communities of origin. But cultural mindsets can change. We no longer assume that battered women belong in their homes. Outside the child welfare world attitudes about abused and neglected children seem to be changing, and there is increasing recognition of the idea that parenting is more about bonding than about blood. We need to bring new ways of thinking into the child welfare world, and into the social work schools that train our future child welfare workers.

There are of course risks that the state, as representative of the larger community, will not do its intervention job right. But there are greater risks involved in continuing to abdicate any community responsibility for our nation's children—in continuing to see the children suffering abuse and neglect as *not* belonging to all of us.

NOTES

INTRODUCTION

1. "Maltreatment" is used throughout the book to include the concepts of abuse *and* neglect, and without regard to whether any active malfeasance on the parent's part is involved.

2. See Sheila Ards and Ronald B. Mincy, "Neighborhood Ecology," in *When Drug Addicts Have Children*, ed. Douglas J. Besharov (Washington, D.C.: Child Welfare League of America, 1994), at 33.

3. I worked with the NAACP Legal Defense and Educational Fund, Inc., from 1968 to 1972, then founded the Legal Action Center, an organization focused on helping those with drug and criminal histories fight discrimination, obtain employment and other opportunities, and receive appropriate treatment services. I directed the Center until 1977, when I joined the Harvard Law School Faculty, and I have continued to serve on the Center's Board of Directors. I also worked for the President's Commission on Law Enforcement and Administration of Justice, the Legal Aid Society of the District of Columbia, and the Vera Institute of Justice, during the periods 1966–68, and 1972–73.

4. See chapter 1. See also Elizabeth Bartholet, *Family Bonds: Adoption and the Politics of Parenting* (Boston: Houghton Mifflin, 1993); a new edition, *Family Bonds: Adoption, Infertility, and the New World of Child Production*, is forthcoming from Beacon Press (Fall 1999).

5. See *In re Clausen*, 502 N.W.2d 649 (Mich. 1993), stay denied sub nom. De-Boer by Darrow v. DeBoer, 509 U.S. 938 (1993); *In re B.G.C.*, 496 N.W. 2d 239 (Iowa 1992).

6. The Baby Jessica case led directly to the formation of a group now known as Hear My Voice, located in Ann Arbor, Michigan. The Baby Richard case, involving similar issues, led to the formation of Kids Help in Chicago, Illinois.

7. See Adam Pertman, "The Adoption Revolution: 'Day 1: A Private Matter No Longer,'" *The Boston Globe*, March 8, 1998, pp. A1, A34–35.

8. See, e.g., Richard Barth, "Abusive and Neglecting Parents and the Care of Their Children," in *All Our Families: New Policies for a New Century*, ed.

Mary Ann Mason, Arlene Skolnick, and Stephen D. Sugarman (New York: Oxford University Press, 1998).

9. See the *Howard M. Metzenbaum Multiethnic Placement Act of 1994*, 42 U.S.C. §§622(b)(9), 5115a, Pub. L. No. 103–382, §§551–554, 108 Stat. 4056, as amended by the Removal of Barriers to Interethnic Adoption Provisions of the *Small Business Job Protection Act of 1996*, 42 U.S.C. §§671, 674, 1996B, Pub. L. 104–188, §1808, 110 Stat. 1903.

10. *Adoption and Safe Families Act of 1997*, Pub. L. 105–89, November 19, 1997, 111 Stat. 2115 (codified as amended in scattered sections of 42 U.S.C.A.) (West Supp. 1998).

11. See, e.g., Duncan Lindsey, *The Welfare of Children* (New York: Oxford University Press, 1994), chap. 8.

12. See President Clinton's Executive Memorandum 12/14/96; U.S. Department of Health and Human Services, *Adoption 2002: A Response to the Presidential Executive Memorandum on Adoption*, Washington, D.C., 2/14/97.

13. The number of children in foster care grew an average of 24,000 per year from 1987 to 1998, rising from 280,000 to 520,000. It grew an average of 20,800 per year in the ten-year period 1988 to 1998, and an average of 18,000 per year in the five-year period 1993 to 1998. Data provided by Penelope L. Maza, Senior Policy Research Analyst, Children's Bureau, U.S. Department of Health and Human Services, Washington, D.C., by e-mail, March 18, 1999, drawn from reports of the U.S. Department of Health and Human Services, the federal Voluntary Cooperative Information System, and the American Public Human Services Association (formerly the American Public Welfare Association).

14. Adoption Assistance and Child Welfare Act of 1980, Pub. L. 96–272, 94 Stat. 500 (1980) (codified in scattered sections of 42 U.S.C. (1994)).

CHAPTER 1. THE INHERITED TRADITION: PARENTING RIGHTS AND STATE WRONGS

1. See generally Reva B. Siegle, "The Rule of Love: Wife Beating as Prerogative and Privacy," *Yale Law Journal* 105 (1996), at 2117.

2. See generally Duncan Lindsey, *The Welfare of Children* (New York: Oxford University Press, 1994), describing the child welfare system in the United States as a "residual service system," serving only the disadvantaged and at risk, rather than all families with children.

3. Temporary Assistance for Needy Families (TANF) was passed in the *Personal Responsibility and Work Opportunity Reconciliation Act of 1996*, Pub. L. No. 104–93, 110 Stat. 2105 (1996), codified in scattered sections of the U.S.C.A. starting at §601.

4. See C. Henry Kempe et al., "The Battered Child Syndrome," *Journal of the American Medical Association* 13 (1962), at 105.

5. See generally Lindsey, *The Welfare of Children*; Neil Gilbert, "International Perspectives and Trends," chap. 1 in *Combating Child Abuse: Comparative Perspectives on Reporting Systems and Placement Trends* (New York: Oxford University Press, 1997).

6. 489 U.S. 189, 212 (1989).

7. See, e.g., Gilbert, "International Perspectives and Trends," in *Combating Child Abuse*; Martha Minow, "What Ever Happened to Children's Rights?," *Minnesota Law Review* 80 (1995), at 267, 294.

8. See Cynthia Godsoe, "Visions of Parent, Child and State Played out in Child Protection Policy and Practice" (Harvard Law School, 1996); Henrietta Hill, "'. . . The Best We Have To Give . . .': Optimism and Challenge for the Duty on States to Protect Children from Familial Abuse" (Harvard Law School, 1996). On file with author.

9. Article 19 reads:

1. States parties shall take all appropriate legislative, administrative, social and educational measures to protect the child from all forms of physical or mental violence, injury or abuse, neglect or negligent treatment, maltreatment or exploitation, including sexual abuse, while in the care of parent(s), legal guardian(s) or any other person who has the care of the child.

2. Such protective measures should, as appropriate, include effective procedures for the establishment of social programmes to provide necessary support for the child and for those who have the care of the child, as well as for other forms of prevention and for identification, reporting, referral, investigation, treatment, and follow-up of instances of child maltreatment described heretofore, and, as appropriate, for judicial involvement.

10. See generally on the Convention, Henrietta Hill, "'. . . The Best We Have to Give . . .'"

11. Proceedings of the Conference on the Care of Dependent Children (1909). See generally Nancy Morawetz, "Welfare Litigation to Prevent Homelessness," *N.Y.U. Review of Law and Social Change* 16 (1989), at 457, 473–76.

12. See also revised and updated versions of these works in *The Best Interests of the Child: The Least Detrimental Alternative*, by Joseph Goldstein, Albert J. Solnit, Sonya Goldstein, and the late Anna Freud (New York: The Free Press, 1996).

13. State intervention was found justified only in cases of death, or disappearance of the caretaker, or serious bodily injury or threat thereof. As of the 1996 publication, n. 12 above, not even sexual abuse was sufficient to justify intervention.

14. See, e.g., Michael Wald, "Thinking About Public Policy Toward Abuse and Neglect of Children: A Review of Before the Best Interests of the Child," *Michigan Law Review* 78 (1980), at 645.

15. *Santosky v. Kramer*, 455 U.S. 745 (1982). See also, e.g., *Stanley v. Illinois*, 405 U.S. 645 (1972).

16. In *Smith v. Organization of Foster Families for Equality and Reform*, 431 U.S. 816 (1997), the Supreme Court found that even assuming foster parents have some constitutional rights they are of a lesser order than biological parents' rights, and denied the foster parent any hearing right prior to removal of a child.

17. Elizabeth Bartholet, "What's Wrong with Adoption Law?" *The International Journal of Children's Rights* 4 (1996), at 263.

18. The Adoption Assistance and Child Welfare Act of 1980, Pub. L. 96–272, 94 Stat. 500 (1980) (codified as amended in 42 U.S.C. §§ 620–628 (1994)).

19. This was passed as part of the Omnibus Budget Reconciliation Act of 1993, Pub. L. 103–66, 107 Stat. 649, 649–56 (1993).

20. Pub. L. No. 105–89, 111 Stat. 2115 (1997) (codified in 42 U.S.C.A. §§673(b), 678, 679(b)). Under this new "Safe and Stable Families Act," reunification services are "time-limited," and funding is expanded to cover postadoption services.

CHAPTER 2. THE POLITICS

1. Deborah Daro, *Confronting Child Abuse: Research for Effective Program Design* (New York: Free Press, 1988), at 149–98; Lisbeth B. Schorr, *Common Purpose: Strengthening Families and Neighborhoods to Rebuild America* (New York: Anchor Books, 1997), at 4, 40–47, and *Within Our Reach: Breaking the Cycle of Disadvantage* (New York: Anchor Books, 1998), at 270–273.

2. See "The Impact on Children" in chapter 3.

3. See, e.g., Diane Bernard, "The Dark Side of Family Preservation," *Affilia* 7, no. 2 (Summer 1992), at 92, 156–159 (voicing feminist concerns that conservatives support family preservation precisely because it is consonant with conservative values).

4. See Lela B. Costin, Jacob Karger, and David Stoesz, *The Politics of Child Abuse in America* (New York: Oxford Unversity Press, 1996), at 118–132 ("In the family preservation approach, liberal welfare professionals found common ground with the religious right," at 121).

5. See "Family Preservation in its Infinite Variety: The Storm" in chapter 5.

6. See chapter 1, text at n. 19, and n. 19.

7. Costin, Karger, and Stoesz, *The Politics of Child Abuse in America*, at 129.

8. See generally Eve S. Buzawa and Carl G. Buzawa, *Domestic Violence: The Criminal Justice Response*, 2d ed. (Thousand Oaks, CA: Sage Publications,

1996); Elizabeth Schneider, *Battered Women, Feminist Lawmaking, and Legal Discourse* (Cambridge: Harvard Press, forthcoming).

9. Many think the evidence on mandatory arrest policies indicates that they have a significant deterrent effect, while others think the case not proven. The research so far indicates that the impact depends on the socio-economic circumstances of the perpetrator: men with more to lose seem to be deterred, while those with less to lose—the unemployed, for example—seem less concerned with the threat of arrest. But those who see little to lose from a simple arrest would more likely be deterred if they knew that arrest would be followed by prompt prosecution, conviction, and punishment.

10. See authorities cited in n. 8 above; see also Ann Jones, *Next Time She'll Be Dead: Battering and How to Stop It* (Boston: Beacon Press, 1994).

11. A recent and important national survey of child maltreatment found that 65 percent of the maltreated children had been maltreated by a female, whereas 54 percent had been maltreated by a male. Of children who were maltreated by their birth parents, the majority (75 percent) were maltreated by their mothers and a sizable minority (46 percent) were maltreated by their fathers (some children were maltreated by both parents). Children were more often neglected by female perpetrators (87 percent by female versus 43 percent by males), and children were more often abused by males (67 percent by males versus 40 percent by females). U.S. Department of Health and Human Services, Administration for Children and Families, Administration on Children, Youth and Families, National Center on Child Abuse and Neglect, "Executive Summary of the Third National Incidence Study of Child Abuse and Neglect (NIS-3)" (Washington, D.C., September, 1996), at 13. See also U.S. Department of Health and Human Services, Administration for Children and Families, Administration on Children, Youth and Families, National Center on Child Abuse and Neglect, "The Third National Incidence Study of Child Abuse and Neglect, Final Report (NIS-3)" (Washington, D.C., September, 1996), at 6–10 to 6–11 (women responsible for 78 percent of fatal and 75 percent of serious outcomes; men and women have comparable rates of child homicide). See National Research Council and Institute of Medicine, *Violence in Families: Assessing Prevention and Treatment Programs* (Washington, D.C.: National Academy Press, 1998), at 42.

12. See Richard J. Gelles and Murray A. Strauss, *Intimate Violence* (New York: Simon and Schuster, 1988), at 20–25.

13. See n. 1 above.

14. Mary B. Larner, Carol S. Stevenson, and Richard E. Behrman, "Protecting Children from Abuse and Neglect: Analysis and Recommendations," *The Future of Children, Protecting Children From Abuse and Neglect*

8, no. 1 (Spring 1998), at 7; Mark E. Courtney, "The Costs of Child Protection in the Context of Welfare Reform," *The Future of Children, Protecting Children From Abuse and Neglect* 8, no. 1 (Spring 1998), at 88, 94.

15. See Martha Minow and Richard Weissbourd, "Social Movements for Children," *Daedalus* 122 (1993), at 1 (analyzing why social movements for children generally fail); Minow, "What Ever Happened to Children's Rights?," *Minnesota Law Review* 80 (1995), at 267, 295 (left and right support for family autonomy).

CHAPTER 3. MODERN-DAY ORPHANS

1. The U.S. Advisory Board on Child Abuse and Neglect, *Child Abuse and Neglect: Critical First Steps in Response to a National Emergency* (Washington, D.C.: U.S. Government Printing Office, 1990) [hereafter *Child Abuse and Neglect: Critical First Steps*].

2. See Robert W. ten Bensel, "Children in a World of Violence," in *The Battered Child*, 5th ed., ed. Mary Edna Helfer et al. (Chicago: University of Chicago Press, 1997) [hereafter Helfer, *The Battered Child*], at 3ff.

3. *Child Abuse and Neglect: Critical First Steps,* at viii.

4. Federal law defines child maltreatment for certain purposes as "the physical or mental injury, sexual abuse or exploitation, or negligent treatment of a child under 18 by a person responsible for the child's welfare under circumstances which indicate that the child's health or welfare is threatened thereby." Child Abuse Prevention and Treatment Act (CAPTA), Pub. L. No. 93–247, 88 Stat. 4 (codified as amended at 42 U.S.C. §§5101–5106,(1994)), §5106g(4). This definition is fairly standard, but state law will vary significantly in defining more particularly the meaning of the terms. CAPTA was amended in 1996 to require that states at a minimum must classify as child abuse or neglect recent acts or failures to act by parents or "caretakers" resulting in death, serious physical or emotional harm, sexual abuse or exploitation, or acts or failures to act presenting an imminent risk of serious harm. Child Abuse Prevention and Treatment Act, Pub. L. No. 104–235, 110 Stat. 3063 (1996).

5. See generally Julie B. Wilson, "Abused and Neglected Children: How Many? How Serious the Maltreatment? What Share Could Be Reached Only Through Coercive Intervention?" paper prepared for the Executive Session, New Paradigms for Child Protective Services, May 16–18, 1996, John F. Kennedy School of Government, Harvard University, Cambridge, MA [hereafter Wilson, "Abused and Neglected Children"].

6. This NIS estimate used a definition of maltreatment specifying danger to health or safety, and included maltreatment cases known to community sources (teachers, health care professionals, other service providers), as well as CPS authorities. See U.S. Department of Health and Human Services, National Center on Child Abuse and Neglect (NCCAN), *Child Maltreatment 1994: Reports from the States to the National Child Abuse and Neglect Data System*, Washington, D.C., 1994 [hereafter NCCAN, *Child Maltreatment, 1994*]; National Research Council and Institute of Medicine, *Violence in Families: Assessing Prevention and Treatment Programs* (Washington, D.C.: National Academy Press, 1998), at 12 [hereafter NRCIM, *Violence in Families*].

7. See Wilson, "Abused and Neglected Children," at 12–13; National Committee to Prevent Child Abuse (NCPCA), "Current Trends in Child Abuse Reporting and Fatalities: The Results of the 1997 Annual Fifty-State Survey," Chicago, IL (1998) (3,195,000 children reported in 1997)[hereafter NCPCA, "Current Trends in Child Abuse Reporting," 1998]; The American Professional Society on the Abuse of Children, *Handbook on Child Maltreatment* (1996)[hereafter APSAC, *Handbook on Child Maltreatment*, 1996].

8. See Douglas Besharov, "Fixing Child Protection," *Philanthropy* (Winter 1998) [hereafter Besharov, "Fixing Child Protection"], at 19 (1986 study shows professionals with duty to report still failing to report half the maltreated children they saw).

9. NCPCA, "Current Trends in Child Abuse Reporting," 1998 (forty-one percent of children who died between 1995 and 1997 had prior or current contact with CPS). See also Wilson, "Abused and Neglected Children," at 16, discussing Wiese and Daro, "Current Trends in Child Abuse Reporting and Fatalities: The Results of the 1994 Annual Fifty-State Survey," National Committee to Prevent Child Abuse (April 1995).

10. U.S. Department of Health and Human Services, Administration for Children and Families, Administration on Children, Youth and Families, National Center on Child Abuse and Neglect, "Executive Summary of the Third National Incidence Study of Child Abuse and Neglect (NIS-3)" (Washington, D.C., September 1996), at 16. See also Lela B. Costin, Howard Jacob Karger, and David Stoesz, *The Politics of Child Abuse in America* (New York: Oxford University Press, 1996), at 136 (only half of all maltreatment cases come to the attention of authorities).

11. Family Impact Seminar, "Child Abuse Prevention: New Partnerships for Protecting Children and Supporting Families" (February 21, 1997), at 11.

12. See Wilson, "Abused and Neglected Children," at 15.

13. Patrick A. Curtis et al., *Child Abuse and Neglect: A Look at the States* (Washington, D.C.: Child Welfare League of America, 1995), at 12.

14. The Edna McConnell Clark Foundation, "Program for Children, Strategy Statement" (March 1996), at 9.

15. Diane J. English, "The Extent and Consequences of Child Mal-

treatment," *The Future of Children, Protecting Children From Abuse and Neglect* 8, no. 1 (Spring 1998), at 43.

16. See Wilson, "Abused and Neglected Children," at 8. CPS reports indicate that from 1987 to 1996 the total number of children reported to CPS increased 41 percent, and from 1988 to 1997 the rate of child fatalities due to maltreatment increased 20 percent. NCPCA, "Current Trends in Child Abuse Reporting," 1997 and 1998.

17. See Wilson, "Abused and Neglected Children," at 21.

18. Coramae Richey Mann, "Maternal Filicide of Preschoolers," in Anna V. Wilson, ed., *Homicide: The Victim/Offender Connection* (Cincinnati, OH: Anderson Publishing Co., 1993), at 227.

19. The National Center on Addiction and Substance Abuse at Columbia University, "No Safe Haven: Children of Substance-Abusing Parents," New York, January 1999 [hereafter CASA Report], at 16.

20. See Wilson, "Abused and Neglected Children," at 10. The fact that state definitions of maltreatment have generally narrowed over the years is another indicator that reports reflect actual increases in maltreatment.

21. "Researchers Identify Risk Factors for Infants Most Likely to be Homicide Victims," *New England Journal of Medicine* (October 22, 1998).

22. NCPCA, "Current Trends in Child Abuse Reporting," 1998; APSAC, *Handbook on Child Maltreatment*, 1996.

23. NCPCA, "Current Trends in Child Abuse Reporting," 1998, APSAC, *Handbook on Child Maltreatment*, 1996. See also NCCAN, *Child Maltreatment*, 1994 for the comparable NIS-3 breakdown of maltreatment categories (55 percent neglect, 25 percent physical abuse). See chapter 10, n. 7, on issue of whether race is a factor in official report rates or actual incidence rates apart from poverty.

24. National Council of Juvenile and Family Court Judges, *Resource Guidelines: Improving Court Practice in Child Abuse and Neglect Cases*, Reno, NV, 1995.

25. Jill D. Berrick et al., *The Tender Years: Toward Developmentally Sensitive Child Welfare Services for Very Young Children* (New York: Oxford University Press, 1998), at 122 [hereafter Berrick, *The Tender Years*]. See also Costin, Karger, and Stoesz, *The Politics of Child Abuse in America* (1996), at 136 (increasingly the CPS caseload is limited to the most dysfunctional families where children are at greatest risk of serious bodily harm).

26. See nn. 4 and 24, above, and CASA Report, at 1.

27. Cecilia Zalkind, *Stolen Futures, A Report on Preventing Foster Care Placement in New Jersey,* Association for Children of New Jersey (1994), at 13, 17, 18.

28. Deborah Daro, *Confronting Child Abuse: Research for Effective Program Design* (New York: Free Press, 1988), at 34.

29. National Institute of Justice Research Preview, "The Cycle of Violence Revisited," February 1996; Cathy Spatz Widom's research reported on in Office of Juvenile Justice and Delinquency Prevention, U.S. Department of Justice, *Juvenile Justice Bulletin*, August 1997, at 3; Hendrika Cantwell, "The Neglect of Child Neglect," in Helfer, *The Battered Child*, at 347.

30. See Ann H. Cohn and Deborah Daro, "Is Treatment Too Late: What Ten Years of Evaluative Research Tell Us," *Child Abuse and Neglect* 11 (1987), at 433, 438.

31. See NCPCA, "Current Trends in Child Abuse Reporting," 1998 (44 percent died from neglect, 51 percent from abuse, and 5 percent from multiple forms of maltreatment); Jill Duerr Berrick, "Child Neglect: Definition, Incidence," in *Outcomes in Child Welfare Research Review*, vol. 2, ed. Jill Duerr Berrick, Richard P. Barth, and Neil Gilbert (New York: Columbia University Press, 1997), at 1ff (significant impact in terms of emotional damage, cognitive deficits; risk of death greater than from other forms of maltreatment); James M. Gaudin and Howard Dubowitz, "Family Functioning in Neglectful Families: Recent Research," in *Child Welfare Research Review*, vol. 2, ed. Berrick, Barth, and Gilbert, at 28ff (40 percent of maltreatment-related child fatalities due to neglect; other serious consequences); Diane J. English, "The Extent and Consequences of Child Maltreatment," *The Future of Children, Protecting Children from Abuse and Neglect* 8, no. 1 (Spring 1998), at 48 (neglect accounts for 37 percent of deaths, abuse and neglect combined for an additional 15 percent).

32. See John R. Schuerman, "Best Interests and Family Preservation in America," Discussion Paper, The Chapin Hall Center for Children at the University of Chicago, October 1996, at 7 (substance abuse and chronic neglect dominate CPS caseloads, with substance abuse often central to the neglect problem).

33. Press release of the National Center on Addiction and Substance Abuse at Columbia University: "CASA Releases Report, *No Safe Haven: Children of Substance Abusing Parents*," January 11, 1999, and CASA Report, at 3.

34. CASA Report, at i.

35. CASA Report, at ii, 4, 13.

36. Reliable figures are hard to come by, since official reports fail to reflect the actual level of drug involvement, but recent research designed to assess the relationship between drug abuse and child maltreatment supports these estimates. See generally Sidney Gardner and Nancy Young, "The Implications of Alcohol and Other Drug-related Problems for Community-wide Family Support Systems," paper prepared for the Executive Session: New Paradigms for Child Protective Services, John F. Kennedy School of Government, Harvard University, Cambridge, MA, November 1996, at 1 ("In discussions with more than two dozen senior-level officials and line

workers in child protective services agencies over the past five years, we
have never had anyone disagree with the high end of the 40–80% range,
*and the most common response is a nod when the figure 80% is mentioned, as
if to say, 'sure, we all know that'* " [emphasis added]). A recent survey in San
Diego, CA found evidence of substance abuse in 79 percent of the cases.
Bridgett A. Besinger, Ann F. Garland, Alan J. Litrownik, and John A. Land-
sverk, "Caregiver Substance Abuse Among Maltreated Children Placed in
Out-of-Home Care," *Child Welfare* 78, no. 2 (March/April 1999), at 221,
232, 235. An important national study found that 80–99 percent of child removal cases were drug-related. Muskie Institute of Public Affairs, *Kinship
Care in America, A National Policy Study* (1995) [hereafter Muskie, *Kinship
Care*], at 4. A 1989 study of children in California found that 88 percent of
the children referred to child welfare came from families with substance
abuse problems. R. P. Barth et al., *From Child Abuse to Permanency Planning: Child Welfare Services Pathways and Placements* (Hawthorne, NY: Aldine deGruyter, 1994), at 6. A 1997 GAO Report says that the number of
CPS cases involving substance abuse can range from 20 to 90 percent, and
that 75 percent of confirmed child maltreatment cases in New York City
had involved substance abuse by a parent or caregiver. U.S. General Accounting Office, *Parental Substance Abuse: Implications for Children, the
Child Welfare System, and Foster Care Outcomes*, Report No. T-HEHS-98–
40, Washington, D.C., October 28, 1997; U.S. General Accounting Office,
Foster Care: Parental Drug Abuse Has Alarming Impact on Young Children,
Washington, D.C., 1994 (78 percent of children in foster care had parents
with substance abuse problems). See also Charlotte McCullough, "The
Child Welfare Response," in *The Future of Children, Drug Exposed Infants* 1,
no. 3 (Spring 1991), at 61, 62 (chemical dependence the dominant characteristic in CPS caseloads, with almost 90 percent of caretakers reported for
child abuse in 22 states and D.C. being "active substance abusers," and nationwide estimates showing between 30 and 90 percent of confirmed child
abuse cases and three-fourths of child abuse fatalities in some cities involving families with drug and alcohol abuse); Diane J. English, "The Extent
and Consequences of Child Maltreatment," *The Future of Children, Protecting Children from Abuse and Neglect* 8, no. 1 (Spring 1998), at 39, 47 (50–
80 percent). The North American Council on Adoptable Children (NA-
CAC) cites estimates that over half of the children entering foster care were
prenatally exposed to cocaine, and that in more than 75 percent of the
cases of children entering care alcohol and drug abuse were factors. NA-
CAC, *A Framework for Foster Care Reform* (November 1996), at 3.

37. NCPCA, "Current Trends in Child Abuse Reporting," 1998.

38. CASA Report, at ii, 13, appendix D at 165–166.

39. See generally Deanna S. Gomby and Patricia H. Shiono, "Estimating the Number of Substance-Exposed Infants," in *The Future of Children, Drug Exposed Infants*, 1, no. 1 (Spring 1991), at 17, 22–24, as updated by Shiono, "Prevalence of Drug-Exposed Infants" in *Revisiting the Issues, The Future of Children* 6, no. 2 (Summer/Fall 1996), at 159–63 [hereafter *Future of Children*, 1991 and 1996]; CASA Report at ii, 13.

40. See The Evan B. Donaldson Adoption Institute, *Synthesis of Conference Findings, Adoption and Prenatal Alcohol and Prenatal Alcohol Exposure*, <http://www.adoptioninstitute.org/proed/pserjw3.html> (1998) [hereafter Donaldson, *Synthesis*], citing Brady, Posner, Lang, and Rosati 1994, Chasnoff 1989 (11 percent of all newborns yearly, or 459,690, exposed to illicit drugs in womb), Gomby and Shiono 1991 (more than 739,000 women each year use one or more illegal drugs during pregnancy). See also CASA Report, at 17 (noting dramatic increase in prenatal exposure, and finding one-half million born annually exposed to cocaine or other illicit drugs prenatally); Ira Chasnoff, Amy Anson, and Kai Moss Iaukea, *Understanding the Drug-Exposed Child: Approaches to Behavior and Learning* (Chicago: Imprint Publications, 1998) [hereafter Chasnoff, *Understanding the Drug-Exposed Child*] (NIDA 1994 data indicate up to 221,000 per year, or 5.5 percent, exposed to illicit drugs, and if alcohol and tobacco added figure is well over 1.5 million), at 1–2.

41. CASA Report, at 44.

42. See *Future of Children*, 1991 and 1996; Sheila Ards and Ronald B. Mincy, "Neighborhood Ecology," in *When Drug Addicts Have Children*, ed. Douglas J. Besharov (Washington, D.C.: Child Welfare League of America, 1994), at 33ff.

43. Future of Children 1991 and 1996; "Cocaine harm to fetus is less than expected," *Boston Globe*, October 28, 1998, col. 2, p. A11, reporting on recent research by Barry Lester, psychologist at Brown University. See note 51 below. Rates are highly variable for different racial groups with respect to different substances. Rates of cocaine use during pregnancy are much higher among African-American women than among white women, while rates of marijuana use are higher among whites.

44. *Behavioral Studies of Drug-Exposed Offspring*, National Institute on Drug Abuse Research Monograph Series (1996), at 19.

45. A 1997 governmental report indicates that while 2.3 percent of all pregnant women ages 12 to 44 reported using an illicit drug in the past month, the use rates for alcohol in the past month were 21.2 percent and for tobacco were 21.5 percent, Substance Abuse and Mental Health Services Administration, *Substance Abuse Among Women in the United States* (1997) [hereafter SAMHSA, 1997], at v, 5–6. According to the National Institute on Drug Abuse, an estimated 45,000 or 1.1 percent of mothers inhaled or injected cocaine at least once during pregnancy in 1994, 757,000 or 18.8 percent drank alcohol, and 820,000 or 20.4 percent smoked tobacco. U.S. Department of Health and Human Services, National Institute of Drug Abuse, National Pregnancy and Health Survey (Rockville, MD, 1994). Another estimate indicates 200,000 children are born each year who have been prenatally exposed to drugs, 800,000 prenatally exposed to alcohol, and 800,000 prenatally exposed to cigarettes. *Adopted Child* 16, no. 11 (November 1997), at 3.

The Donaldson Adoption Institute Synthesis of conference findings, n. 40 above, reported that over 2 million infants are prenatally exposed to alcohol yearly; 0.13 to 0.22 percent of newborns are affected by fetal alcohol syndrome (FAS), a set of serious birth defects caused by significant alcohol use during pregnancy; many more are born suffering less serious alcohol-related birth defects. See also CASA Report, at 17 (636,000 women drink during pregnancy, with 137,000 of them drinking frequently or heavily). On certain Native American reservations the rates of alcohol abuse during pregnancy are reported to be much higher. See Michael Dorris, *The Broken Cord* (New York: Harper and Row, 1989), at 164–179.

46. SAMHSA, 1997, at 5.1 (citations omitted).

47. See, e.g., "Cocaine Before Birth," *The Harvard Mental Health Letter* 15, no. 6 (December 1998), at 1–2 [hereafter *Harvard Mental Health*, "Cocaine"].

48. Gary A. Emmett, "What Happened to the 'Crack Babies?'" *Drug Policy Analysis Bulletin* no. 4 (February 1998), at 2 [hereafter Emmett, "Crack Babies?" 1998], at 1.

49. See *Harvard Mental Health*, "Cocaine," at 1 ("vascular accidents" may occur in utero, leaving "literally holes in the brain," which "may result in any outcome from no apparent damage to permanent and severe motor or developmental delay . . . cerebral palsy and/or mental retardation").

50. See *Harvard Mental Health*, "Cocaine," at 2.

51. Barry Lester, et al., "Cocaine Exposure and Children: The Meaning of Subtle Effects," *Science* 282 (1998), at 633–634.

52. Chasnoff, *Understanding the Drug-Exposed Child*, at 10.

53. "Long-Term Neurodevelopmental Risks in Children Exposed in Utero to Cocaine: The Toronto Adoption Study," *Annals of the New York Academy of Science* 846, no. 2 (June 21, 1998).

54. Chasnoff, *Understanding the Drug-Exposed Child*, at 10–17.

55. See CASA Report, at 22, text at nn. 135–136 and authorities cited in nn. 135–136.

56. Emmett, "Crack Babies?" at 2.

57. Richard Barth, "Long-Term In-Home Services," in Besharov, *When Drug Addicts Have Children*, at 175–176.

58. Berrick, *The Tender Years*, at 113–114.

59. MaryLee Allen and Jamila Larson, *Healing the Whole Family: A Look at Family Care Programs* (Washington, D.C.: Children's Defense Fund, 1998), at 44; Gardner and Young, *The Implications of Alcohol and Other Drug-related Problems for Community-wide Family Support Systems*, at 14.

60. R. P. Barth and D. Brooks, "Outcomes for Drug-Exposed Children Eight Years After Adoption," in *Adoption and Prenatal Alcohol and Drug Exposure: The Research, Policy and Practice Challenges*, ed. R. Barth, D. Brodzinsky, and M. Freundlich (Washington, D.C.: Child Welfare League of America, in press), at 22. See also CASA Report, at 19 (noting in a study of prenatally exposed children that 30.2 percent were reported as abused or neglected within six years, twice the rate among all children living in the area).

61. National Association of State Alcohol and Drug Abuse Directors, Special Report, no. 1, 1995, "Substance Abuse Among Parents," at iii.

62. U.S. Department of Health and Human Services, Substance Abuse and Mental Health Services Administration, Office of Applied Studies, Rockville, MD, "Preliminary Results from the 1996 National Household Survey on Drug Abuse," DHHS Publication No. (SMA) 97–3149, July 1997.

63. Barry Zuckerman, "Effects on Parents and Children," in Besharov, *When Drug Addicts Have Children*, at 52.

64. Judy Howard, "Barriers to Successful Intervention," in Besharov, *When Drug Addicts Have Children*, at 92–93.

65. SAMHSA, 1997, at 6–1.

66. CASA Report, at 3 (substance abuse and addiction almost guaranteed to lead to neglect); Dan Bays, "Substance Abuse and Child Abuse: Impact of Addiction on the Child," Pediatric Clinics of North America, 37, no. 4 (August 1990) at 897.

67. CASA Report, at 15.

68. Howard, "Barriers to Successful Intervention," in Besharov, *When Drug Addicts Have Children*, at 98.

69. National Institute of Justice Research Preview, *Drugs, Alcohol, and Domestic Violence in Memphis* (October 1997).

70. CASA Report, at 14.

71. Besharov, "Fixing Child Protection," at 2.

72. Michael Massing, *The Fix* (New York: Simon and Schuster, 1998), at 41.

73. Lisa Newmark and Inessa Chevtchinskaia, "Parental Drug Testing in Child Abuse and Neglect Cases: Major Findings," The Urban Institute, Washington, D.C., 1995.

74. Chasnoff, *Understanding the Drug-Exposed Child*, at 6, citing D. R. Griffith, "The effects of perinatal cocaine exposure on infant neurobehavior and early maternal-infant interactions," in *Drugs, Alcohol, Pregnancy and Parenting*, ed. Chasnoff (Lancaster, UK: Kluwer Academic Publishers, 1988).

75. Besharov, *When Drug Addicts Have Children*, at xi.

76. Bays, "Substance Abuse," at 892.

77. Zuckerman, "Effects on Parents and Children," in Besharov, *When Drug Addicts Have Children*, at 50.

78. CASA Report, at ii and 21, iii, iv–v, 6, and 23.

79. Barth, "Long-Term In-Home Services," in Besharov, *When Drug Addicts Have Children*, at 183.

80. U.S. General Accounting Office, Health Education and Human Services Division, "Foster Care: Parental Drug Abuse Has Alarming Impact on Young Children," Washington, D.C., 1994.

81. Berrick, *The Tender Years*, at 35–37.

82. See *Drug Abuse Treatment Outcome Study* (DATOS), ed. D. Dwayne Simpson and Susan J. Curry, Special Issue of *Psychology of Addictive Behaviors* (Journal of Division 50 of the American Psychological Association), 11, no. 4 (December 1997) [hereafter DATOS], at 241 ("Clinical impressions indicate that . . . psychological problems associated with cocaine-crack clients are more severe and multidimensional than those associated with opiods").

83. CASA Report, at 19 (relapse a common event in the lifelong process of recovery); Besharov, *When Drug Addicts Have Children*, at ix, xiii (even with the best treatment services available most crack addicts can't be freed of addiction; crack drug addiction must be understood as chronic, relapsing disorder); Judy Howard, "Chronic Drug Users as Parents," *Hastings Law Journal* 43 (1992), at 645 (addiction a "chronic, relapsing disorder," addicts have limited prospects for successful treatment, majority won't become drug-free even after extensive treatment course, and only small percentage able to become and remain drug-free, with no ability to predict which during author's own three-year research project). See also Nancy Young and Sidney Gardner, *Implementing Welfare Reform: Solutions to the Substance Abuse Problem* (Washington, D.C.: Drug Strategies, 1997) (age a major factor affecting treatment outcome, with older (over 30) more likely to succeed).

At a recent conference Ira J. Chasnoff, one of the nation's preeminent experts on drugs and their impact on children, noted that in his study of cocaine/poly-drug using mothers and their offspring, 100 percent of the mothers had relapsed into drug or alcohol use within six years. See generally *Adoption and Prenatal Alcohol and Drug Exposure: The Research, Policy and Practice Challenges*, a conference held October 24–25, 1997, in Alexandria, Virginia, sponsored by the Evan B. Donaldson Adoption Institute, Chasnoff presentation, October 24, 1997. See also Janet Chiancone, "Research Basics: Substance Abuse Treatment in Child Welfare: A Guide for Lawyers Representing Children and Families," ABA Child Law Practice 17, no. 6 (August 1998), at 92 (crack-cocaine hardest to treat, citing one study finding that even in treatment most continued to use drugs, with only 15 percent of mothers remaining abstinent).

84. See DATOS, 1997, at 213, 276, 321.

85. *Children '98: America's Promise—Children Need Protection and Care More Than Ever* (Washington, D.C.: Child Welfare League of America, 1998). See Clarice Dibble Walker, Patricia Zangrill, and Jacqueline Marie Smith, "Parental Drug Abuse and African-American Children in Foster Care," in *Child Welfare Research Review*, vol. 1, ed. Richard Barth, Jill D. Berrick, and Neil Gilbert (New York: Columbia University Press, 1994) at 109, 117–19 (after two years in foster care, 28 percent of children of drug abusers discharged vs. 51 percent of children of nonabusers; of those discharged, 36.6 percent of children of drug abusers reunified vs. 60.6 percent of children of nonabusers); R. P. Barth, "Revisiting the Issues: Adoption of Drug-exposed Children," *The Future of Children, Adoption* 3, no. 1 (Spring 1993), at 168 (these infants remain in foster care far longer than older children even though drug involvement a poor predictor of reunification).

86. CASA Report, at 16.

87. Institute for Children and National Center for Policy Analysis, "The State of the Children: An Examination of Government-Run Foster Care," 1997 (as of end of fiscal 1996, 526,112 children in substitute care).

88. See Introduction, n. 13; T. Tatara, *Voluntary Cooperative System* (Washington, D.C.: American Public Welfare Association, 1997).

89. See generally Mark E. Courtney, "Factors Associated with Entry Into Group Care," in *Child Welfare Research Review*, vol. 1 (1994), ed. Barth, Berrick, and Gilbert, at 185, 187. See also Allen and Larson, *Healing the Whole Family*, at 44 (infants remain in care about one-third longer than children in any other age group); F. Wulczyn, A. Harden, and R. Goerge, *An Update from the Multistate Foster Care Data Archive: Foster Care Dynamics 1983–1994* (Chicago, IL: The Chapin Hall Center for Children at the University of Chicago, 1997), at 45–46 (infants have high rates of entry and long stays in foster care).

90. Child Welfare League of America, "Child Abuse and Neglect: A Look at the States, 1997 CWLA Stat Book," Washington, D.C., at 123; see Wulczyn, Harden, and Goerge, *Update from the Multistate Foster Care Data*, at 64; North American Council on Adoptable Children, "Adoptalk," (Fall, 1998), at 1.

91. Peter Gibbs, "The Forgotten Children," *Boston Globe*, March 25, 1998, p. A19.

92. Richard Barth, "Abusive and Neglecting Parents and the Care of Their

Children," in *All Our Families: New Policies for a New Century*, ed. M. A. Mason, A. Skolnick, and S. D. Sugarman (New York: Oxford University Press, 1998), 217–235 [hereafter Barth, "Abusive and Neglecting Parents"] (30 percent of children entering foster care in 1983 and later reunified with parents had reentered foster care by end of 1993); Berrick, *The Tender Years*, at xiii (30 percent of infants in California study returned to their parents are revictimized).

93. R. P. Barth and D. L. Blackwell, "Death Rates Among California's Foster Care and Former Foster Care Populations," *Child and Youth Services Review* 20, no. 7 (1998), at 577, 601.

94. Berrick, *The Tender Years*, at 115.

95. Berrick, *The Tender Years*, at 117–119.

96. Richard Barth, "Permanent Placements for Young Children Placed in Foster Care: A proposal for a child welfare services performance standard," *Child and Youth Services Review* 19, no. 8 (1997), at 615, 622–623 [hereafter Barth, "Permanent Placements"]; see also Barth, "After Child Protection, What is the Guiding Principle of Child Welfare Services: Permanency, Family Continuity, or Productive Development," The Fedele F. and Iris M. Fauri Memorial Lecture Series on Child Welfare, The University of Michigan School of Social Work, Ann Arbor, MI, December 11, 1995 [hereafter Barth, "After Child Protection"], at 9 (after six years in foster care, one-sixth of children placed as infants had had five or more placements).

97. Barth, "After Child Protection," at 9–10, citation omitted.

98. See Besharov, *When Drug Addicts Have Children*, at xi (disproportionate share of infant foster placements in underclass neighborhoods, saturated by drugs, crime, and deep poverty, where families are under constant psychological, social, and financial bombardment, and where families are isolated and have minimal support). On negative impact of devastated neighborhood environment, see also Introduction, text at n. 2 and n. 2.

99. David Armstrong, "DSS lets criminals give care: 115 offenders cleared to be foster parents," *Boston Globe*, April 28, 1996, Metro/Region, p. 1, and "DSS to curb foster care by criminals: Serious offenders to be barred from state human service jobs," *Boston Globe*, April 29, 1996, Metro/Region, p. 1.

100. Michael Grunwald, "Welfare mother, foster parent: Dual role of many questioned," *Boston Globe*, April 5, 1997, Metro/Region, p. A1.

101. Doris Sue Wong, "Tighter rules set for foster parents," *Boston Globe*, September 27, 1998, pp. A1, A14.

102. Mark E. Courtney, "The Costs of Child Protection in the Context of Welfare Reform," *The Future of Children, Protecting Children From Abuse and Neglect* 8, no. 1 (Spring 1998), at 88, 93.

103. Jill Duerr Berrick, "When Children Cannot Remain Home: Foster Fam-

ily Care and Kinship Care," *The Future of Children, Protecting Children From Abuse and Neglect* 8, no. 1 (Spring 1998), at 72, 75.

104. Interview with attorney with adoption unit, Massachusetts Department of Social Services, Boston, MA, May 7, 1997.

105. On kinship care see generally June Melvin Mickens and Debra Ratterman Baker, *Making Good Decisions About Kinship Care* (Washington, D.C.: American Bar Association, 1997) [hereafter Mickens and Baker, *Making Good Decisions*]; Marianne Takas, *Kinship Care and Family Preservation: Options for States in Legal and Policy Development* (Washington, D.C.: American Bar Association Center on Children and the Law, 1994); Jill D. Berrick, *Assessing Quality of Care in Kinship and Foster Family Care for Santa Clara County Social Services Agency* (May 1996); *Child Welfare Journal, Special Issue on Kinship Care*, ed. Wilson and Chipungu (September/October 1996); U.S. Department of Health and Human Services, *Informal and Formal Kinship Care* (1997); Muskie Institute of Public Affairs, *Kinship Care in America, A National Policy Study* (1995) [hereafter Muskie Institute, *Kinship Care*].

106. Barth, "Abusive and Neglecting Parents," at 73.

107. Personal Responsibility and Work Opportunity Reconciliation Act of 1996, Pub. L. No. 104–193, §505,110 Stat. 2105, 2278 (1996)(codified at 42 U.S.C. §671(a) (18)).

108. CASA Report, at 37.

109. CASA Report, at 12 ("Kinship care—usually by grandmothers or aunts—is complicated by the fact that substance abuse that afflicts parents often burns through the ties that bind their families, leaving what had been a network of caring relatives in ashes. When children do enter kinship care, some mothers continue their alcohol and drug abuse and visit the child at their convenience."); Muskie Institute, *Kinship Care* (biological parent may have continued access, and child often at similar risk with relatives as with parents); Charlotte McCullough, "Revisiting the Issues, Drug-Exposed Infants," in *The Future of Children, Health Care Reform* 3, no. 2 (Summer/Fall 1993), at 211 (not unusual for parents to live in same household with the guardian-relative and the child).

110. See Muskie Institute, *Kinship Care*, at 38 (in several communities studied, relatives selected automatically without consideration of best interests of child); Mickens and Baker, *Making Good Decisions*, at 9. See generally Barth, "Permanent Placements," at 622.

111. Charlene Ingram, "Kinship Care: From Last Resort to First Choice," *Child Welfare, Special Issue on Kinship Care*, ed. Dana B. Wilson and Sandra S. Chipungu, 75, no. 5 (September 1, 1996), at 550, 553, citing Berrick's 1994 study.

112. NACAC, "A Framework for Foster Care Reform," (November 1996), at 14.

113. Joe Sexton and Rachel L. Swarns, "A Slide into Peril, With No One to Catch Her," *New York Times*, November 15, 1997, pp. A1 and A17; Felicia R. Lee, "At Funeral, 2 Worn Dolls Left Behind," *New York Times*, November 15, 1997, p. A17; Joe Sexton, "Schools Are Faulted in Death of Girl in Abuse Case," *New York Times*, November 11, 1997, p. A27.

114. See Jill Berrick, "Group Care for Children in California: Trends in the 1990's," *Child and Youth Care Forum* 22, no. 1 (February 1993).

115. Mary-Lou Weisman, "When Parents Are Not in the Best Interests of the Child," *Atlantic Monthly*, July 1994.

116. See, e.g., Victor Groze and Daniela Heana, "A Follow-Up Study of Adopted Children from Romania," *Child and Adolescent Social Work Journal* 13, no. 6, at 511 (December 1996); Sharon Marcovitch, Laura Cesaroni, Wendy Roberts, and Cathy Swanson, "Romanian Adoption: Parents' Dreams, Nightmares, and Realities," *Child Welfare* 74, no. 5 (September/October 1995), at 993; Sharon A. Cermak and Lisa A. Daunhauer, "Sensory Processing in the Postinstitutionalized Child," *American Journal of Occupational Therapy* 51, no. 7 (July/August 1997), at 500; Deborah A. Frank, Perri E. Klass, Felton Earls, and Leon Eisenberg, "Infants and Young Children in Orphanages: One View From Pediatrics and Child Psychiatry," *Pediatrics* 97, no. 4 (April 1996), at 569; L. Albers, D. Johnson, M. Hostetter, S. Iverson, and L. Miller, "Health of Children Adopted From the Former Soviet Union and Eastern Europe: Comparison with Pre-Adoptive Medical Records," *Journal of the American Medical Association*, 278, no. 11 (1997), at 922–924; M. Talbot, "Attachment Theory: The Ultimate Experiment," *New York Times Magazine*, May 24, 1998; M. Terwogt, J. Schene, W. Koops, "Concepts of Emotion in Institutionalized Children," *Journal of Child Psychology and Psychiatry* 31, no. 7 (1990), at 1131–1143; "Special Edition: Your Child," *Newsweek*, vol. 129, March 22, 1997, at 6, 28, 38.

117. See, e.g., Rima Shore, *Rethinking the Brain: New Insights Into Early Development* (New York: Families and Work Institute, 1997).

118. See Berrick, *The Tender Years*, at 86.

119. Berrick, *The Tender Years*, at 83.

120. Mark E. Courtney, "The Costs of Child Protection in the Context of Welfare Reform," *The Future of Children, Protecting Children From Abuse and Neglect* 8, no. 1 (Spring 1998), at 88, 93.

121. Robert Karen, *Becoming Attached* (New York: Warner Books, 1994) (see generally and at 440 discussing history of developmental psychology, with changes over the years but consensus on the core essentials of attachment theory).

122. Malcolm Gladwell, "Damaged: Why do some people turn into violent criminals? New evidence suggests that it may all be in the brain," *The New Yorker*, February 24 and March 3, 1997, at 140 [hereafter Gladwell, "Damaged"]; Shore, *Rethinking the Brain*.

123. Gladwell, "Damaged," at 132–140, 142; Lewis D. Mallovic and V. Webb, "Child Abuse, Juvenile Delinquency, and Violent Criminality," in *Child Maltreatment*, ed. D. Cicchetti and V. Carlson (Cambridge: Cambridge University Press, 1989), at 707–721.

124. See Thomas McDonald et al., *Assessing the Long-Term Effects of Foster Care, A Research Synthesis* (Washington, D.C.: Child Welfare League of America, 1996)[hereafter McDonald, *Assessing the Long-Term Effects of Foster Care*], at 132.

125. National Research Council, *Understanding Child Abuse and Neglect* (National Academy Press, 1993), at 223 (about 30 percent). By contrast only 2–4 percent of the general population will maltreat their children. National Research Council, *Violence in Families*, at 46.

126. Deborah Daro, "Child Maltreatment Research," in *Child Abuse, Child Development, and Social Policy, Advances in Applied Developmental Psychology*, vol. 8, ed. Dante Cicchetti and Sheree L. Toth (Norwood, NJ: Ablex Publishing Corporation, 1993) (Minnesota Mother-Child Project, most significant prospective study on cycle of violence, shows that of mothers abused as children, 34 percent abused their children, 6 percent evidenced other problematic parenting behavior, and 30 percent engaged in "borderline caretaking," a total of 70 percent, as compared to the control group in which only one of thirty-five was a maltreating parent); APSAC, *Handbook on Child Maltreatment*, 1996.

127. National Research Council, *Understanding Child Abuse and Neglect*, at 93. See also Daro, *Confronting Child Abuse*, at 53 (of all causal factors of maltreatment, childhood abuse of parent the most consistently cited). See generally Steven Krugman, "Trauma in the Family: Perspectives on the Intergenerational Transmission of Violence," in *Psychological Trauma*, ed. Bessel van der Kolk (Washington, D.C.: American Psychiatric Press, 1987), at 127–151.

128. Gladwell, "Damaged," at 144–145.

129. Jane Waldfogel, *The Future of Child Protection: How to Break the Cycle of Abuse and Neglect* (Cambridge, MA: Harvard University Press, 1998), at 11 and n. 30, citing Wiese and Daro, *Current Trends in Reporting*, 1994, p. 11 (only 5 percent of children reported to CPS are removed from their homes, and only 14 percent of those in substantiated cases of maltreatment) [hereafter Waldfogel, *Future of Child Protection*]. *Violence in Families*, at 106 (1–25% of substantiated cases result in removal).

130. Waldfogel, *Future of Child Protection*, at 51 and nn. 28–30. A court-appointed panel in New York City found that 43 percent of maltreated chil-

dren who entered the child welfare system were again maltreated by their families. *Child Protection Report* 23, no. 22 (October 23, 1997), at 185.

131. See n. 92 above.

132. See Michael Wald, J. M. Carlsmith and P. H. Leiderman, *Protecting Abused and Neglected Children* (Stanford, CA: Stanford University Press, 1988); Richard P. Barth and Marianne Berry, "Implications of Research on the Welfare of Children Under Permanency Planning," in *Child Welfare Review*, vol. 1, ed. Richard Barth, Jill Duerr Berrick, and Neil Gilbert (New York: Columbia University Press, 1994)[hereafter Barth, "Implications of Research on the Welfare of Children"], at 323–68; McDonald, "Assessing the Long-Term Effects of Foster Care," at 67, 137, 149; Michael Bohman and Soren Sigvardsson, "Outcomes in Adoption: Lessons from Longitudinal Studies," in *The Psychology of Adoption,* ed. David Brodzinsky and Marshall D. Schecter (New York: Oxford University Press, 1990), at 93, 100–106; John Triseliotis and Malcolm Hill, "Contrasting Adoption, Foster Care and Residential Rearing," in Brodzinsky and Schecter, eds., *The Psychology of Adoption,* at 107–120; Richard P. Barth and Marianne Berry, *Adoption and Disruption: Rates, Risks and Responses* (Hawthorne: Aldine De Gruyter, 1988), at 23–41; Elizabeth Bartholet, *Family Bonds: Adoption and the Politics of Parenting* (New York: Houghton Mifflin, 1993), at 79 and nn. 31–33 [a new edition, *Family Bonds: Adoption, Infertility, and the New World of Child Production,* is forthcoming from Beacon Press (Fall 1999)]. See also John R. Schuerman and Julia H. Littell, "Problems and Prospects in Society's Response to Abuse and Neglect," The Chapin Hall Center for Children at the University of Chicago, Discussion Paper No. 053, at 95, 59, n. 55 (abuse and neglect recidivism rates ten times higher in original families as compared to foster families). See chapter 8, text at nn. 4, 7–8 and nn. 4, 7–8 for additional studies on adoption adjustment.

133. Barth, "Implications of Research on the Welfare of Children," at 333–34.

134. See, e.g., William Feigelman and Arnold Silverman, *Chosen Children* (New York: Praeger, 1983), at 92–93, and Richard D. Barth et al., "Predicting Adoption Disruptions," *Social Work* 33 (1988), at 227.

CHAPTER 4. UNDERINTERVENTION VS. OVERINTERVENTION

1. Julie Wilson of the John F. Kennedy School of Government prepared a paper addressing these issues for the Executive Session on New Paradigms for Child Protective Services, at the John F. Kennedy School of Government. This Executive Session project focused on the Community Partnership concept, with its emphasis on diverting cases from the CPS system to a community-based system of services. (See chapter 6.) Ms. Wilson concluded that, contrary to the underlying assumption of Community Partnership advocates, only a limited portion of the current CPS caseload could be safely diverted, with one-third to two-thirds continuing to require coercive CPS intervention. She noted further that any reduction in the CPS caseload should depend on whether community agencies had the necessary resources available, and whether they had some coercive authority. See Julie B. Wilson, "Abused and Neglected Children: How Many? How Serious the Maltreatment? What Share Could Be Reached Only Through Coercive Intervention?" paper prepared for the Executive Session: New Paradigms for Child Protective Services, John F. Kennedy School of Government, Harvard University, Cambridge, MA, May 16–18, 1996, at 29–30.

2. See National Research Council and Institute of Medicine, *Violence in Families: Assessing Prevention and Treatment Programs* (Washington, D.C.: National Academy Press, 1998) [hereafter NRCIM, *Violence in Families*], chap. 5, "Legal Interventions," noting the limited use of criminal law and other legal interventions as compared to social service interventions, in cases of child maltreatment, and contrasting this to the treatment of domestic violence.

3. Richard J. Gelles and Murray A. Strauss, *Intimate Violence* (New York: Simon and Schuster, 1988), chap. 2, text at n. 12.

4. See American Bar Association Center on Children and the Law, "The Prosecution of Child Sexual and Physical Abuse Cases" (1993) (disproportionately more sexual abuse prosecutions); and NRCIM, *Violence in Families*, at 160 (increase in legal interventions in sex abuse area since 1980s earns grudging respect by child welfare professionals due to apparent success).

5. U.S. Department of Health and Human Services, Administration for Children and Families, Administration on Children, Youth and Families, National Center on Child Abuse and Neglect, *Executive Summary of the Third National Incidence Study of Child Abuse and Neglect (NIS-3)* (Washington, D.C., September 1996), at 16.

6. The Edna McConnell Clark Foundation Program for Children, "Strategy Statement," March 1996, at 9.

7. National Committee to Prevent Child Abuse (NCPCA), "Current Trends in Child Abuse Reporting and Fatalities: The Results of the 1997 Annual Fifty-State Survey," Chicago, IL, 1998.

8. Diane J. English, "The Extent and Consequences of Child Maltreatment," *The Future of Children, Protecting Children From Abuse and Neglect* 8, no. 1 (Spring 1998), at 49 (40–60 percent of cases).

9. John R. Schuerman, "Best Interests and Family Preservation in America," Discussion Paper, The Chapin Hall Center for Children at the University of Chicago, October 1997, at 6–7.

10. T. Tatara, "Recent Rise in Substitute Care Population," in *Child Welfare Research Review*, vol. 1, ed. Richard Barth, Jill D. Berrick, and Neil Gilbert (New York: Columbia University Press, 1994), at 126, 141. See also chapter 3, text at n. 129 and n. 129 above for percentages of maltreatment cases in which children were removed.

11. Cecilia Zalkind, *Stolen Futures, A Report on Preventing Foster Care Placement in New Jersey*, Association for Children of New Jersey (1994), at 1–3, 5–7, 35.

12. Diego Ribadeneira, "Judge returns 'Andy' to birth parents: Foster couple is denied a goodbye to abused child, 3," *Boston Globe*, October 14, 1992, pp. 1, 20; Sally Jacobs, "Decision on child by DSS decried," *Boston Globe*, September 30, 1992, pp. 20, 26.

13. "Federal Adoption Policy," Hearing before the Subcommittee on Human Resources of the Committee on Ways and Means, House of Representatives, 104th Congress, 1st Session, 5/10/95 [hereafter 5/10/95 Hearing]; "Barriers to Adoption," Hearing before the same Subcommittee, 104th Congress, 2nd Session, 6/27/96 [hereafter 6/27/96 Hearing].

14. 5/10/95 Hearing, at 141.

15. 6/27/96 Hearing, at 27, 33.

16. 6/27/96 Hearing, at 33.

17. 6/27/96 Hearing, at 59, 61.

18. John McCormick, "Chicago Hope: Exclusive: How a judge bucked the system by putting children first," *Newsweek*, March 24, 1997, at 68.

19. See chapter 3, text at n. 130 and n. 130 above. See generally Michael Wald and Sophia Cohen, "Preventing Child Abuse," *Family Law Quarterly*, no. 2 (Summer 1986).

20. Ibid, at 281, n. 1 (little research indicating any prevention services programs work except intensive home visitation programs of kind discussed in chapter 7 below; parenting skill programs in particular show little likelihood of working).

21. Anne Harris Cohn and Deborah Daro, "Is Treatment Too Late: What Ten Years of Evaluative Research Tell Us," *Child Abuse and Neglect* 11 (1987), at 433–442, 440, 87.

22. NCRIM, *Violence in Families*, at 105–106, 118–119, 292.

23. See, e.g., Wald and Woolverton, "Risk Assessment: The Emperor's New Clothes?" *Child Welfare* 69, no. 6 (November/December 1990), at 503ff (family preservation services might be most appropriate for families most amenable to change, whereas in the most serious cases of abuse the children might benefit from foster placement and parental rights termination, rather than services).

24. Robert M. Goerge, Fred H. Wulczyn, and Allen W. Harden, *An Update from the Multistate Foster Care Data Archive: Foster Care Dynamics 1983–*

1994 (Chicago, IL: Chapin Hall Center for Children at the University of Chicago, 1997); R. P. Barth et al., *From Child Abuse to Permanency Planning: Child Welfare Services Pathways and Placements* (Hawthorne, NY: Aldine deGruyter, 1994), at 154 (less than 10 percent of children in foster care are adopted per year, while roughly 50–65 percent are reunified with their families, and others are relegated to continued foster care).

CHAPTER 5. TRADITIONAL PROGRAMS WEATHER THE STORM

1. See, e.g., Jacquelyn McCroskey and William Meezan, "Family- Centered Services: Approaches and Effectiveness," *The Future of Children, Protecting Children From Abuse and Neglect* 8, no. 1 (Spring 1998), at 54, 62–63: "Workers usually carry caseloads of only two to six families at a time, see families from 4 to 20 hours per week, and can be reached by the family 24 hours per day. Families are almost always seen in their homes, on a flexible schedule designed to encourage participation by all family members."
2. Andrew Gottesman and Cameron McWhirter, "In the end, everyone failed Joseph," in the series, "Killing our children. 16 Dead in 1993," *Chicago Tribune*, April 20, 1993, North Sports Final Edition, p. 1.; Margaret Lowrie, "Chicago Asking Questions About Death of Young Boy," *CNN News*, Transcript no. 344–2, April 22, 1993; Andrew Gottesman and Cameron McWhirter, "Report: System Doomed Joseph," in the series, "Killing our children. 55 Dead in 1993," *Chicago Tribune*, October 27, 1993, North Sports Final Edition, p. 1; Bob Greene, "'It Doesn't Matter Joseph,'" *Chicago Tribune*, October 31, 1993, Final Edition, p. 1.
3. See Rachel Swarms, "3 Years After a Girl's Murder, 5 Siblings Lack Stable Homes," *New York Times*, August 4, 1998, New York Region, Late Edition, p. A1; Nina Bernstein and Frank Bruni, "Seven Warnings: She Suffered in Plain Sight, But Alarms Were Ignored," *New York Times*, December 24, 1995.
4. New York State Commission on Child Abuse, "Report to Governor Pataki," November 22, 1996, at 4.
5. Marcia Robinson Lowry, "2 Commentary," "Four Commentaries: How We Can Better Protect Children from Abuse and Neglect," *The Future of Children, Protecting Children From Abuse and Neglect* 8, no. 1 (Spring 1998), at 123, 124. See also Nina Bernstein, "Almost a Fatality," *New York Times*, December 14, 1995, Late Edition, p. B12 ("When the police found her last May, the child, called Marisol in the lawsuit . . . was a starving 4-year-old, naked beneath a urine-soaked sheet. Her front teeth had been knocked out, her feet scalded, her body covered by bruises and cigar burns. One leg bone was splintered, large clumps of her hair were missing, and she had been sexually abused.")

6. Patrick T. Murphy, *Wasted: The Plight of America's Unwanted Children* (Chicago: Ivan R. Dee, 1997), at 13, 181.

7. See, e.g., Carol S. Bevan, *Too Little, Too Early, Too Late* (1996), sponsored by the National Council for Adoption.

8. See Introduction, n. 6 above, discussing Hear My Voice and Kids Help.

9. See, e.g., Francine Jacobs, "Calling a Truce: Family Preservation Services and Evaluation," in *Evaluating Family Preservation Services: A Guide for State Administrators*, ed. Francice Jacobs et al., forthcoming (1999) (describes Wave 1 of IFPS research, characterized by inadequate success criteria and no controls, followed by Wave 2, characterized by more extensive success criteria and controls, and showing no success on any criteria, and notes that Wave 3 consists of major reputable studies that are now in progress); Kathleen Wells and Elizabeth Tracy, "Reorienting Intensive Family Preservation Services in Relation to Public Child Welfare Practice," *Child Welfare* 75, no. 6 (1996), at 667–692 (reviews research, finding no success in preventing placement demonstrated, and notes that only studies that assessed the impact on children's safety found no differences between IFPS and regular child welfare services programs); Julia H. Littell, John R. Schuerman, and Amy Chak, "What Works Best for Whom in Family Preservation? Relationships Between Service Characteristics and Outcomes for Selected Subgroups of Families," Discussion Paper No. 054, Chapin Hall Center for Children at the University of Chicago, November 1994 (family preservation programs providing increased services in Illinois had no impact on placement rates or subsequent maltreatment rates); National Research Council and Institute of Medicine, *Violence in Families: Assessing Prevention and Treatment Programs* (Washington, D.C.: National Academy Press, 1998) [hereafter NRCIM, *Violence in Families*], 105–106, 119, 303 (major review of all social science research in area finds little evidence of IFPS programs reducing placement or improving child welfare); William Meezan and Jacquelyn McCroskey, "Improving Family Functioning Through Family Preservation Services: Results of the LA Experiment," *Family Preservation Journal* 1, no. 2 (1996) (finding no differences between experimental and control groups in removal rates, and that, while caseworkers and families believed services produced modest improvements in the family's functioning, these apparent changes were not sustained over time).

Julia H. Littell and John A. Schuerman, *A Synthesis of Research on Family Preservation and Family Reunification Programs*, a report prepared for the U.S. Dept. of Health and Human Services as part of the National Evaluation of Family Preservation Services (Washington, D.C., 1995), pulls together the research to date for purposes of a major national evaluation of family preservation being conducted by Chapin Hall, Westat, Inc., and James Bell and Associates. The review concludes that that there is no evidence that family *preservation* programs reduce placement or maltreatment rates, although they may produce modest, short-term improvements in some aspects of the child's and the family's functioning. It concludes that the very limited research on family *reunification* programs includes few controlled studies, and leaves it unclear whether intensive services programs increase the rates at which children return home, lessen the chance of the child subsequently being maltreated, or reduce the risk of the child reentering foster care. Tina Rzepnicki, John Schuerman, and Penny Johnson, "Facing Uncertainty: Reuniting High-Risk Families," in *Child Welfare Research Review*, vol. 2, ed. J. D. Berrick et al. (New York: Columbia University Press, 1997), reviews programs that provide special services designed to promote reunification and finds limited evidence that they are successful in inducing more reunification, noting a 30 percent reentry rate after two years of reunification, which is no better than the general reentry rate.

10. Peter H. Rossi, *Evaluating Family Preservation Programs: A Report to The Edna McConnell Clark Foundation* (1991). Rossi challenged the emphasis on placement prevention and expressed skepticism about the assumptions underlying IFPS programs that family preservation would promote children's well-being. Clark's then president, Peter Bell, expressed his own limited enthusiasm for Rossi's conclusions in a foreword to the report, noting that while helping children and families in outcome terms (as measured, e.g., by maltreatment rates) was of course part of the IFPS goal, another real goal was simply to change policy so as to keep families together. See also Rossi, "Strategies for Evaluation," in *Reforming Child Welfare through Demonstration and Evaluation*, ed. Douglas Besharov et al. (Tarrytown, NY: Pergamon Press, 1992) (research should shift from the focus on placement rates to a focus on child and family outcomes).

11. Chapter 3, text at n. 130 and n. 130.

12. See n. 9 above. See also Richard P. Barth, "The Juvenile Court and Dependency Cases," *The Future of Children, The Juvenile Court* 6, no. 3 (1996), at 100, 103 (Illinois IFPS program had 39 percent substantiated child abuse report rate and 32 percent reentry rate within two years).

13. Richard J. Gelles, *The Book of David: How Preserving Families Can Cost Children's Lives* (New York: Basic Books, 1996), at 126–127, 148 [hereafter Gelles, *The Book of David*]; Wells and Tracy, "Reorienting Intensive Family Preservation Services"; NRCIM, Violence in Families, at 105, 108. Ironically, as this critique has been mounted, some IFPS programs have actually *reduced* the period of services to a mere four weeks. R. P. Barth et al., *From Child Abuse to Permanency Planning: Child Welfare Services Pathways and Placements* (Hawthorne, NY: Aldine deGruyter, 1994), at 265.

14. Clark Foundation consultant Peter Rossi pointed this out in his 1992

"Strategies for Evaluation," noting that placements might well be reduced given that a placement moratorium is part of the program protocol.

15. See Massachusetts Special Commission on Foster Care, Final Report, vol. 1 (February 1993), at 121–122 (family preservation structured so that service providers have incentive not to report abuse and neglect, because if child removed will count as a failure); NRCIM, *Violence in Families*, at 303 (IFPS may result in child endangerment).

16. Gelles, *The Book of David*, at 127.

17. This was passed as part of the Omnibus Budget Reconciliation Act of 1993, Pub. L. 103–66, 107 Stat. 312, 649.

18. See chapter 1, text at n. 20 and n. 20. The 1993 legislation had required an evaluation of family preservation, which should be available by the time this new funding expires.

19. The Federal Personal Responsibility and Work Opportunity Act of 1996, Pub. L. 105–33, amending 42 U.S.C., §671(a).

20. I have told much of the story summarized in this section in more detail in Elizabeth Bartholet, "Where Do Black Children Belong? The Politics of Race Matching in Adoption," *University of Pennsylvania Law Review* 139 (1991), at 1163 [hereafter "Where Do Black Children Belong?"]; "Race Separatism in the Family: More on the Transracial Adoption Debate," *Duke Journal of Gender Law and Policy* 2 (Spring 1995), at 99 [hereafter "Race Separatism in the Family"]; "Private Race Preferences in Family Formation," *Yale Law Journal* 107 (May 1998), at 2351 [hereafter "Private Race Preferences"]; written testimony at hearing on Implementation of the 1996 Interethnic Adoption Amendments to the Multi-Ethnic Placement Act of 1994, before the Subcommittee on Human Resources of the Committee on Ways and Means, U.S. House of Representatives, September 15, 1998 [hereafter MEPA Implementation Hearing].

21. The Indian Child Welfare Act (ICWA) of 1978, Pub. L. 95–608, 92 Stat. 3069, 25 U.S.C. 1901, Section 102(f) ("No termination of parental rights may be ordered in such proceeding in the absence of a determination, supported by evidence beyond a reasonable doubt, including testimony of qualified expert witnesses, that the custody of the child by the parent or Indian custodian is likely to result in serious emotional or physical damage to the child.") See also Section 102(e) ("No foster care placement may be ordered in such proceeding in the absence of a determination, supported by clear and convincing evidence, including testimony of qualified expert witnesses, that the continued custody of the child by the parent or Indian custodian is likely to result in serious emotional or physical damage to the child.")

22. See Sonya Witt, "Failing Indian Children: The Indian Child Welfare Act in Practice" (Harvard Law School, 1994), at 23 and nn. 65, 67 (on file with author).

23. *60 Minutes*, "Simple as Black and White," CBS News, October 25, 1992.

24. See Bartholet, "Where Do Black Children Belong?" at 1191–1193.

25. See, e.g., Richard Barth, "Effects of Age and Race on the Odds of Adoption Vs. Remaining in Out-of-Home Care," *Child Welfare* (March/April 1997), at 285–308 (black children in out-of-home care in California four times less likely to be adopted, with race the only factor explaining differential rate); Bartholet, "Where Do Black Children Belong?" at 1201–1206.

26. See, e.g., Bartholet, "Where Do Black Children Belong?" documenting the nature and impact of race-matching policies, summarizing the social science findings, and analyzing the applicable law. This article helped trigger significant debate in the legal and the political arenas. See R. Richard Banks, "The Color of Desire: Fulfilling Adoptive Parents' Racial Preferences Through Discriminatory State Action," *Yale Law Journal* 107 (1998), at 987.

27. See, e.g., Elizabeth Bartholet, "In foster-care limbo," Op-Ed, *Boston Globe*, March 17, 1992, p. 17, col. 1.; Bartholet, "Adoption is about family, not race," *Chicago Tribune*, November 9, 1993, p. 23; "Adopting across racial lines," Editorials, *Boston Globe*, Friday, March 18, 1994, p. 12; "Equal-opportunity adoptions," Editorials, *Boston Globe*, Thursday, April 21, 1994, p. 18; Randall Kennedy, "Let love, not color be the key to adoption," Op-Ed, *Boston Sunday Globe*, July 21, 1996, p. C2; Randall Kennedy, "Kids Need Parents—Of Any Race," *Wall Street Journal*, November 9, 1992, p. A18; "All in the Family," Editorial, *New Republic*, January 24, 1994, pp. 6–7.

28. See, e.g., Heidi Durrow, "Mothering Across the Color Line: White Women, 'Black Babies,'" *Yale Journal of Law and Feminism* 7 (1995), at 227.

29. Kirsten Albrecht, a biracial transracial adoptee, founded this organization, located in Los Angeles, California.

30. Bartholet, "Race Separatism in the Family," at 102–103.

31. Written testimony of Professor Richard P. Barth, The University of North Carolina at Chapel Hill School of Social Work, before the Subcommittee on Human Resources of the Committee on Ways and Means, U.S. House of Representatives, September 15, 1998, citing R. P. Barth, D. Brooks, and S. Iyer, *Adoption Demographics in California* (Berkeley, CA: University of California at Berkeley, School of Social Welfare, Child Welfare Resource Center, 1996), and D. Brooks and R. P. Barth, "Parental Preferences for Adoptable Children and Agency Responses to Those Preferences," unpublished manuscript available from the authors.

32. See generally for arguments rebutting the claims of same-race placement advocates, Bartholet, "Race Separatism in the Family," and "Private Race Preferences."

33. See the Howard M. Metzenbaum Multiethnic Placement Act of 1994, 42 U.S.C. §§622(b)(9), 5115a, Pub. L. No. 103–382, §§551–554, 108 Stat. 4056, as amended by the Removal of Barriers to Interethnic Adoption Provisions of the Small Business Job Protection Act of 1996, 42 U.S.C. §§671, 674, 1996b, Pub. L. 104–188, §1808, 110 Stat. 1903.

34. The Removal of Barriers to Interethnic Adoption Provisions of the Small Business Job Protection Act of 1996, 42 U.S.C. §§671, 674, 1996b, Pub. L. 104–188, §1808, 110 Stat. 1903.

35. *In re: Bridget R.*, 41 Cal. App. 4th 1483, 49 Cal. Rptr. 2d 507 (1996), cert. denied, 117 S.Ct. 1460 (1997).

36. The National Committee for Adoption has been active in these efforts.

37. Administration on Children, Youth and Families, "Information Memorandum: Guidance for Federal Legislation—The Small Business Job Protection Act of 1996 (P. L. 104–88), Section 1808, "Removal of Barriers to Interethnic Adoption," ACYF-1M-CB-97–04, at 4 (U.S. Department of Health and Human Services, Washington, D.C., June 5, 1997).

38. Administration on Children, Youth and Families, "Information Memorandum: Information on Implementation of Federal Legislation—Questions and Answers that Clarify the Practice and Implementation of Section 471(a)(18) of title IV-E of the Social Security Act," ACYF-1M-CB-98–03 (U.S. Department of Health and Human Services, Washington, D.C., May 11, 1998), at 22.

39. See Bartholet, "Where Do Black Children Belong?" at 1183–1200 for detailed description of race-matching policies.

40. See, e.g., Ruth G. McRoy, Zena Oglesby, and Helen Grape, "Achieving Same-Race Placements for African-American Children: Culturally Sensitive Practice Approaches," *Child Welfare* 76, no. 1 (1997), at 85–104; Leslie Doty Hollingsworth, "Promoting Same-Race Adoption for Children of Color," *Social Work* 43, no. 2 (March 1998), at 106.

41. Howard M. Metzenbaum, Multiethnic Placement Act of 1994, 42 U.S.C. §622(b)(9), Pub. L. 103–382, §552, 108 Stat. 4056.

42. The North American Council on Adoptable Children, with support from The Annie E. Casey Foundation, "Shortening Children's Stays: Innovative Permanency Planning Programs," (April 1997).

43. The Stuart Foundations, Report by the Adoption and Race Work Group, "Adoption and Race: Implementing the Multiethnic Placement Act of 1994 and the Interethnic Adoption Provisions" (1997).

44. Letter from Elizabeth Bartholet to Richard P. Barth, June 27, 1996, on file with the author.

45. See chapter 3, text at n. 99 and n. 99.

46. See James Breay, "Who Are the Waiting Children?" Office of Field Support Services, Massachusetts Department of Social Services (1991).

47. MEPA Implementation Hearing, supra n. 20.
48. Written testimony of Kirsten Albrecht, Esq., President, Transracial Adoption Group, MEPA Implementation Hearing.
49. Written testimony of Patrick T. Murphy, Cook County Public Guardian, MEPA Implementation Hearing.
50. Written testimony of Professor Randall Kennedy, Harvard Law School, MEPA Implementation Hearing.
51. Organizations that have been active opposing racial barriers include the National Council for Adoption (NCFA) in Washington, D.C., and the National Committee to End Racism in America's Child Care System, Inc., in Taylor, Michigan. NCFA is a nonprofit organization whose membership includes adoption agencies and adoption professionals, which has been active in various advocacy efforts. The National Committee is a small nonprofit with limited resources, organized by foster parents, which has helped educate foster parents and others as to their legal rights to challenge racial barriers to adoption. The American Civil Liberties Union, the Public Interest Law Center in Philadelphia, PA, and the Institute for Justice in Washington, D.C., have handled lawsuits challenging racial matching policies. Numerous law professors, lawyers, social scientists, foster and adoptive parents, and other interested individuals, have given their support to the effort to eliminate racial barriers in adoption by testifying in connection with state and federal legislative efforts, testifying as experts in court proceedings, and engaging in various forms of advocacy.

CHAPTER 6. "NEW" PROGRAMS PROMOTE TRADITIONAL IDEAS

1. U.S. Advisory Board on Child Abuse and Neglect, "Neighbors Helping Neighbors: A New National Strategy for the Protection of Children," Washington, D.C., 1993, at 30–31, 39.
2. American Humane Association (AHA), *Protecting Children* 12, no. 3 (1996).
3. AHA, Children's Division, with the support of The Edna McConnell Clark Foundation, 1997.
4. AHA, Children's Division, 1997 Roundtable Series of conferences held in California, Michigan, and Pennsylvania.
5. See, e.g., "Children and Families in Crisis," in *The State of America's Children, Yearbook 1997* (Washington, D.C.: The Children's Defense Fund, 1997), at 57–58.
6. See Mark Hardin, "Family Group Conferences in Child Abuse and Neglect Cases: Learning from the Experience of New Zealand," ABA Center on Children and the Law (1996), at 3; author's telephone conversation with Mark Hardin, January 28, 1999.

7. AHA, "Family Group Decision Making: Assessing the Promise and Implementing the Practice," November 3–4, 1997, Philadelphia, PA.

8. See, e.g., reports cited in nn. 2–4 above. A randomized controlled trial of FGDM outcomes is planned in the United Kingdom, with dissemination of results scheduled for the fall of 2001. AHA, *Protecting Children* 14, no. 4 (1998), at 33.

9. See generally The Center for the Study of Social Policy for The Edna McConnell Clark Foundation, "Community Partnerships for Protecting Children: The Initiative's Theory of Change" (October 1996), at 3.

10. The Edna McConnell Clark Foundation, "Program for Children, Strategy Statement" (March 1996).

11. National Conference of State Legislatures, "New Directions for Child Protection Services: Supporting Children, Families and Communities Through Legislative Reform" (1997).

12. Jane Waldfogel, "Rethinking the Paradigm for Child Protection," *The Future of Children, Protecting Children From Abuse and Neglect* 8, no. 1 (Spring 1998), at 104 (describing implementation in Missouri, Florida, and Iowa). See also Jane Waldfogel, *The Future of Child Protection: How to Break the Cycle of Abuse and Neglect* (Cambridge, MA: Harvard University Press, 1998)(promoting community partnerships as the new paradigm for child protection) [hereafter Waldfogel, *Future of Child Protection*].

13. See Sidney Gardner and Nancy K. Young, "The Implications of Alcohol and Other Drug-related Problems for Community-wide Family Support Systems," and Julie B. Wilson, "Abused and Neglected Children: How Many? How Serious the Maltreatment? What Share Could Be Reached Only Through Coercive Intervention?" (both papers prepared for the Executive Session meeting, John F. Kennedy School of Government, Harvard University, Cambridge, MA, May 16–18, 1996).

14. Frank Farrow, "Child Protection: Building Community Partnerships, Getting From Here to There," The Executive Session on Child Protection, John F. Kennedy School of Government, Harvard University, Cambridge, MA (1997) [hereafter Farrow, "Child Protection: Building Community Partnerships"], at 38–39.

15. Mary B. Larner, Carol S. Stevenson, and Richard E. Behrman, "Protecting Children from Abuse and Neglect: Analysis and Recommendations," *The Future of Children, Protecting Children From Abuse and Neglect* 8, no. 12 (Spring 1998), at 11; Waldfogel, "Rethinking the Paradigm for Child Protection," at 113; Waldfogel, *Future of Child Protection*, at 150.

16. Richard P. Barth, "The Juvenile Court and Dependency Cases," *The Future of Children, The Juvenile Court* (Winter 1996), at 100, 101.

17. Farrow, "Child Protection: Building Community Partnerships," at 36.

18. See Introduction, text at n. 2 and n. 2, above.

CHAPTER 7. INTERVENING EARLY WITH HOME VISITATION

1. See U. S. Dept. Of Health and Human Services, Administration for Children and Families, U.S. Advisory Board on Child Abuse and Neglect, "Recommendations for Change IIIG," in *Creating Caring Communities: Blueprint for an Effective Federal Policy on Child Abuse and Neglect, 2nd Report* (Washington, D.C., September 15, 1991), at 141–146. See also U.S. Advisory Board on Child Abuse and Neglect, "Neighbors Helping Neighbors" (Washington, D.C., 1993), at 68 (supporting universal home visitation). C. Henry Kempe, whose work on the "battered child syndrome" was largely responsible for reviving interest in the maltreatment problem in an earlier era, had also recommended universal health visitation. See Jane D. Gray, Christy A. Cutler, Janet G. Dean, and C. Henry Kempe, "Prediction and Prevention of Child Abuse and Neglect," *Journal of Social Issues* 35, no. 2 (1979). On home visiting generally, see "Home Visiting," *The Future of Children* 3, no. 3, (Winter 1993) [hereafter *Home Visiting, The Future of Children*].
2. National Committee to Prevent Child Abuse (NCPCA), "Current Trends in Child Abuse Reporting and Fatalities: The Results of the 1997 Annual Fifty-State Survey" (Chicago, IL, 1998).
3. The Massachusetts Children Trust Fund helped achieve passage of legislation providing for a $5 million home visiting program for all first-time teenage mothers with newborns, starting in 1998. Doris Sue Wong, "Welcome Visits: $5m Program Aims to Help Teenage New Parents Cope," *Boston Globe*, February 27, 1998, p. B1.
4. See generally U.S. General Accounting Office, Report to the Chairman, Subcommittee on Labor, Health and Human Services, Education, and Related Agencies, Committee on Appropriations, U.S. Senate, *Home Visiting: A Promising Early Intervention Strategy for at-Risk Families* (Washington, D.C., 1990), at 18 and throughout (describing universal home visitation systems for new parents in Great Britain and Denmark, noting similar programs in a number of other countries in Europe and Scandinavia, and pointing out that number of visits varies and is often quite limited); see also Sheila B. Kamerman and Alfred J. Kahn, "Home Health Visiting in Europe," in *Home Visiting, The Future of Children*, at 39.
5. Deborah Daro, Research Director, National Committee to Prevent Child Abuse, divides families into three categories for purposes of thinking about home visitation's potential: consumer families, which are capable on their own of taking advantage of the many services available in the community; dependent families, which are not, but can be helped by home visitation and other active outreach programs; and broken families, which may be beyond the reach of even such outreach. Daro, "Child Maltreatment Research: Implications for Program Design," in *Child Abuse, Child Develop-*

ment and Social Policy: Advances in Applied Developmental Psychology, vol.
8, ed. Dante Cicchetti and Sheree L. Toth (Norwood, NJ: 1993), at 331, 356–
361 [hereafter Daro, "Child Maltreatment Research"].

6. National Research Council and Institute of Medicine, *Violence in Families: Assessing Prevention and Treatment Programs* (National Academy
Press, 1998) [hereafter NRCIM, *Violence in Families*], at 222 (calling home
visitation "one of the most promising interventions for prevention of child
abuse or neglect"). See generally at 220–223, 301–303, assessing all the
home visitation research.

7. *Intensive Home Visitation: A Randomized Trial, Follow-up and Risk Assessment Study of Hawaii's Healthy Start Program, Final Report* (June 15, 1996)
[hereafter *Intensive Home Visitation, Final Report*], at viii, xi. An earlier report on the 1987–91 results indicated that among the high-risk families in
the Healthy Start program, confirmed rates of abuse and neglect were 1.9
percent, whereas the comparable rate for the at-risk family group not
served by Healthy Start was 5.0, with the actual rate in the families not
served probably much higher than this reported rate. Ralph B. Earle, "Helping To Prevent Child Abuse—and Future Criminal Consequences: Hawaii
Healthy Start," National Institute of Justice, Program Focus (October
1995), at 9.

8. David L. Olds et al., "Long-term Effects of Home Visitation on Maternal
Life Course and Child Abuse and Neglect, Fifteen Year Follow-up of a Randomized Trial," *Journal of the American Medical Association* 278, no. 8 (August 27, 1997) [hereafter Olds, "Long-term Effects of Home Visitation"], at
637–643.

9. David L. Olds et al., "Long-term Effects of Nurse Home Visitation on
Children's Criminal and Antisocial Behavior, 15 Year Follow-up of a Randomized Controlled Trial," *Journal of the American Medical Association*
280, no. 14 (October 14, 1998), at 1238ff.

10. Harriet Kitzman, David Olds, et al., "Effect of Prenatal and Infancy
Home Visitation by Nurses on Pregnancy, Outcomes, Childhood Injuries,
and Repeated Childbearing, A Randomized Controlled Trial," *Journal of
the American Medical Association* 278, no. 8 (August 27, 1997), at 644–652.

11. See Olds and Kitzman, "Review of Research in Home Visiting for Pregnant Women and Parents of Young Children," in *Home Visiting, The Future
of Children,* at 53; Neil B. Guterman, "Early Prevention of Physical Child
Abuse and Neglect: Existing Evidence and Future Direction," *Child Maltreatment* 2, no. 1 (February 1997)[hereafter Guterman, "Early Prevention
of Physical Child Abuse and Neglect"], at 12–34 (home visitation may serve
to monitor, and thus increase maltreatment reports, as a result of its very
effectiveness).

12. One estimate says the cost of providing the kind of intensive home visi-

tation services involved in Olds's Elmira program for all of the 4.2 million children born each year would be as much as $9.2 billion for just the first year of visits. Another estimate indicates that it would cost $7800 per family to provide the full five years of service involved in Hawaii's Healthy Start Program. See Deanna S. Gomby, Carol S. Larson, Eugene M. Lewit, and Richard E. Behrman, "Home Visiting: Analysis and Recommendations," in *Home Visiting, The Future of Children*, at 6, 19, 13.

13. Olds, "Long-term Effects of Home Visitation," at 642.

14. See W. Steven Barnett, "Economic Evaluation of Home Visiting Programs," in *Home Visiting, The Future of Children*, at 93, 104–105 (concluding Olds's estimate of cost savings is conservative, at least for programs targeting low-income families). Olds is engaged in a follow-up cost benefit analysis which will include savings related to reduction in family size, use of welfare, incidence of child abuse and neglect, and maternal criminality fifteen years after the birth of the first child. Olds, "Long-term Effects of Home Visitation," at 642. See also Deborah Daro, *Confronting Child Abuse: Research for Effective Program Design* (New York: Free Press, 1998) [hereafter Daro, *Confronting Child Abuse*], at 149 (arguing that compared to current intervention efforts after child maltreatment has occurred early intervention is cost effective).

15. See Daro, *Confronting Child Abuse*, at 145 (noting tension between universal home visitation and family autonomy tradition in the United States).

16. See Daro, "Child Maltreatment Research." See n. 5 above.

17. During a presentation in early 1997 on home visiting, Daro discussed the difficulty of engaging the highest risk families, noting that programs were able to get some to cooperate, but not enough; about 5 percent of the families that are offered services refuse outright, while many others initially participate, then drop out. Conference on "Responding to Child Maltreatment," San Diego, California, January 29, 1997. See also *Intensive Home Visitation, Final Report*, at xiii (noting that a sizeable number of potential participants never fully engaged in Healthy Start services, calling this a problem endemic to the prevention field).

18. But see Hillary Rodham Clinton, *It Takes A Village and Other Lessons Children Teach Us* (New York: Simon & Schuster, 1996), at 81 ("While Healthy Start operates on a consensual basis, states might also consider making public welfare or medical benefits contingent on agreement to allow home visits or to participate in other forms of parent education.")

19. Robert Halpern, "The Societal Context of Home Visiting and Related Services for Families in Poverty," in *Home Visiting, The Future of Children* [hereafter Halpern, "The Societal Context of Home Visiting"], at 158, 165.

20. Daro, "Child Maltreatment Research," at 359–361 (these families exhibit extreme disorganization, substance abuse, and violent behavior; they have

been very poor candidates for prevention and treatment services, so they may not be helped by home visitation).

21. NCRIM, *Violence in Families*, at 302. See also Guterman, "Early Prevention of Physical Child Abuse and Neglect," whose review of all home visitation research indicates that it is better not to limit visitation to high-risk families, since this might exclude those most apt to benefit from support services and include those least likely to. Robert Halpern questions the ability of home visiting to transform what he calls "multiply vulnerable families" living in an "extremely depleted, socially isolated community." Robert Halpern, "The Societal Context of Home Visiting and Related Services for Families in Poverty," in *Home Visiting, The Future of Children*, at 165, 168.

22. Craig T. Ramey and Sharon Landesman Ramey, "Home Visiting Programs and the Health and Development of Young Children," in *Home Visiting, The Future of Children*, at 129, 133; Richard P. Barth, "An Experimental Evaluation of In-Home Child Abuse Prevention Services," *Child Abuse & Neglect* 15 (1991), at 363–375. See also evaluations discussed at the Workshop on Revisiting Home Visiting, sponsored by the Board on Children, Youth, and Families, National Research Council/Institute of Medicine, March 8–9, 1999, Washington, D.C., discussed in *Home Visiting: Recent Program Evaluations, The Future of Children* 9, no. 1 (Spring/Summer 1999) (concluding that only David Olds's programs have demonstrated through adequate research the impact on child maltreatment).

23. See chapter 4, text at n. 21 and n. 21, and chapter 5, text at nn. 9, 11–12 and nn. 9, 11–12.

24. Olds's own program experienced this kind of dilution in the transition from a model demonstration program to a community services program administered by local government agencies. See NCRIM, *Violence in Families*, at 221.

25. These pressures may be reflected in the debate within the field over whether home visitors should be health care or child welfare professionals, or should instead be paraprofessionals selected from within the community to be served. Paraprofessionals may save costs, and they are often seen as more capable than professional outsiders of working closely and empathically with parents in their own communities. But professional outsiders may be more capable of sticking to the goals defined by their training, and their professional distance may enable them to better perform both the support and the surveillance aspects of their job.

CHAPTER 8. TAKING ADOPTION SERIOUSLY

1. The U.S. Department of Health and Human Services reports that adoptions increased from 1996 to 1997 by more than 10 percent, from 27,761 to

31,031, still leaving more than 100,000 children identified as waiting for adoption <http://www.acf.dhhs/gov/programs/cb/special/ado-pincen.htm> (1999). See also North American Council on Adoptable Chldren, *Adoptalk*, Winter 1999, at 1 (projecting adoptions of at least 36,000 children in 1998).

2. Written Testimony of Olivia A. Golden, Assistant Secretary for Children and Families, U.S. Department of Health and Human Services, before the Subcommittee on Human Resources Committee on Ways and Means, United States House of Representatives, Washington, D.C., September 15, 1998, at 3–4; Madelyn Freundlich, "Supply and Demand: The Forces Shaping the Future of Infant Adoption," *Adoption Quarterly* 2, no. 1 (1998), at 37.

3. See chapter 3, above, text at nn. 132–134 and nn. 132–134.

4. See, e.g., Elizabeth Bartholet, *Family Bonds: Adoption & The Politics of Parenting* (Boston: Houghton Mifflin, 1993) [hereafter Bartholet, *Family Bonds*], at 174–181 (a new edition, *Family Bonds: Adoption, Infertility, and the New World of Child Production,* is forthcoming from Beacon Press); Peter Benson, Anu R. Sharma, Eugene C. Roehlkepartain, *Growing Up Adopted: A Portrait of Adolescents & Their Families* (Minneapolis, MN: Search Institute, 1994); "Research Literature Survey, Adoption: Long Term Outcomes," *Adoption Access* 1, no. 3 (1998), at 1–2. Two more recent studies confirm the earlier findings. See Barbara Maugham, Stephan Collishaw, and Andrew Pickles, "School Achievement and Adult Qualifications Among Adoptees: A Longitudinal Study," *Journal of Child Psychology and Psychiatry* 39, no. 5 (1998), at 669–685 (those in adopted group do better on educational measures than group raised by birth parents and do comparably with general population group); see DiAnne Borders, Lynda K. Black, and B. Kay Pasley, "Are Adopted Children and Their Parents at Greater Risk for Negative Outcomes," *Family Relations* 47, no. 3 (1998), at 237–241 (those in adopted group do comparably with matched control group from general population on variety of measures of satisfaction, well-being and behavior).

5. See, e.g., Edwin J. Delattre, "Victims to Victimizers," in *When Drug Addicts Have Children,* ed. Douglas Besharov (Washington, D.C.: Child Welfare League of America, 1994), at 65 (impact on children of drug-abusing parents, devastated neighborhoods so great, and absence of parenting during early childhood so destructive of ability to become person capable of empathy and civilized conduct, that long-term group homes best solution for many); Richard B. McKenzie, ed., *Rethinking Orphanages for the 21st Century: A Search for Reform of the Nation's Child Welfare System,* published by the Center of the American Experiment (Thousand Oaks, CA: Sage Publications, 1998) (resurgence of orphanages or group homes likely because many children hard to place or unavailable for placement).

6. See chapter 9, text at nn. 14–16 and nn. 14–16 below.

7. See Elizabeth Bartholet, "International Adoption: Overview," chapter 10 in *Adoption Law and Practice* (New York: Matthew Bender, 1998), Suppl. 1998, at 10–16 to 10–18 and nn. 17–19.

8. See n. 4, above; William Feigelman and Arnold Silverman, *Chosen Children* (New York: Praeger, 1983), at 92–93. See also Rebecca Helgeson, "The Brain Game," *Adoptive Families*, July/Aug 1997 (discussing negative impact on brain of neglect as comparable to orphanage experience, in terms of intellectual and emotional damage, together with evidence that good nurturing in adoptive home can help children recover, and concluding that adoption by age 4–6 months key).

9. U.S. State Department, Bureau of Consular Affairs, "Immigrant Visas Issued to Orphans Coming to the U.S.," Fiscal Year 1998 (Washington, D.C.) (15,774 intercountry adoptions in U.S. in 1998). <http://travel.state.gov/orphans_numbers.html>, at 2.

10. *Vital Health Statistics, Fertility, Family Planning, and Women's Health: New Data from the 1995 National Survey of Family Growth*, U.S. Dept. of Health and Human Services, May 1977, at 4, 7 [hereafter *1995 National Survey*].

11. Ibid, at 8.

12. See generally Bartholet, *Family Bonds*.

13. An important national survey of women conducted in 1987 reveals white and black women adopting at similar rates overall (1.8 and 1.5 percent, respectively), but at significantly different rates when adoption is broken down between related and unrelated adoptions, with blacks adopting a related child at a higher rate (0.6 compared with 0.2 percent), and whites adopting an unrelated child at a higher rate (1.4 as compared with 0.8 percent). Christine A. Bachrach, Patricia Adams, Soledad Sambrano, and Kathryn A. London, "Adoption in the 1980's," *Advance Data*, Vital Health Statistics of the National Center for Health Statistics, no. 181 (January 5, 1990), at 4. A more recent survey shows that of women age 18 to 44, 0.9 percent of whites have ever adopted, as compared to 1 percent of blacks. The percentages of those "currently seeking to adopt" are 0.7 percent for whites and 1.8 percent for blacks; the percentages of those who have actually applied to an agency are 0.1 percent for whites, and 0.2 percent for blacks. *1995 National Survey*, at 75–76.

14. See James Breay, "Who are the Waiting Children?," Office of Field Support Services, Massachusetts Department of Social Services, table 3.3 (1991).

15. Child Abuse Intervention Strategic Planning Meeting, October 20–21, 1997, sponsored by National Institute of Justice, Washington, D.C.

16. See generally Sheree L. Toth and Dante Cicchetti, "Child Maltreatment:

Where Do We Go from Here in our Treatment of Victims?" in *Child Abuse, Child Development, and Social Policy, Advances in Applied Developmental Psychology*, vol. 8, ed. Cicchetti and Toth (Norwood, NJ: Ablex Publishing Corporation, 1993), at 399 (noting limited treatment available for child victims, as compared to adult perpetrators, and difficulty of doing effective therapy when child is subject to ongoing abuse or in uncertain, impermanent foster situation).

17. Richard Barth, "After Child Protection, What Is the Guiding Principle of Child Welfare Services: Permanency, Family Continuity, or Productive Development?" The Fedele F. And Iris M. Fauri Memorial Lecture Series on Child Welfare, The University of Michigan School of Social Work, Ann Arbor, MI (December 11, 1995), at 5–8, 7, 8, 10, 11–12 (citations deleted).

18. Richard Barth, "Abusive and Neglecting Parents and the Care of Their Children," in *All Our Families: New Policies for a New Century*, ed. Mary Ann Mason, Arlene Skolnick, and Stephen D. Sugarman (New York: Oxford University Press, 1998), at 24, 26–28.

19. Adoption Assistance Provisions of the Small Job Protection Act of 1996, 26 U.S.C. 23 et seq., Pub. L. 104–188, §1807, 110 Stat. 1899.

20. See Ada Schmidt-Tieszen and Thomas P. McDonald, "Children Who Wait: Long Term Foster Care or Adoption?", *Children and Youth Services Review* 20, nos. 1/2 (1998), at 25–26.

21. The federal government's "Adoption 2002" project is supposed to issue "guidelines for state legislation" during the summer of 1999 to encourage states to reform their laws in line with the President's Adoption 2002 Initiative and with ASFA.

22. See generally Linda Katz, "Concurrent Planning: Fifteen Years Later," *Adoptalk*, Spring 1996, at 12–13; L. Katz, N. Spoonemore, C. Robinson, "Concurrent Planning: From Permanency Planning to Permanency Action," Lutheran Social Services of Washington and Idaho, Mountlake Terrace, WA, 1994.

23. See, e.g., N.Y. State Department of Social Services, ABA Center on Children and the Law, "Termination Barriers: Speeding Adoption in New York State Through Reducing Delays in Termination of Parental Rights Cases, Final Report, June 1989 to May 1991" (1991) (finding an increase in adoption rates and reductions in average time in foster care by one year and four months in Onondaga County and by one year in Chemung County, resulting in a savings in foster care costs of $2 million and $250,000 respectively). The ABA expanded the project and later reported that it had increased adoptions by 400 percent in Niagara County and 333 percent in Seneca County, and reduced average time in foster care in Niagara by nearly one year and in Seneca County by one year and eight months. This was reported to equate with savings in foster care costs of at least

$1,260,000 in Niagara County and $126,000 in Seneca County. The ABA project was recently expanded to include St. Lawrence County, where a reduction of time in foster care of two years and four months was achieved, with related cost savings of $500,000. Author telephone interview with Ann Marie Lancour, January 22, 1999.

24. See Mark Hardin and Robert Lancour, *Early Termination of Parental Rights: Developing Appropriate Statutory Grounds*, published by the American Bar Association, with the support of The Edna McConnell Clark Foundation (1996) [hereafter Hardin and Lancour, *Early Termination of Parental Rights*].

25. *Protecting the Children of New York: A Plan of Action for the Administration of Children's Services*, The Honorable Rudolph W. Giuliani, Mayor of the City of New York, Nicholas Scoppetta, Commissioner, December 19, 1996.

26. Patricia Schene, "Expedited Permanency Planning in Colorado, An Evaluation Prepared for the Colorado Department of Human Services" (December 1998), at 47, 56 (more than 80 percent of children in permanent homes at 12 months in counties implementing the plan).

27. See, e.g., *The Illinois Permanency Initiative of 1997*, enacted prior to ASFA, and codified in part as The Children and Family Services Act, 20 ILCS 505 and in part as a section of The Juvenile Court Act of 1987, 705 ILCS 405/1–2. This law clarified that family reunification is not necessary in cases when not reasonable, i.e., cases in which child or sibling of child is abandoned, tortured, or chronically abused, and emphasized that concurrent planning should be considered as soon as evident that parent cannot or will not correct conditions that resulted in placement.

28. Texas Family Code, Annotated, §§162.015, 162.308 (Vernon 1996).

29. See Elizabeth Bartholet, "Where Do Black Children Belong? The Politics of Race Matching in Adoption," *University of Pennsylvania Law Review* vol. 139, 1163 (1991), at 1239–1240, 1252.

30. See the Howard M. Metzenbaum Multiethnic Placement Act of 1994, 42 U.S.C. §§622(b)(9), Pub. L. No. 103–382, §552, 108 Stat. 4056.

31. The Secretary of the U.S. Department of Health and Human Services is required to submit a report on substance abuse issues in child welfare as well as on kinship care.

32. The new "Expedited Permanency Planning" program in Colorado, discussed in text at n. 26 above, may help illustrate the meaning of the new permanency focus. This program sets permanency within 12 months of removal from home as the goal, and uses concurrent planning, and recruitment of fost-adopt and relative homes as methods. An early report on implementation indicates that it has doubled adoption rates, but this means pushing them from only 4 percent to 8 percent, while sending 66 percent

home, giving custody of 6 percent to another parent, and placing 17 percent with relatives. Patricia Schene, "Expedited Permanency Planning in
Colorado: A Preliminary Evaluation of Implementation in Jefferson and
Boulder Counties," report on initial findings presented to the Colorado Department of Human Services and the Colorado State Legislature (October
1996), at 37.

33. See Hardin and Lancour, *Early Termination of Parental Rights*, at 2.

34. Ibid, at 11.

35. See report cited in n. 23 above.

36. Linda Katz and Chris Robinson, "Foster Care Drift: A Risk- Assessment
Matrix," *Child Welfare* 70, no. 3 (May/June 1991), at 349–50.

CHAPTER 9. SUBSTANCE ABUSE

1. Richard Barth, "Long-Term In-Home Services," in *When Drug Addicts
Have Children*, ed. Douglas J. Besharov (Washington, D.C.: Child Welfare
League of America, 1994) [hereafter Besharov, *When Drug Addicts Have
Children*, 1994], at 175, 176 (noting dramatic shift recently away from placing drug-involved children in long-term foster care, toward keeping them
at home where they typically receive little or nothing in the way of services;
describing children as at high risk of abuse and neglect, and with limited
prospects for good outcomes, which depend on intensive nurturing and
services).

2. The National Center on Addiction and Substance Abuse at Columbia
University, "No Safe Haven: Children of Substance- Abusing Parents"
(New York: January 1999) [hereafter CASA Report], at 35.

3. See, e.g., Richard P. Barth, "The Juvenile Court and Dependency Cases,"
The Future of Children, The Juvenile Court 6, no. 3 (1996), at 103–104 (of
drug-exposed children, half of those who go into foster care go after having been first sent home and then subjected to abuse or neglect).

4. CASA Report, at iv.

5. U.S. General Accounting Office, Report to the Chairman, Committee on
Finance, U.S. Senate, "Foster Care, Agencies Face Challenges Securing Stable Homes for Children of Substance Abusers," Report No. GAO /HEHS-
98–182, (Washington, D.C., September, 1998) [hereafter GAO, "Foster Care
1998"], at 17.

6. See, e.g., Jan Bays, "Substance Abuse and Child Abuse: Impact of Addiction on the Child," *Pediatric Clinics of North America* 37, no. 4 (August
1990) [hereafter Bays, "Substance Abuse and Child Abuse"], 881–904, at
889 (author, who is director of child abuse programs at health care center
in Portland, Oregon, says high percentage of drug addicts abused as children and raised in homes where drugs a problem); Karen Ingersoll, Kath-

ryn Dawson, and Deborah Haller, "Family Functioning of Perinatal Substance Abusers in Treatment," *Journal of Psychoactive Drugs* 28, no. 1 (January-March 1996) [hereafter Ingersoll, Dawson, and Haller, "Family Functioning"], at 62, 69 (many studies have found that pregnant and parent addicts' families of origin are pathological, with women raised suffering from abuse, neglect, and parental addiction problems); CASA Report, at 3, 20–21 (same).

7. Ira Chasnoff, Amy Anson, and Kai Moss Iaukea, *Understanding the Drug-Exposed Child: Approaches to Behavior and Learning* (Chicago: Imprint Publications, 1998), at 2.

8. See, e.g., Gary A. Emmett, "What Happened to 'Crack Babies'?" *Drug Policy Analysis Bulletin*, no. 4 (February 1998) [hereafter Emmett, "Crack Babies"]; Linda C. Mayes, Richard H. Granger, Marc H. Bornstein, and Barry Zuckerman, "Commentary, The Problem of Prenatal Cocaine Exposure," *Journal of American Medical Association* 267, no. 3 (1992).

9. See, e.g., Emmett, "Crack Babies," at 1 ("current research demonstrates that by the time the child reaches age five, the effect of the disastrous social situation that [the children of] many crack cocaine users share with other economically deprived children washes out any measurable effect of the cocaine itself on . . . school performance;" crack babies' home and social situation more devastating to future development than crack exposure); *Behavioral Studies of Drug-Exposed Offspring*, National Institute on Drug Abuse Research Monograph Series (1996), at 212 (research showing no major differences between cocaine-exposed and control groups in preschool and school-aged children likely reflects all the other damage that the control group suffers—"The central question for outcomes . . . is whether or not the possible increased incidence of impairments . . . is uniquely different from that seen in children from dysfunctional or multirisk families not affected by substance abuse"—and noting also that continued parental cocaine use postnatally may affect outcomes).

10. *The Harvard Mental Health Letter*, "Cocaine Before Birth," 13, no. 6 (December 1998), at 3 [hereafter *Harvard Mental Health*].

11. "It is obviously not good for a child to be exposed to cocaine in the womb, but by far the greater risk is being born to or raised by a crack addict." *Harvard Mental Health*, at 3–4.

12. Barry Zuckerman, "Drug-Exposed Infants: Understanding the Medical Risk," *The Future of Children, Drug Exposed Infants* 1, no. 3 (Spring 1991), at 25, 34–35. See also Carol Seval Brooks, Barry Zuckerman, Amy Bamforth, Jean Cole, and Margot Kaplan-Sanoff, "Clinical Issues Related to Substance-Involved Mothers and Their Infants," *Infant Mental Health Journal* 15, no. 2 (Summer 1994).

13. Diana Kronstadt, "Complex Development Issues of Parental Drug Expo-

sure," *The Future of Children, Drug Exposed Infants* 1, no. 3 (Spring 1991), at 36, 44.

14. See generally *Adoption and Prenatal Alcohol and Drug Exposure: The Research, Policy and Practice Challenges*, a conference held October 24–25, 1997, in Alexandria, Virginia, sponsored by the Evan B. Donaldson Adoption Institute, and see "Prenatal Substance Exposure, Select Bibliography," prepared for same <http://www.adoptioninstitute.org/ proed/pserjw3.html>; see also Richard Barth, "Adoption of Drug- Exposed Children," *Child and Youth Services Review* 13, nos. 5/6 (1991) (these children are adoptable); NIDA, *Behavioral Studies of Drug-Exposed Offspring*, at 194 (developmental outcome likely to be function of "how the caregiving environment responds to the behavioral constellation of the infant"); Barry Zuckerman, "Effects on Parents and Children," in Besharov, *When Drug Addicts Have Children*, 1994 (child's social environment key); A. Orney, V. Michailevskaya, and I. Lukashov, "The Developmental Outcome of Children Born to Heroin Dependent Mothers Raised at Home or Adopted," *Child Abuse & Neglect* 20, no. 5 (1996), at 385–396 (developmental delays suffered by children born to heroin-dependent mothers attributed primarily to severe environmental deprivation and fact that one or both parents addicted). Ira J. Chasnoff, D. R. Griffith, et al., "Cocaine/Polydrug Use in Pregnancy: Two Year Follow Up," *Pediatrics* 89, no. 2 (February 1992), at 284–289 (finding that prognosis for children exposed prenatally to cocaine and other drugs varied depending on environment, with those not in multiple placements or not living with drug-affected mothers displaying fewer problems).

15. Orney, Michailevskaya, and Lukashov, "Developmental Outcome of Children Born to Heroin Dependent Mothers."

16. See presentations and discussions at the Donaldson Conference in n. 14, above. See also Susan Edelstein, *Children with Prenatal Alcohol and/or Other Drug Exposure: Weighing the Risks of Adoption* (Washington, D.C.: Child Welfare League of America, 1995); Richard P. Barth, "Outcomes for Drug-Exposed and Non Drug-Exposed Adopted Children at Four and Eight Years" (paper presented at the Donaldson Conference, n. 14 above (finding some but relatively limited differences between the two groups in terms of disabilities, ADHD, functioning, parental satisfaction with adoption). A recent study of parents who adopted drug-exposed children found very high levels of satisfaction—84 percent were "very satisfied" and 12 percent were "satisfied"—a proportion quite similar to that found among parents who adopted non-drug-exposed children. Richard Barth, "Revisiting the Issues: Adoption of Drug Exposed Children," *The Future of Children, Adoption* 3, no. 1 (1993).

17. See generally chapter 3 above for discussion of some of the problems associated with these kinds of substitute parenting arrangements. See Pamela

M. Wallace and Harolyn M. E. Belcher, "Drug Exposed Children and the Foster Care System: In the Best Interests of the Child?," *Journal of Child & Adolescent Substance Abuse* 7, no. 1 (1997), at 19, 30 (noting limitations of foster care environment for prenatally exposed children). Even then, research indicates that drug-exposed children placed at birth, whether with kin or nonkin foster parents, do better than children not placed at birth. D. Brooks and R. P. Barth, "Characteristics and Outcomes of Drug-Exposed and Non Drug-Exposed Children in Kinship and Non-Relative Foster Care," *Children and Youth Services Review* 20, no. 6 (1998), at 475–501.

18. See, e.g., Clarice Dibble Walker, Patricia Zangrillo, and Jacqueline Marie Smith, "Parental Drug Abuse and African-American Children in Foster Care," in *Child Welfare Research Review*, Vol. 1, ed. Richard Barth et al. (New York: Columbia University Press, 1994), at 109, 111–112 (in parental drug abuse cases primary reason for placement was neglect and not abuse, with typical cases involving serious level of neglect, e.g., no school, grossly limited supervision and food).

19. See Sidney Gardner and Nancy Young, "The Implications of Alcohol and Other Drug-related Problems for Community-wide Family Support Systems"(paper prepared for the Executive Session: New Paradigms for Child Protective Services, John F. Kennedy School of Government, Harvard University, Cambridge, MA, November 1996). See discussion of Executive Session process in chapter 6, above.

20. See Frank Farrow, "Child Protection: Building Community Partnerships: Getting from Here to There" (paper prepared for the Executive Session: New Paradigms for Child Protective Services, John F. Kennedy School of Government, Harvard University, Cambridge, MA, November 1996).

21. See, e.g., *Psychology of Addictive Behaviors*, ed. D. Dwayne Simpson and Susan J. Curry, *Journal of Division 50 of the American Psychological Association, Special Issue: Drug Abuse Treatment Outcome Study* (DATOS), 11, no. 4 (December 1997) [hereafter DATOS, 1997], at 219–220 (legal pressure correlates with longer periods in treatment); *Treatment for Drug-Exposed Women and Their Children: Advances in Research Methodology*, National Institute on Drug Abuse Research Monograph Series (1996), at 14, 55, 115 (coercive pressure of legal involvement useful in recruitment and retention, shown by several studies); Nancy Young and Sidney Gardner, *Implementing Welfare Reform: Solutions to the Substance Abuse Problem* (Washington, D.C.: Drug Strategies, 1997) (studies indicate that threat of sanctions, including child removal, useful in motivating treatment and rehabilitation); "Developments in the Law—Alternatives to Incarceration," *Harvard Law Review* 111 (1998), at 1863, 1904, 1919 (use of legal pressure found useful in inducing treatment compliance); Jennifer Trone and Douglas Young, "Bridg-

ing Drug Treatment and Criminal Justice," Vera Institute of Justice (1996); Bays, "Substance Abuse and Child Abuse," at 900 (need combination of compassion and coercive control model because "compassion alone has made no inroads against the addictive power of drugs like cocaine, amphetamine, or heroin"); CASA Report ("many who work in the field of addiction argue that serious consequences are sometimes necessary to get the serious attention of addicts who do not want to address their problem"), at 8; see also 29. See also Emmett, "Crack Babies," 1998, at 2 ("the most successful intervention [for cocaine using parents] has involved intensive teaching of mothering skills combined with drug rehabilitation and the prospect of imprisonment if the course was not finished"); Sonya Steven and Ann Stiehm Ahlstrom, "Perspective From a Minnesota County Attorney's Office," *The Future of Children, Drug Exposed Infants* 1, no. 3 (Spring 1991) [hereafter Steven, "Perspective From a Minnesota County Attorney's Office"], at 93ff (claim for success of program threatening civil commitment and child removal, for refusals to engage in treatment). Welfare reform has led to the creation of programs in some areas requiring drug addicts to participate in treatment as a condition of receiving welfare benefits, a development that is seen by many as promising. See Legal Action Center, "Making Welfare Reform Work: Tools for Confronting Alcohol and Drug Problems Among Welfare Recipients" (1997).

22. Some two hundred women were prosecuted as of 1998. Lawrence J. Nelson and Mary Faith Marshall, *Ethical and Legal Analyses of Three Coercive Policies Aimed at Substance Abuse By Pregnant Women*, project funded by the Substance Abuse Policy Research Program at the Robert Wood Johnson Foundation (1998)[hereafter Nelson and Marshall, *Ethical and Legal Analyses of Three Coercive Policies*], at 37. In some cases prosecutors have relied on the drugs being passed on to the live baby through the umbilical cord after birth, but before the cord was cut, in an effort to avoid the legal issue as to whether harm to the unborn baby can trigger prosecution.

23. See *Whitner v. South Carolina*, 492 S. E.2d 777 (1996), cert. denied, 118 S.Ct. 1857 (1998); see "State Decision on Pregnant Moms Allowed to Stand," *Of Substance: A Newsletter for the Substance Abuse Treatment Community* 19, no. 3 (May/June 1998), at 1 (The Legal Action Center, New York).

24. See Steven, "Perspective From a Minnesota County Attorney's Office," at 93ff.

25. State supreme courts addressing the issue have so far held that child removal could not be premised solely on the mother's prenatal drug or alcohol use. See *In re Valerie D.*, 613 A.2d. 748 (Conn. 1992) (drugs); *In the Matter of the Appeal in Pima City*, 183 Ariz. 546, 905 P.2d. 255 (1995) (alcohol).

26. See The Legal Aid Society, Juvenile Rights Division, "Position Paper:

Governmental Action in Cases of In Utero Drug or Alcohol Exposure: The Role and Responsibilities of Child Protective Authorities and the Family Court," December 1997, attached as Appendix B to Nelson and Marshall, *Ethical and Legal Analyses of Three Coercive Policies.*

27. See, e.g., California Welfare and Inst. Code sect. 361.5(b)(12); GAO, Foster Care 1998, at Appendix V, 85–89, "Summary of State Termination of Parental Rights Laws Related to Parental Substance Abuse."

28. See e.g., CASA Report, at 7–8 and in Section V, "Promising Innovations: Family Drug Courts," at 61–75. On the San Diego program see also *The Dependency Court Recovery Project, Project Summary and Current Highlights* (November 1998). See also GAO, Foster Care 1998, at 28–32 ("Initiatives Seek to Improve Prospects for Recovery and Family Reunification").

29. See chapter 8 text at n. 34 and n. 34 and text at n. 27 and n. 27 above.

30. See text at n. 21 above, and n. 21.

31. See Inger, Dawson, and Haller, "Family Functioning," at 68–69, study of addicted pregnant women and parents in intensive outpatient treatment, one of the only studies to assess value of treatment in terms of parenting, shows no improvement, finding this "of particular concern to programs that hope to prevent or minimize damage to children living with addicted mothers." See also Julia H. Littell, John R. Schuerman, and Amy Chak, "Cocaine Abuse," Discussion Paper 054 in "What Works Best for Whom in Family Preservation," The Chapin Hall Center for Children at the University of Chicago (1994), at 19ff (family preservation programs resulted in very high percentage getting drug treatment, but ultimately neither that or other services had impact on subsequent maltreatment or placement rates).

32. *Planned Parenthood v. Casey,* 112 S.Ct. 2791 (1992).

33. See Bays, "Substance Abuse and Child Abuse," at 895 (drug abusers tend not to follow through on ordered treatment even when at risk of losing child); *Marisol v. Giuliani,* Case Record Review: Reports 1, 2, and 3, prepared by Marisol Joint Case Review Team, August 12, 1997, September 5, 1997, and December 1997 (revealing that in overwhelming percentage of cases lack of cooperation by addicted parents key to failure to receive services, rather than limited availability of services, Report 2, at 53, Report 3, at 12, 170–171); GAO, Foster Care 1998, at 18 (resistance to entering treatment and high drop out rate). A 1997 governmental report found no research providing empirical support for claimed relationship between barriers to treatment for women and their use of treatment resources. Substance Abuse and Mental Health Services Administration, "Substance Abuse Among Women in the United States" (1997), at 7–1.

34. CASA Report, at 2; see also at 5–6, 36.

35. DATOS, 1997, at 212–13, 321.

36. See chapter 3, text at nn. 82–84 and nn. 82–84 above. See also U.S. General Accounting Office, "Care and Protection Services: Complex Challenges Require New Strategies" (Washington, D.C., 1997), at 9–10 (drug treatment services too limited, but even when provided, relapse rates high).

37. Center for Substance Abuse Prevention, "Pregnant and Postpartum Women and Their Infants (PPWI) Demonstration Program Findings, Executive Summary," unpublished report on file with the author, October 1996 (research report on federally funded demonstration programs serving drug-abusing parents finds that programs specially targeted for this population have enormous difficulty retaining clients); NIDA, *Treatment for Drug-Exposed Women*, at 52–53, 69 (reporting on NIDA-funded demonstration programs, finding that even in model programs offering range of services for mother and child, together with provision for children to live with mother, recruitment and retention extraordinarily difficult); Judy Howard, "Barriers to Successful Intervention," in Besharov, *When Drug Addicts Have Children*, 1994, at 91ff (report on research on two-year intensive early intervention program, using home visitors, with drug-abusing mothers, which helped with access to drug treatment of both residential and outpatient variety, found that only about 15 percent remained abstinent for one year, and they could not predict which would); Martha Morrison Dore and Joan M. Dorris, "Preventing Child Placement in Substance-Abusing Families: Research-Informed Practice," *Child Welfare* 78, no. 4 (July/August 1998), at 407, 420–421 (research shows that in demonstration treatment program for mothers and children, with mothers under pressure from CPS in background, one-third of original 138 referred agreed to accept treatment and able to complete treatment regimen; noted extensive needs of mothers and significant developmental delays in children and related importance of providing intensive support over significant period of time for mothers and special care for children, and warned that achieving sobriety "is a series of forward and backward steps.") See also Ingersoll, Dawson, and Haller, "Family Functioning."

38. See Robert Apsler, "The Need for Better Research," in Besharov, *When Drug Addicts Have Children*, 1994, at 101ff (limited research showing any success, with only exceptions being studies of (1) highly motivated heroin addicts in methadone treatment with auxiliary services programs, and (2) those in long-term therapeutic residential communities).

CHAPTER 10. RACE, POVERTY, AND HISTORIC INJUSTICE

1. See Lela B. Costin, Jacob Karger, and David Stoesz, *The Politics of Child Abuse in America* (New York: Oxford University Press, 1996), at 145–151.

2. U.S. Department of Health and Human Services, "Executive Summary of the Third National Incidence Study of Child Abuse and Neglect (NIS-3)" (Washington, D.C., September 1996) [hereafter Executive Summary NIS-3], at 10.

3. National Research Council and Institute of Medicine, *Violence in Families: Assessing Prevention and Treatment Programs* (Washington, D.C.: National Academy Press, 1998), at 43.

4. Richard Barth, "Abusive and Neglecting Parents and the Care of Their Children," in *All Our Families: New Policies for a New Century*, ed. Mary Ann Mason, Arlene Skolnick, and Stephen D. Sugarman (New York: Oxford University Press, 1998), at 223.

5. See Diana J. English, "The Extent and Consequences of Child Maltreatment," *The Future of Children, Protecting Children From Abuse and Neglect* 8, no. 1 (Spring 1998), at 39, 47, citing the Third National Incidence Study.

6. English, "Extent of Child Maltreatment," at 47.

7. Note that the statistics discussed above come from the NIS-3 incidence study, and see chapter 3 discussing comparison between incidence studies and reported abuse rates. There is more of a dispute today as to whether there is any difference in maltreatment or removal rates between racial groups that is not explained by economic differences, and there is evidence indicating that poverty is in any event a more powerful determinant than race or ethnicity. Jane Waldfogel, *The Future of Child Protection: How to Break the Cycle of Abuse and Neglect* (Cambridge, MA: Harvard University Press, 1998), at 10–12. The NIS-3 study found no significant race differences in maltreatment incidence, concluding that the disproportionate numbers of minority race children in the CPS and foster care population result from disproportionate attention by system decision-makers. Executive Summary, NIS-3, at 7. But see, e.g., R. P. Barth and D. L. Blackwell, "Death Rates Among California's Foster Care and Former Foster Care Populations," *Children and Youth Services Review* 20, no. 7 (1998), at 577–605 (death rates for black children significantly higher than for white and hispanic children in foster, former foster, and general populations); U.S. Advisory Board on Child Abuse and Neglect, "A Nation's Shame" (Washington, D.C., 1995), at 25 (black fatality rate from abuse and neglect two to three times that of other ethnic groups).

8. See Patricia A. Schene, "Past, Present, and Future Roles of Child Protective Services," *The Future of Children, Protecting Children From Abuse and Neglect* 8, no. 1 (Spring 1998), at 23, 25; Andrea Warren, "The Orphan Train, All Aboard for the Largest Migration of Children in History," *Special to Washington Post*, November 11, 1998, p. H1.

9. Human Rights and Equal Opportunity Commission of Australia, "Bringing them Home: Report of the National Inquiry into the Separation of Aboriginal and Torres Strait Islander Children from Their Families," April 1997, Reconciliation and Social Justice Library. <http://www.austlii.edu.au/au/special/rsjproject/rsjlibrary/hreoc/stolen/prelim.html>.

10. Clifford Krauss, "Argentine Kidnapping Inquiry Stepped Up, 2 More 'Dirty War' Officers are Held; Judge Has 30 Suspects," *The New York Times*, December 31, 1998, International, p. A9; Tina Rosenberg, "What Did You Do in the War, Mama?," *The New York Times Magazine*, February 7, 1999, at 52.

11. Captain Richard Pratt, formerly of the Carlisle Indian School, was quoted as saying that such schools "Kill the Indian in him, and save the man." Jane Salodof, "A New School Bridges Two Worlds, Indians are Prepared for Ivy League Colleges and Tribal Life," *The New York Times*, November 29, 1998, National, p. 32.

INDEX

Abandoned Infants Assistance Act
(AIA), 210
abandonment of children, 64, 65,
104, 197
abortion and fetal rights, 229–30
abuse of children. *See* maltreatment
of children
adoption: coercive use of, in Australia, Argentina, and El Salvador,
237; in concurrent planning programs, 18, 189–90, 200–201; court
decisions concerning, 22; of drug-
exposed children, 216, 223, 227;
effects of, on children, 60, 81, 97,
110, 157, 177–79, 216; federal policies on, 14–15, 23–24, 118, 122, 125,
129, 158, 176, 186–89, 193–94; financial support for, 47, 88, 125,
186, 189; following foster and institutional care, 47, 82, 85, 88–89, 118,
154, 176–77, 178, 179, 189–91, 201;
growing support for, 7, 26, 118,
176; historical development of, 25,
180, 236; of infants, 177, 179, 180,
216, 223; international, 127, 180,
182, 236; need for expanded use of,
23–24, 50, 97, 159, 163, 183, 203–4,
241; number of children involved
in, 25, 176–77, 180; openness arrangements in, 156, 179; opposition to expanded use of, 26, 45,
188, 202; race matching and, 47,
123–25, 126, 129, 131, 134, 138, 182,

186–87; recruitment of parents
for, 127, 134, 180–83, 192–93, 201,
241–42; reluctance of child welfare
system to use, 14, 26, 102, 177, 188,
202; of special needs children, 125,
179, 182–83, 186, 189, 242; transracial, 45, 123–24, 125, 126–27, 129,
182, 188
Adoption and Race Work Group
(California), 135–36
Adoption and Safe Families Act
(ASFA): adoption encouraged by,
14, 24, 118, 183, 188–89; compromises and loopholes in, 14–15, 26–
27, 122, 123, 158, 193–96, 198, 203,
218–19; enactment of, 23, 49, 55,
105; family preservation policies
limited by, 42, 105, 188; margin-
alization of substance abuse problem in, 122, 197–98, 217–18; permanency as priority in, 190, 198;
safety as priority in, 197
Adoption Assistance and Child Welfare Act, 25–26, 42, 46, 188
Adoption 2002 program, 25, 118, 176
Adoptive Families of America
(AFA), 130
Africa, communal responsibility for
children in, 2, 181
African-American adults: as adoptive parents, 127, 138–39, 181–82; as
foster parents, 92, 138–39, 181; and
interracial family relationships,

ACKNOWLEDGMENTS

This book was made possible by the generous support of the Harvard Law School, the Robert Wood Johnson Foundation, and Dr. Joseph Puma. I want to thank Dean Robert Clark for granting me a two-year leave from teaching and for the generous institutional support provided during this period. I want to thank the Robert Wood Johnson Foundation for the extraordinarily generous grants which made it possible for me to take the teaching leave in order to devote myself to this project, and Dr. Robert Hughes, Vice President of the Robert Wood Johnson Foundation, for his faith in the project. I want to thank Dr. Joseph Puma, whose early belief in and generous individual support for the project helped make everything that followed possible.

I am also deeply grateful to the many friends and colleagues who read and commented on drafts of the manuscript. I am particularly indebted to Richard P. Barth, Frank A. Daniels Professor, Jordan Institute for Families at the University of North Carolina School of Social Work, both for his own work, which I find invaluable, and for his extraordinarily helpful comments, and to Lynn A. Girton, Chief Counsel at the Volunteer Lawyers Project of the Boston Bar Association, for her wise perspective, informed by a lifetime of legal services work on behalf of impoverished clients, and for her advice and suggestions. I also want to thank for their generosity in giving of their time, and for their comments: Cassie Bevan, Howard Davidson, Jonathan Davis, Charles Fried, Gerald Frug, Alec Gray, Joan Hollinger, Peter Hutt, Alexandra Lowe, Michael Meltsner, Martha Minow, Robert Mnookin, Patrick Murphy, William Pierce, and Michael Wald.

Many others gave of their knowledge and time in interviews that were important to my understanding of the issues, including Marylee Allen, Director, Child Welfare and Mental Health Division, Children's Defense Fund, Washington, D.C.; members of Richard Barth's research group at the Center for Social Services Research at the School of Social Welfare, University of California, Berkeley; Suzin Bartley, Executive Director, Children's Trust Fund, Boston; Madelyn Freundlich, Executive Director, The Evan B. Donaldson Adoption Institute, New York City; Linda Gibbs, Deputy Commissioner, Administration for Children's Services, New York City; Sarah Greenblatt, Director, National Resource Center for Permanency Planning,

New York City; Mark Hardin, Director of Child Welfare, American Bar Association Center on Children and the Law, Washington, D.C.; Francis X. Hartmann, Executive Director, Program in Criminal Justice Policy and Management at the Malcolm Wiener Center for Social Policy, John F. Kennedy School of Government, Harvard University; Professor Fran Jacobs, Associate Professor and Chair, Eliot-Pearson Department of Child Development, Tufts University; Ann Marie Lancour, Skills Training Director, American Bar Association Center on Children and the Law, Washington, D.C.; Mark Moore, Professor of Criminal Justice Policy and Management, John F. Kennedy School of Government, Harvard University; Susan Notkin, Director of the Program for Children, The Edna McConnell Clark Foundation, New York City; Theodora Ooms, Executive Director, Family Impact Seminar, Washington, D.C.; Sister Mary Paul, Director of Clinical Services, Center for Family Life, Sunset Park, Brooklyn, New York; Patricia Schene, Consultant in Children and Family Services, Littleton, Colorado; Jane Waldfogel, Associate Professor of Social Work and Public Affairs at Columbia University School of Social Work, New York City; Richard Wexler, Member of the Board of Directors of the National Coalition for Child Protection Reform, Alexandria, Virginia; Elizabeth White, attorney, Massachusetts Department of Social Services, Boston; and Barry Zuckerman, Chief of Pediatrics at Boston Medical Center and Professor and Chairman of Pediatrics at Boston University School of Medicine.

I also want to thank those at Beacon Press who did such a spectacular job in connection with the production of this book. Special thanks go to Helene Atwan, Beacon's director and my editor, whose enthusiasm, insight, imagination, and humor made the publication process a genuine pleasure. Thanks also to Susan Meigs and Matt Seccombe for their wonderful work editing the final manuscript and indexing the book, respectively.

And thanks to Lindy Hess, for invaluable advice about the publication process, and to my agent Faith Childs. Thanks to Robert Cunningham and Penny Peoples, who helped me get started finding support for this project. Thanks to Emma Clark and Jessica Dubin for their assistance with documentation. And thanks finally to my assistant Lisa Skop, whose unfailingly cheerful spirit and extraordinary dedication to this project, from its initial stages through the final details of production, have been absolutely central to the enterprise.